Free Video  Free Video

Essential Test Tips Video from Trivium Test Prep

Dear Customer,

Thank you for purchasing from Trivium Test Prep! We're honored to help you prepare for your AP exam.

To show our appreciation, we're offering a **FREE *AP World History Essential Test Tips* Video by Trivium Test Prep.*** Our video includes 35 test preparation strategies that will make you successful on the AP exam. All we ask is that you email us your feedback and describe your experience with our product. Amazing, awful, or just so-so: we want to hear what you have to say!

To receive your **FREE *AP World History Essential Test Tips* Video**, please email us at 5star@triviumtestprep.com. Include "Free 5 Star" in the subject line and the following information in your email:

1. The title of the product you purchased.
2. Your rating from 1 – 5 (with 5 being the best).
3. Your feedback about the product, including how our materials helped you meet your goals and ways in which we can improve our products.
4. Your full name and shipping address so we can send your **FREE *AP World History Essential Test Tips* Video**.

If you have any questions or concerns please feel free to contact us directly at 5star@triviumtestprep.com.

Thank you!

– Trivium Test Prep Team

*To get access to the free video please email us at 5star@triviumtestprep.com, and please follow the instructions above.

AP World History Review Book 2021-2022

Study Guide with Practice Test Questions for the Advanced Placement Exam

Copyright © 2020 by Accepted, Inc.

ISBN-13: 9781635309812

ALL RIGHTS RESERVED. By purchase of this book, you have been licensed one copy for personal use only. No part of this work may be reproduced, redistributed, or used in any form or by any means without prior written permission of the publisher and copyright owner. Accepted, Inc.; Trivium Test Prep; Cirrus Test Prep; and Ascencia Test Prep are all imprints of Trivium Test Prep, LLC.

The College Board was not involved in the creation or production of this product, is not in any way affiliated with Accepted, Inc., and does not sponsor or endorse this product. All test names (and their acronyms) are trademarks of their respective owners. This study guide is for general information only and does not claim endorsement by any third party.

Printed in the United States of America.

Table of Contents

Introduction i

PART I: REVIEW   **1**

**1: Early Civilizations
and the Great Empires** 3
Paleolithic and Neolithic Eras 3
Middle East and Egypt 4
India 6
China 7
The Americas 8
Answer Key 11

**2: Civilization, Culture,
and Religion** 13
Great Empires 13
World Religions 18
Answer Key 22

**3: Feudalism through
the Era of Expansion** 23
The Middle Ages in Europe 23
The Islamic World 26
Conflict and Cultural Exchange 28
Empires in Transition 32

Mesoamerican and
Andean Civiliztions 36
Answer Key 38

4: Globalization 39
The European Renaissance 39
Colonization of the
Western Hemisphere 40
Armed Conflicts 43
Answer Key 48

5: The Age of Revolutions 49
Revolution 49
European Division 53
Conflict in the Balkans 54
Imperialism 55
Industrial Revolution 59
Answer Key 62

6: Global Conflict 63
Pre-Revolutionary Russia 63
World War I 64
Change in the Middle East 66
Russian Revolution 67

Change in East Asia 69
World War II 71
The Cold War 75
Decolonization 78
Post-Cold War World 82
Answer Key 87

PART II: TEST YOUR KNOWLEDGE — 91

7: Practice Test One 93
Selected-Response Questions 93
Free-Response Questions 102
Answer Key 107

8: Practice Test Two 113
Selected-Response Questions 113
Free-Response Questions 122
Answer Key 125

9: Practice Test Three 131
Selected-Response Questions 131
Free-Response Questions 140
Answer Key 143

10: Practice Test Four 149
Selected-Response Questions 149
Free Response Questions 158
Answer Key 163

Appendix: Sample Essays 169
Prompt One:
The Impact of Disease 69
Prompt Two: Continuity
and Change over Time 172
Document-Based Questions 175

Introduction

Congratulations on choosing to take the AP World History exam! By purchasing this book, you've taken a big step toward scoring high on your exam and obtaining college credit.

This guide will provide you with a detailed overview of the AP World History exam so you know exactly what to expect on test day. We'll take you through all the concepts covered on the tests and give you the opportunity to test your knowledge with practice questions. Even if it's been a while since you last took a major test, don't worry; we'll make sure you're more than ready!

What is AP World History?

The Advanced Placement (AP) World History course is a college-level class for high school students. It culminates in the AP World History exam, offered by the College Board. Students are not required to take the class to take the exam, but it helps. Most US and Canadian universities offer college credit for high AP test scores.

AP World History covers the historical development of the entire world from the earliest historical periods. The course spans the earliest stages of human development to the modern world and includes significant information on Asia, Africa, Latin America, and Oceania.

The breadth of the course poses challenges for both students and teachers. Most college-level world history textbooks will provide an appropriate review tool for this subject, particularly if you are planning to take the test without having taken the course. This text provides a review of important trends in world history. It should not stand alone if you have not taken the AP World History class in school.

What's on the AP World History Exam?

The Advanced Placement World History test consists of fifty-five multiple choice questions, three short-answer questions, one document-based question (DBQ), and one essay. The test is three hours and fifteen minutes long.

\multicolumn{4}{c}{Overview of the AP World History Exam}			
Question Type	Number of Questions	Percentage of Test	Time
Multiple choice	55	40%	55 minutes
Short answer	3	20%	40 minutes
DBQ	1	25%	60 minutes
Long essay	1	15%	40 minutes
Total	**55 multiple choice, 3 short answer, 2 essays**		**3 hours, 15 minutes**

There are fifty-five multiple choice questions, making up 40 percent of your total grade. You'll have fifty-five minutes in total for this portion of the test. Each of the nine historical themes of the test will be included on the multiple choice portion of the examination: Global Tapestry, Networks of Exchange, Land-Based Empires, Transoceanic Interconnections, Revolutions, Consequences of Industrialization, Global Conflict, Cold War and Decolonization, and Globalization.

What's on the AP World History Exam?		
Category	Concepts	Percentage of Test
Global Tapestry c. 1200 – c. 1450	▶ formation, expansion, and decline of states (Africa, Afro-Eurasia, East Asia, Europe, South and Southeast Asia, the Americas) ▶ global belief systems (religions)	8 – 10%
Networks of Exchange c. 1200 – c. 1450	▶ Silk Roads, Trans-Saharan trade routes, Indian Ocean trade network ▶ Mongol Empire, cross-cultural interactions	8 – 10%
Land-Based Empires c. 1450 – c. 1750	Manchu, Mughal, Safavid, Ottoman Empires	12 – 15%
Transoceanic Interconnections c. 1450 – c. 1750	▶ Scientific Revolution and technological innovation ▶ the Columbian Exchange ▶ maritime empires and challenges to hierarchy	12 – 15%

Category	Concepts	Percentage of Test
Revolutions c. 1750 – c. 1900	▶ the Enlightenment ▶ the development of nation-states ▶ the Industrial Revolution	12 – 15%
Consequences of Industrialization c. 1750 – c. 1900	▶ imperialism and resistance to it ▶ migration ▶ growth of the global economy	12 – 15%
Global Conflict c. 1900 – present	▶ World War I, interwar period ▶ World War II ▶ mass atrocities	8 – 10%
Cold War and Decolonization c. 1900 – present	▶ causes of the Cold War, spread of communism ▶ decolonization in Africa and Asia ▶ end of the Cold War	8 – 10%
Globalization c. 1900 – present	▶ technological, environmental, health, and economic change ▶ international institutions ▶ reform movements	8 – 10%
Total	**55 multiple-choice questions**	**55 minutes**

FREE-RESPONSE QUESTIONS

The free response portion of the examination takes up the majority of the test time. First, you must respond to three short answer questions. You will have forty minutes to read and respond to the short answer questions, which involve analyzing historical perspectives and sources. You may read primary or secondary sources, or review maps, charts, or other materials. The short answers make up 20 percent of your score.

What's on the Short Answer Portion of the AP World History Exam?	
Question	Topic
Short Answer 1	▶ discuss historical developments and processes between 1200 and 2001 ▶ analyze a secondary source
Short Answer 2	▶ discuss historical developments and processes between 1200 and 2001 ▶ analyze a primary source

What's on the Short Answer Portion of the AP World History Exam? (continued)	
QUESTION	TOPIC
Short Answer 3	▶ analyze developments and processes during a time period ▶ choose between two questions (addressing 1200–1750 or 1750–2001) ▶ no source to analyze (free response)
Total	**40 minutes, 20% of test**

The next portion of the test includes two essays. The first is a document-based question (DBQ). You have one hour to complete your DBQ, including fifteen minutes of reading time. You will have seven documents to assess. Analyze the information and synthesize it into an essay supported by the historical evidence. The DBQ covers a time period between 1450 – 2001.

Finally, the long essay focuses on historical change or continuity, with a forty minute writing period. You will be able to choose from among three periods: 1200 – 1750, 1450 – 1900, or 1750 – 2001. There are no sources to study or analyze; the essay is free response.

What's on the Free-Response Portion of the AP World History Exam?			
QUESTION TYPE	TOPICS	PERCENTAGE OF TEST	TIME
Document-based question (DBQ)	▶ analyze 7 historical documents ▶ form argument supported by historical sources ▶ time period covered: 1450 – 2001	25%	60 minutes
Long essay	▶ form argument supported by historical sources ▶ choose from 3 questions ▶ time period covered: 1450 – 2001	15%	40 minutes
Total		**40%**	**1 hour, 40 minutes**

For a high-scoring test, you need to do well on both the essay questions and the multiple choice questions. Plan to spend the first few minutes of each writing block planning your essay with a brief outline or some simple notes. This will help you to stay on track and focused throughout the essay. Practice will help you to write well under time pressure.

How is the AP World History Exam Scored?

The test is scored on a scale of 1 to 5. A score of 5 is extremely well qualified to receive college credit, while a score of 1 is not qualified to receive college credit. Scores of 4 to 5 are widely accepted by colleges and universities; however, scores of 3 or lower may provide less credit or none at all. Review the AP policies at your college or university to better understand scoring requirements and credit offered.

Students take the AP World History Examination in May; scores are typically available on your online account in July. You can have your scores sent to the college of your choosing, or, if you're testing after your junior year, simply wait until you're ready to apply to the colleges of your choice.

Multiple-choice questions are graded by computer. You receive one point for each correct answer. There are no penalties for an incorrect answer or a skipped question. You should, if you're unsure, guess. Even the most random guess provides you a one in four chance of a point. If you can narrow down the choices just a bit, your chances increase and, along with them, your possible test score.

Free-response questions are graded by human graders, typically high school and college instructors working with the College Board. Your short answer, DBQ, and long essay responses will be scored. Those scores are combined with your multiple-choice score to create a composite score. The composite score is then scaled onto the five-point scale, resulting in your final score. See the College Board website for details.

About This Guide

This guide will help you to master the most important test topics and also develop critical test-taking skills. We have built features into our books to prepare you for your tests and increase your score. Along with a detailed summary of the format, content, and scoring of the AP exam, we offer an in-depth overview of the content knowledge required to pass the exam. In the review you'll find sidebars that provide interesting information, highlight key concepts, and review content so that you can solidify your understanding of the exam's concepts. You can also test your knowledge with sample questions throughout the text and practice questions that reflect the content and format of the exams. We're pleased you've chosen Accepted, Inc. to be a part of your journey!

PART I
Review

For the AP World History exam, you will be expected to understand how world societies and civilizations have been shaped by historical trends. These include conflict, technology, and religion; ideologies like nationalism, totalitarianism, and other political philosophies; economic movements like impact of trade within and between cultures, industrialization, and the market economy; and major demographic trends.

Specific questions may ask about the classical civilizations in Europe and Asia, their transformation from 300 – 1450 CE, European developments from the Renaissance through the Enlightenment, colonization, trade, and other global interactions from 1200 – 1750 CE, the consequences of nationalism and European imperialism from 1750 – 1900 CE, the causes and consequences of the First and Second World Wars (like decolonization and the rise of the Soviet Union), and the important developments of the post-Cold War world (such as globalization and fundamentalism).

CHAPTER ONE
Early Civilizations and the Great Empires
Before 600 BCE

Paleolithic and Neolithic Eras

The earliest humans were hunter-gatherers until the development of agriculture in about 11,000 BCE 60,000 – 70,000 years ago, early humans began migrating from Africa, gradually spreading out across the continents in several waves of migration throughout Europe and Asia, eventually into Australia, the Pacific Islands, and the Americas.

Early human history begins with the **PALEOLITHIC ERA**, the period before agricultural development and settled communities. During this period, early **HOMINIDS** exhibited the use of tools, up to and including our ancestors, *Homo sapiens sapiens*. Other early hominids included *Australopithecus*, from which *Homo habilis*, *Homo neanderthalensis*, *Homo erectus*, and others descended. In fact, there is some evidence that *Homo sapiens sapiens* and *Homo neanderthalensis* may have coexisted. All are now extinct, save for us, *Homo sapiens*.

During the Paleolithic Era, human technology was rudimentary, based on stone; hence, the term **STONE AGE** describes this period before metalworking was invented. Between approximately 11,000 – 10,500 BCE, humans began changing their behavior; they started settled communities, developed agricultural practices, and began domesticating animals. Notable technological developments occurred: humans began to create tools, weapons, and other objects made of metal. Furthermore, all species of human except *Homo sapiens sapiens* became extinct. This transition marked the beginning of the **NEOLITHIC PERIOD**, characterized by behavioral and technological change like the invention of the wheel. During the **BRONZE AGE**, humans began working with copper and tin, creating stronger tools and weapons.

Middle East and Egypt

Beginning in the Near East, settled societies organized into larger centralized communities characterized by early social stratification and rule of law; the earliest known examples of these were in the **Fertile Crescent**, the area in North Africa and Southwest Asia stretching from Egypt through the Levant and into Mesopotamia.

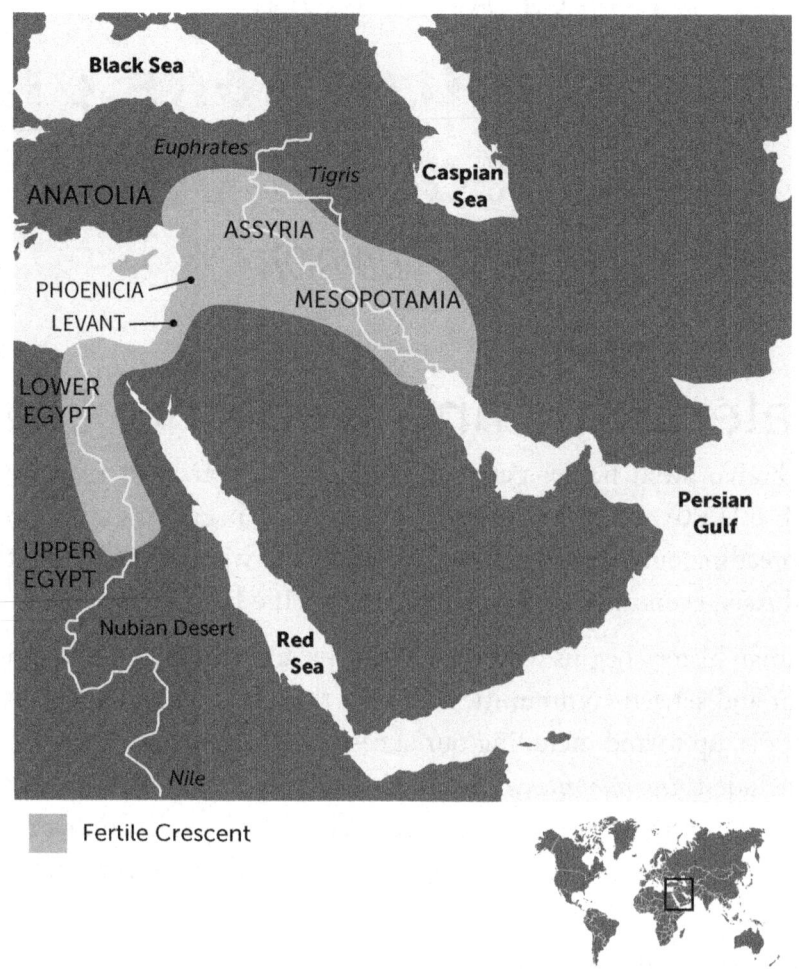

Figure 1.1. Fertile Crescent

Around 2,500 BCE (or possibly earlier) the **Sumerians** emerged in the Near East (eventually expanding into parts of Mesopotamia); developing irrigation and advanced agriculture, they were able to support settled areas that developed into city-states and eventually major cities like Uruk.

They also developed **cuneiform**, the earliest known example of writing to use characters to form words; early education, literary and artistic developments resulted such as the early poetry of *The Epic of Gilgamesh* and architectural achievements like ziggurats. Sumer featured city-states, the potter's wheel, early astronomy and mathematics, and religious thought. More advanced governance and administration was facilitated by the written language of cuneiform.

Eventually the Sumerians were overcome by Semitic-speaking, nomadic peoples in the Fertile Crescent: the result was the **AKKADIAN EMPIRE**, which grew to encompass much of the Levant, Mesopotamia, and parts of Persia. One of its major legacies was the Semitic Akkadian language, which adopted cuneiform.

Around the eighteenth century BCE, the Akkadians had given way to **BABYLONIA** in Southern Mesopotamia and **ASSYRIA** in the north. These two civilizations would develop roughly concurrently and remain at odds, with Babylonia eventually coming under Assyrian domination until the final defeat of Assyria by Babylonia in 612 BCE in the battle of **NINEVEH**, the Assyrian capital.

> **DID YOU KNOW?**
> Settled communities needed the reliable sources of food and fresh water a temperate climate could provide. Surpluses of food allowed for cultural and civilizational development, not just survival.

Before its defeat, Assyria had developed as a powerful city-state in northern Mesopotamia. The Assyrians had based much of their culture on the Sumerian and Akkadian legacies, contributing unique sculpture and jewelry, establishing military dominance, and playing an important role in regional trade. At odds with Babylonia over the centuries, the Assyrian Empire had grown to encompass most of the Fertile Crescent. The Assyrian identity persists to this day among the (widely persecuted) Assyrian people in Iraq, Syria, Turkey, and Iran.

Around 1200 BCE during a time of instability in Mesopotamia, the region became vulnerable to the **HITTITES** from Anatolia. The Hittites had developed in the Bronze Age but flourished in the **IRON AGE**, developing expertise in metallurgy to create strong weapons; they also mastered horsemanship and invented chariots. These technological developments made the Hittites a strong military power and a threat to both the Assyrians and later the Egyptians (see below); not only did these empires risk losing land but they also lost control of trade routes throughout the Fertile Crescent. Eventually Assyria grew strong enough to overcome the Hittites.

Like Assyria, Babylonia inherited the Akkadian language and used the Sumerian language in religious settings; it also inherited other elements of Sumerian civilization and developed them further. In the eighteenth century BCE, King Hammurabi in Babylonia had developed courts and an early codified rule of law—**THE CODE OF HAMMURABI**—which meted out justice on an equal basis: "an eye for an eye, a tooth for a tooth."

Babylonia continued settled, urban development supported by organized agriculture, warfare, administration and justice; **BABYLON** became a major ancient city. Babylonia developed more advanced astronomy, medicine, mathematics, philosophy, and art (particularly in working with clay, building bricks, and bas relief).

Furthermore, Babylonian civilization featured literature, developing the Sumerian poetry that was the basis for *the Epic of Gilgamesh* into the extended work we know today. (In fact, according to the Smithsonian, more lines from the epic have been discovered in stone fragments in Iraq as recently as 2011.) After the fall of Nineveh, Babylonia would control Mesopotamia until the fall of Babylon to the Persian Achaemenid Empire in Persia in 539 BCE (see below).

Meanwhile, development had been under way in the **NILE VALLEY** in ancient **EGYPT**. Known for their pyramids, art, and pictorial writing (**HIEROGLYPHS**), the ancient Egyptians emerged as early as 5000 BCE; evidence of Egyptian unity under one monarch, or **PHARAOH**, dates to the First Dynasty, around 3000 BCE

Despite the surrounding Sahara Desert, the fertile land on the banks of the Nile River lent itself to agriculture, and the early Egyptians were able to develop settled communities thanks to agriculture and irrigation. Civilizations developed on the Upper and Lower Nile, unifying under the early dynasties, which established the Egyptian capital at **MEMPHIS**. By the Fourth Dynasty, Egypt's civilizational institutions, written language, art, and architecture were well developed. It was during this period that the famous **PYRAMIDS** were erected at Giza; these structures were actually burial tombs for the Pharaohs Khufu, Khafre and Menkaure circa 2400 – 2500 BCE In addition, the religious framework of ancient Egypt had become established, with a complex mythology of various gods.

Following this period, around 2200 BCE Egypt became increasingly unstable; eventually fighters from the city of Thebes took over, establishing the Eleventh Dynasty. The subsequent Twelfth Dynasty took control of Nubia (now Sudan), an area rich in gold and other materials. Egypt grew in power; it reached its apex during the Eighteenth Dynasty, between 1550 and 1290 BCE Led by the powerful Pharaoh Thutmose III, Egypt expanded into the Levant.

Later, **KING AKHENATEN (AMENHOTEP IV)** abolished the Egyptian religion, establishing a cult of the sun—Aten—linked to himself. During this period Egypt saw a surge of iconoclastic art and sculpture. However, Akhenaten's successors, particularly Ramesses I and Ramesses II, founded the Nineteenth Dynasty and returned traditional values. Under **RAMESSES II**, Egypt battled the aggressive Hittites in the Levant, reaching a stalemate. Egypt eventually fell into decline, losing control of the Levant and eventually falling to Assyria.

QUICK REVIEW
What were the contributions of the early Middle Eastern civilizations? List several.

India

Meanwhile, early civilizations also developed farther east. The **INDUS VALLEY CIVILIZATIONS** flourished in the Indian Subcontinent and Indus and Ganges river basins. The **HARAPPAN** civilization was based in Punjab from around 3000 BCE The major cities of **HARAPPA** and **MOHENJO-DARO** feature grid systems indicative of detailed urban planning; they may be the earliest planned cities in the world. In addition, Harappan objects found in Mesopotamia reveal trade links between the civilizations.

Centuries later, concurrent with the Roman Empire, the **Gupta Empire** emerged in India. During this period, known as the Golden Age of India, the region was economically strong; there was active trade by sea with China, East Africa and the Middle East in spices, ivory, silk, cotton, and iron, which was highly profitable as an export.

The Guptas encouraged music, art, architecture, and Sanskrit literature and philosophy. While practitioners of Hinduism, the empire was tolerant of Buddhists and Jains. Organized administration and rule of law made it possible for **Chandragupta II** to govern a large territory throughout the Subcontinent. However, by 550, invasions from the north by the Huns and internal conflicts within the Subcontinent led to imperial decline.

China

In **China**, the **Shang Dynasty**, the first known dynasty, ruled the **Huang He** or **Yellow River** area around the second millennium BCE and developed the earliest known Chinese writing, which helped unite Chinese-speaking people throughout the region. Like the early civilizations in the Middle East, the Shang Dynasty featured the use of bronze technology, horses, wheeled technology, walled cities, and other advances beyond the Neolithic societies.

DID YOU KNOW?
Shared customs like the use of silkworms, jade, chopsticks, and the practice of Confucianism also indicate early Chinese unity.

Around 1056 BCE the **Zhou Dynasty** emerged. It succeeded the Shang and expanded Chinese civilization to the **Chiang Jiang** (Yangtze River) region. Under the Zhou Dynasty, China developed a social and political infrastructure in which family aristocracies controlled the country, with the capital at **Hao** (near **Xi'an**). Ancestral cults controlled tracts of land throughout the country in a hierarchy similar to later European feudalism, setting the foundation for hierarchical rule and social stratification.

The concept of the **Mandate of Heaven**, in which the emperor had a divine mandate to rule, emerged from the understanding that land was divinely inherited. The unstable period toward the end of the Zhou Dynasty was known as **the Spring and Autumn Period**; during this time **Confucius** lived (c. 551 – 479 BCE). His teachings would be the basis for Confucianism, the foundational Chinese philosophy emphasizing harmony and respect for hierarchy.

Following the chaotic **Warring States Period** (c. 475 – 221 BCE) the short-lived but influential Qin Dynasty emerged, unifying disparate Chinese civilizations and regions under the first Emperor, Qin Shihuangdi. This dynasty (221 – 206 BCE) was characterized by a centralized administration, expanded infrastructure, standardization in weights and measures, standardized writing, a standardized currency, and strict imperial control. The administrative bureaucracy established by the emperor was the foundation of Chinese administration until the twentieth century. In addition, the Emperor constructed the Great Wall of China; Emperor Qin Shihuangdi's tomb is guarded by the famous terracotta figurines. During the Qin Dynasty, China expanded as far south as Vietnam.

Figure 1.2. The Great Wall of China

Despite the short length of the Qin Dynasty, it had a lasting impact on Chinese organization. The Han Dynasty took over in 206 for the next 300 years (206 BCE – 220 CE), retaining Qin administrative organization and adding Confucian ideals of hierarchy and harmony. The Han prized education in the Confucian tradition and the idea that educated men should control administrative government began to take root in China. Women were not included in politics or administration.

The Americas

Prehistoric peoples migrated to the Americas from Asia during the Paleolithic period, and evidence of their presence dates to 13,000 years ago; remnants of the Clovis people dating to this time have been found in New Mexico. Recent findings in Canada suggest, however, that prehistoric peoples may have come to North America even earlier, about 13,300 years ago. Migration from Asia was gradual, probably occurring over hundreds or thousands of years; early humans likely crossed by land from Siberia to Alaska, while some may even have had naval capabilities and arrived by boat. Gradually, humans spread throughout the hemisphere.

From around 1200 BCE, the Olmec civilization developed on the Mexican Gulf Coast. Its massive sculptures reflect complex religious and spiritual beliefs. Later civilizations in Mexico included the Zapotecs, Mixtecs, Toltecs, and Mayas in the Yucatán peninsula. Throughout Mesoamerica, civilizations had developed irrigation to expand and enrich agriculture, similar to developments in the Fertile Crescent.

Meanwhile, in South America, artistic evidence remains of the Chavin, Moche, and Nazca peoples, who preceded the later Inca civilization and empire. The complex Chavin style, which focused on animals, went on to influence Andean art, while the Moche have left behind complicated ceramics comparable to Hellenic artifacts. The construction of the famous Nazca lines, enormous sketches in the ground only visible from the air, remains a mystery.

In North America, the remains of mounds in the Mississippi Valley region may be ancient spiritual structures.

Figure 1.3. Mississippi Mounds

EXAMPLES

1. What is required for a settled community?
   A) domesticated animals
   B) a source of fresh water
   C) technology
   D) weapons

2. The earliest known use of writing to use characters to form words was
   A) cuneiform, developed by the Egyptians.
   B) cuneiform, developed by the Sumerians.
   C) hieroglyphs, developed by the Egyptians.
   D) hieroglyphs, developed by the Sumerians.

3. The Shang and Zhou Dynasties are particularly relevant in Chinese history for their contributions in what?
   A) developing Chinese administration
   B) centralizing Chinese imperial power as symbolized through the terracotta figurines in the imperial tombs
   C) forming a Chinese identity through the development of written language, the Emperor's Mandate of Heaven, and fostering Confucianism
   D) ensuring China's safety by building the Great Wall of China

Answer Key

1. A) is incorrect. While domesticated animals can be a food source or facilitate production, they are not absolutely necessary for food production or surplus.

   B) is correct. Fresh water permits a reliable food source, which allows for settlement; people need not travel in search of food.

   C) is incorrect. While technology is useful and can improve quality of life, it is not absolutely necessary for a settled society.

   D) is incorrect. While weapons are useful for ensuring safety, they are not essential for establishing a settled society.

2. A) is incorrect. The Egyptians did not develop cuneiform.

   B) is correct. The Sumerians developed cuneiform.

   C) is incorrect. While the Egyptians did develop hieroglyphs, they were pictographs, or images that expressed meaning rather than characters that formed written versions of spoken words.

   D) is incorrect. The Sumerians did not develop hieroglyphs.

3. A) is incorrect. These developments occurred under the Qin Dynasty.

   B) is incorrect. The terracotta figurines are found in the tomb of the Qin Emperor Shihuangdi.

   C) is correct. Written Chinese developed under the Shang Dynasty, and the Mandate of Heaven emerged under the Zhou Dynasty; furthermore, traditions like the use of chopsticks also came about during these periods.

   D) is incorrect. Again, construction of the Great Wall of China began during the Qin Dynasty.

CHAPTER TWO
Civilization, Culture, and Religion
~ 600 BCE to 600 CE

Great Empires
PERSIA and GREECE

The **PERSIAN** emperor **CYRUS**, founder of the **ACHAEMENID EMPIRE**, conquered the Babylonians in the sixth century BCE. His son **DARIUS** extended Persian rule from the Indus Valley to Egypt, and north to **ANATOLIA** by about 400 BCE, where the Persians encountered the ancient **GREEKS**. Known for its fundamental impact on Western civilization to this day, neighboring Greek or **HELLENIC CIVILIZATION** included political, philosophical, and mathematical thought; art and architecture; and poetry and theater.

QUICK REVIEW
How is Greek philosophy and its focus on reason important in modern culture?

Greece was comprised of **CITY-STATES** like **ATHENS**, the first known **DEMOCRACY**, and the military state **SPARTA**. Historically these city-states had been rivals; however, they temporarily united to come to the aid of Ionian Greeks in Anatolia under Persian rule and drive Persia from Greece. In Anatolia, the Persian king **XERXES** led two campaigns against Greek forces. The Greeks held the Persians at bay, and much of Greece became unified under Athens following the war. It was during this period, the **GOLDEN AGE** of Greek civilization that much of the Hellenic art, architecture, and philosophy known today emerged.

The term *democracy* comes from the Greek word **DEMOKRATIA**—"people power." It was participatory rather than representative; officials were chosen by groups rather than elected. Athens was the strongest of the many small political bodies (in fact, the word *political* comes from the Greek word **POLIS** meaning "city-state" or "community"). The Persians had been decisively defeated at the battles of **MARATHON** (490 BCE) and **SALAMIS** (480 BCE) around 460 BCE Athens became a revolutionary democracy controlled by the poor and working classes under the Athenian leaders **PERICLES** and **EPHIALTES**.

In this period and into the fourth century BCE, the **Parthenon** was built, as were other masterpieces of ancient Greek sculpture and architecture. **Socrates** began teaching philosophy, influencing later philosophers like **Plato** who founded the Academy where figures like **Aristotle** emerged, establishing the basis for modern western philosophical and political thought. Playwrights like **Sophocles**, **Euripides**, and **Aeschylus** emerged; their work influenced later western literature.

Despite its status as a democracy, Athens was not fully democratic: women did not have a place in politics, and Athenians practiced slavery. Furthermore, those men eligible to participate in political life had to prove that both of their parents were Athenian (the criterion of double descent).

Toward the end of the fifth century BCE, Athens and Sparta were at odds once again during the **Peloponnesian War** (431 – 404 BCE), which involved most of the Hellenic world and ultimately crippled the Athenian democracy permanently. Instability permitted the rise of the northern state of Macedon; later in the fourth century BCE, Philip II of Macedonia was able to take over most of Greece. His son **Alexander** (later known as Alexander the Great) would go on to conquer Persia, spreading Greek civilization throughout much of Western and Central Asia.

ROME

Meanwhile, in Italy, the ancient Romans had begun consolidating their power. The city of **Rome** was founded as early as the eighth century BCE; it became strong thanks to its importance as a trade route for the Greeks and other Mediterranean peoples. Early Roman culture drew from the **Etruscans**, native inhabitants of the Italian peninsula, and the Greeks, from whom it borrowed elements of architecture, art, language, and even religion.

Originally a kingdom, Rome became a republic under **Lucius Junius Brutus** in 509 BCE As a **republic**, Rome elected lawmakers (senators) to the **Senate**. The Romans developed highly advanced infrastructure, including aqueducts and roads, some still in use today. Economically powerful Rome began conquering areas around the Mediterranean with its increasingly powerful military, expanding to westward to North Africa in the **Punic Wars** (264 – 146 BCE) against its rival **Carthage** (in present-day Tunisia). With conquest of territory and expansion of trade came increased slavery, and working class Romans (**Plebeians**) were displaced; at the same time, the wealthy ruling class (**Patricians**) became more powerful and corrupt. Resulting protest movements led by the tribunes **Gaius** and **Tiberius** led to legislative reform and republican stabilization, strengthening the republic by the first century BCE

The increasingly diversified republic, while militarily and economically strong, was still divided between the wealthy ruling class (the **Optimates**, or "the best") and the working, the poor, and the military (now calling themselves **Populare**, "the people," still favoring more democratization). As the Senate weakened due to its own corruption, the **First Triumvirate** of the military leaders **Gaius Julius Caesar** and **Gnaeus Pompeius Magnus (Pompey the Great)**, and the wealthy citizen **Marcus Licinius Crassus** consolidated their rule of the republic. Pompey and Crassus belonged to the Optimate class, while Julius Caesar, a popular military leader, was firmly of the Populare.

Caesar had proven himself in the widely chronicled conquest of **Gaul** (today, France), and was respected and beloved by the military for his personal devotion to his troops. Meanwhile, Crassus was the wealthiest man in Rome, controlling most of the political class; despite his wealth, he was not popular among the Populare and was not regarded as a military leader on the level of Caesar, though he had played a role in the defeat of the widespread slave rebellion led by the gladiator **Spartacus**. Pompey had led successful missions conquering territory for Rome in Syria and elsewhere in the Levant; he also took credit for defeating Spartacus, though he played less of a role than Crassus, causing a rift between the two.

With resentment between Crassus and Pompey over credit for the defeat of Spartacus, Crassus' insecurity over his perception as a military leader, and Caesar's popularity among the Populare, the Triumvirate was short-lived. Crassus was killed fighting the Parthians in Turkey in 53 BCE, at which point Pompey and Caesar declared war upon each other; the two fought in Greece where Pompey was defeated, fled to Egypt, and was assassinated.

Forcing the corrupt Senate to give him control, Caesar began to transition Rome from a republic (if, at that point, in name only) to what would become an empire. Caesar was assassinated by a group of senators led by **Brutus** and **Cassius** in 44 BCE; however, in that short time he had been able to consolidate and centralize imperial control. His cousin, **Marcus Antonius (Mark Antony)**, his friend **Marcus Aemilius Lepidus**, and his nephew **Gaius Octavius Thurinus (Octavian)** defeated Brutus and Cassius two years later at the Battle of Philippi, forming the **Second Triumvirate**.

Lepidus was sent from Rome to Hispania (Spain) and Africa while Mark Antony and Octavian split control of Rome between east and west, respectively. However, the two went to war after Antony became involved with the Egyptian queen **Cleopatra**, upsetting the balance of power; Octavian defeated Antony and Cleopatra, taking control of Rome in 31 BCE He took the name **Augustus Caesar** when the Senate gave him supreme power in 27 BCE, becoming the first Roman emperor and effectively starting the Roman Empire.

At this time, Rome reached the height of its power, and the Mediterranean region enjoyed a period of stability known as the **Pax Romana**. Rome controlled the entire Mediterranean region and lands stretching as far north as Germany and Britain, territory into the Balkans, far into the Middle East, Egypt, North Africa, and Iberia. In this time of relative peace and prosperity, Latin literature flourished, as did art, architecture, philosophy, mathematics, science, and international trade throughout Rome and beyond into Asia and Africa. A series of emperors would follow and Rome remained a major world power, but it would never again reach the height of prosperity and stability that it did under Augustus.

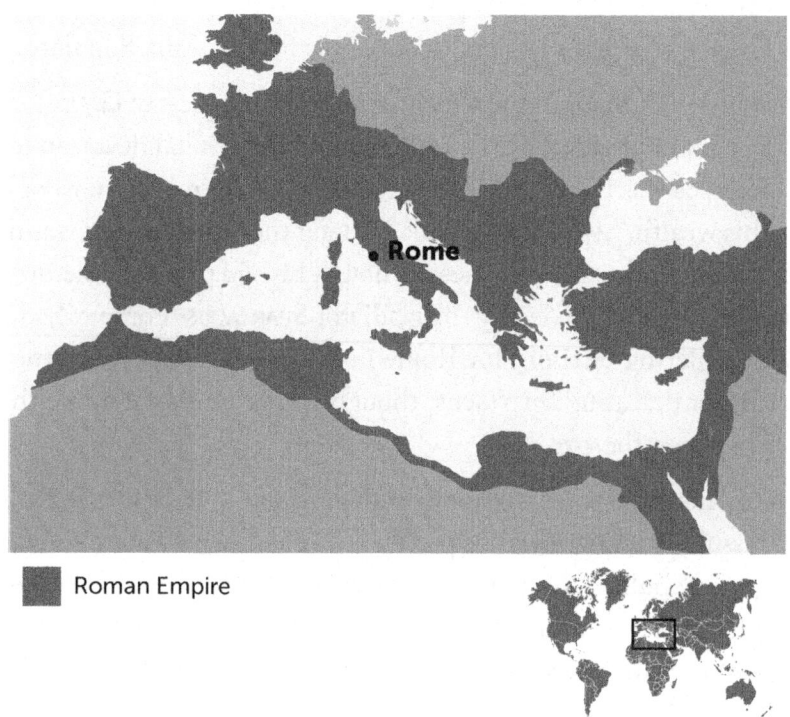

Figure 2.1. *Pax Romana*

It was during the time of Augustus that a Jewish carpenter named Jesus in Palestine began teaching that he was the son of the Jewish God, and that his death would provide salvation for all of humanity. Jesus was eventually crucified; followers of **Jesus Christ**, called Christians, preached his teachings throughout Rome. Despite the persecution of Christians, the concept of forgiveness of sin became popular and **Christianity** would eventually become the official religion of Rome. Christianity's universal appeal and applicability to people of diverse background would allow it to spread quickly.

By 300 CE, Rome was in decline. Following a series of unstable administrations, **Diocletian** (284 – 305 CE) took over as Emperor, effectively dividing the empire into two: the Western Roman Empire and the Eastern Roman Empire. Diocletian reestablished some stability and more effective administration, creating a loose power-sharing agreement throughout the empire. The Christian **Constantine** took over the eastern half of the empire, establishing a new capital at **Constantinople**, Christianity as an official religion, and building the **Hagia Sophia**. However, the ambitious Constantine reconquered the Western Roman Empire and reunited the empire in 324 CE; the capital remained at Constantinople, and the balance of power and stability shifted to the east.

This political shift enabled the western (later, Catholic) Church to gain power in Rome. One of Jesus Christ's followers, Peter, was considered to be the first **Pope**, or leader of Christian ministry. He had been executed in Rome in 67 CE after a lifetime of spreading the religion; ever since, the city has been a base of Christianity and home to the **Vatican**, the seat of the Catholic Church. Over time, the Catholic Church would become one of the most powerful political entities in the world; even today, following several schisms in Christianity, there are around one billion Catholics worldwide.

Figure 2.2. Hagia Sophia

The western part of the Roman Empire gradually fell into disarray: a weakening Rome had created security agreements with different European clans like the **Anglo-Saxons**, the **Franks**, the **Visigoths**, the **Ostrogoths**, and the **Slavs**, among others, to protect its western and northern borders. Eventually, these groups rebelled against the government and what was left of the Roman Empire in the west finally fell. In Western Europe, the last Roman emperor was killed in **476 CE**, marking the end of the empire. The west dissolved into territories controlled by these and other tribes.

> **DID YOU KNOW?**
> These clans and others from Central Asia were able to defeat the Romans in the north and settle in Europe, thanks to their equestrian skills, superior wheels, and iron technology.

Meanwhile the eastern part of the Roman Empire, with its capital at Constantinople, evolved into the unified **Byzantine Empire**. The Byzantine emperor **Justinian** (527 – 565 CE) re-conquered parts of North Africa, Egypt, and Greece, established rule of law, and reinvigorated trade with China. Ultimately, the Byzantines would control varying amounts of land in Anatolia, the Levant, and North Africa until the conquest of Constantinople by the Ottoman Turks in 1453.

He also continued the establishment of Christianity, rebuilding the Hagia Sophia, and eliminating the last vestiges of the Greco-Roman religion and competing Christian sects. However, over time, differences in doctrine between the church in Rome and

Christians in Constantinople would give way to a schism, creating the Roman Catholic Church and the Greek Orthodox Church, as discussed.

During the early Middle Ages in Europe and the Byzantine Empire, the roots of another civilization were developing in the Arabian Peninsula. In the seventh century, the Prophet **MUHAMMAD** began teaching **ISLAM**. Based on the teachings of Judaism and Christianity, Islam presented as the final version of these two religions, evolving its own set of laws and philosophical teachings. Like Christianity, it held universal appeal.

Conversion was (and is) simple, as is practicing the faith; the religion transcends national and ethnic differences; and it offers the possibility of redemption, forgiveness of sins, and a pleasant afterlife. Furthermore, due to ideological similarities, Muslims were willing to accept Jews and Christians as **PEOPLE OF THE BOOK** rather than forcing their conversion, enabling their later conquest of Southwest Asia and facilitating relationships in the region. Leading a small group of followers out of the desert to conquer the Arabian cities of Mecca and Medina, where they would establish the beginnings of the **CALIPHATE**, the political embodiment of the society envisioned in Islam, Muhammad's followers would later come to control Southwest Asia and North Africa.

World Religions

JUDAISM

Judaism was the first **MONOTHEISTIC** religion; its adherents believe in only *one* god. It is believed that God came to the Hebrew Abraham and that the Hebrews – the Jews – were to be God's *chosen people*, to serve as an example to the world. Later, **MOSES** would lead the Jews out of slavery in Egypt, and God gave him **TEN COMMANDMENTS** or laws, the basis of what would become Judeo-Christian and Islamic moral codes. Notably, these moral codes applied to all people, including slaves. In addition to confirming the singular nature of God, the Ten Commandments laid out social rules for an organized society under that one god: to refrain from theft and murder and to honor one's parents, among others. Judaism's holy texts are the **TORAH** and the **TALMUD** (religious and civil law). There are different branches of Judaism with varying teachings, including Orthodox, Conservative and Reform Judaism, among others.

CHRISTIANITY

In Roman Palestine, the Jewish carpenter **JESUS** taught that he was the son of the singular, Jewish God. Christians believe that Jesus came to suffer and die for the sins of mankind so that all mankind may be forgiven for sin. He gained many followers for his teaching; ultimately, he was crucified. Christians believe that Jesus rose from the dead three days later (the **RESURRECTION**) and ascended to heaven. Christians believe that Jesus was miraculously born from a virgin mother (the **VIRGIN MARY**) and believe in the **HOLY TRINITY**, that God is made up of the Father, the Son, and the Holy Spirit, all parts of one God. The **CATHOLIC CHURCH** is led by the Pope and descended from the early western Church that followed the **SCHISM OF 1054**, when theological disagreement divided the Church into the western Catholic Church and **EASTERN ORTHODOX** Christianity. Later in Western Europe, the **PROTESTANT REFORMATION** gave rise to other forms of Protestant, or non-Catholic, Christianity.

ISLAM

Islam is rooted in the Arabian Peninsula. Muslims believe that the angel Gabriel spoke to the **PROPHET MUHAMMAD**, transmitting the literal word of **ALLAH** (God), which was later written down as the **QUR'AN**. Muhammad is considered by Muslims to be the final prophet of the god of the Jews and Christians, and Islam shares similar moral teachings. Islam recognizes leaders like Abraham, Moses, and Jesus, but unlike Christianity, views Jesus as a prophet, not as the son of God. The Prophet Muhammad was a religious, military, and political leader; in conquering the Arabian Peninsula and later other parts of the Middle East, he protected the People of the Book, or Jews and Christians. After his death, discord among his followers resulted in the **SUNNI-SHI'A SCHISM** over his succession and some teachings; to this day, deep divisions remain between many Sunnis and Shi'ites. Like Judaism, Islam also has a book of legal teachings called the **HADITH**.

> **QUICK REVIEW**
> Explain Monotheism. What are the major monotheistic religions and who are their main figures?

HINDUISM

Major tenets of Hindu belief include **REINCARNATION**, or that the universe and its beings undergo endless cycles of rebirth and **KARMA**, that one creates one's own destiny. The soul is reincarnated until it has resolved all karmas, at which point it attains **MOKSHA**, or liberation from the cycle. Hindus believe in multiple divine beings. Religion is based in the **VEDIC SCRIPTURES**; other important texts include the **UPANISHADS**, the **MAHABHARATA**, and the **BHAGAVAD GITA**. Hinduism is the primary religion in India and is intertwined with the **CASTE SYSTEM**, the hierarchical societal structure.

BUDDHISM

In Buddhism, the Prince **SIDDHARTHA GAUTAMA** is said to have renounced worldly goods and lived as an ascetic in what is today northern India, seeking **ENLIGHTENMENT** around the third century BCE. Buddhism teaches that desire – the ego, or self – is the root of suffering, and that giving up or **TRANSCENDING** material obsessions will lead to freedom, or **NIRVANA**—enlightenment. While Buddhism originated in India, it is practiced throughout Asia and the world. The main Buddhist schools of theology are the

> **QUICK REVIEW**
> Compare Hinduism and Buddhism.

Mahayana, which is prevalent in northern and eastern Asia (Korea, parts of China, Mongolia), and **Theravada**, dominant in Southeast Asia and Indian Ocean regions. **Vajrayana** Buddhism is central to Tibetan Buddhism.

CONFUCIANISM

Confucianism teaches obedience and adherence to tradition in order to maintain a harmonious society. Ideally, practicing integrity and respecting wisdom would ensure that authority would be used for beneficial purposes. Confucius himself was a Chinese scholar in the sixth century BCE; his philosophy would go on to inform Chinese culture for centuries.

EXAMPLES

1. The Athenian concept of democracy embraced which of the following?
   A) participatory democracy, in which local groups made decisions directly by vote, permitting the poor to dominate the process rather than the elites
   B) an anonymous electoral process similar to that of the United States in which officials were elected
   C) people of all backgrounds, so that all residents of Athens had a stake in the political process
   D) an educated electorate in order to ensure the best possible decision-making

2. How did Julius Caesar rise to and retain power?
   A) He invaded Rome with his armies from Gaul, and used his military resources to control the Empire.
   B) He was elected president of the Senate by the people thanks to political support throughout the Republic.
   C) He took control of the Senate and maintained control of Rome thanks to his charisma and widespread popularity among the people.
   D) As part of the Triumvirate, he was guaranteed a leadership position and the support of Crassus and Pompey.

3. Following the death of Muhammad, Muslim leadership became so divided that the religious movement eventually became split into Sunnis and Shi'ites. This was due to
   A) disagreement over secession to his place as leader.
   B) disagreement about the importance of conquest.
   C) disagreement over the theological nature of Islam.
   D) disagreement over whether to accept Christians and Jews as *People of the Book*.

4. Which of the following explains why the Eastern Roman Empire remained stable and transitioned to the Byzantine Empire while Rome in Western Europe collapsed?

   A) Feudalism contributed to instability in Western Europe, and so that part of the continent disintegrated into a series of small states.

   B) The schism between the Catholic and Greek Orthodox Churches tore the empire apart.

   C) Muslims entered Constantinople and took it from Christian Roman control.

   D) Imprudent alliances in the West led to Roman collapse, while strong leadership and centralization in the East developed a new empire.

Answer Key

1. **A) is correct.** The Athenian notion of *demokratia*, or people power, was participatory rather than representative.

   B) is incorrect. Voting was not anonymous in Athens.

   C) is incorrect. Only free male Athenians, who could prove Athenian parentage, could take part in the process.

   D) is incorrect. Education was not required to participate.

2. A) is incorrect. While Julius Caesar was a powerful military leader, he did not take power purely through military means. Furthermore, when he came to power, Rome was still nominally a republic, not an empire.

   B) is incorrect. There was no president of the Senate and he was not elected as such.

   C) is correct. The Senate's corruption and weakness, and Caesar's popularity with the plebeians, support of the military, and strong leadership, enabled him to take and retain control.

   D) is incorrect. Caesar, Pompey, and Crassus were rivals and their alliance was one of convenience. Furthermore, both Pompey and Crassus were dead by the time Caesar took power.

3. **A) is correct.** The Meccan elites believed that they should take over leadership of Islam and continue the movement beyond the Arabian Peninsula; however Ali and Fatima, Muhammad's cousin and daughter, believed Ali was Muhammad's rightful successor as his closest living male relative.

   B) is incorrect. All the Muslim leadership believed that they were called to spread Islam beyond the Arabian Peninsula.

   C) is incorrect. While the sides had some differences and while major theological differences eventually did develop between Sunni and Shia Islam, the original break was mainly based on the dispute over succession.

   D) is incorrect. Accepting the People of the Book was not at issue.

4. A) is incorrect. Feudalism actually helped stabilize Western Europe.

   B) is incorrect. The divisions between the Catholic and Greek Orthodox Churches were not integral to the collapse of Rome.

   C) is incorrect. Islam had not yet appeared as a religious movement.

   D) is correct. Security alliances with Germanic and Gothic tribes left Western Rome vulnerable to their attack; meanwhile in the east, centralized power in Constantinople and strong leadership, particularly under Justinian, led to the rise of the powerful Byzantine Empire.

CHAPTER THREE
Feudalism through the Era of Expansion
~ 600 CE to 1450 CE

The Middle Ages in Europe

The Byzantine Empire remained a strong civilization and a place of learning. Constantinople was a commercial center, strategically located at the Dardanelles, connecting Asian trade routes with Europe. Later, missionaries traveled north to Slav-controlled Russia, spreading Christianity and literacy. The ninth-century missionaries Saints Cyril and Methodius are credited with developing what would become the **Cyrillic** alphabet used in many Slavic languages. In 988 CE, the Russian Grand Prince of Kiev, **Vladimir I**, converted to Christianity and ordered his subjects to do so as well. Russian Christianity was influenced by the Byzantine doctrine, what would become Greek Orthodox Christianity.

Despite the chaos in Western Europe, the Church in Rome remained strong, becoming a stabilizing influence. However, differences in doctrine between Rome and Constantinople became too wide to overcome. Beginning in 1054, a series of **schisms** developed in the now-widespread Christian religion between the Roman Catholic Church and the Greek Orthodox Church over matters of doctrine such as the role of the Pope and papal authority, the use of leavened versus unleavened bread in religious services, and some theological concepts. Eventually the two would become entirely separate churches.

In Europe, the early Middle Ages (or **Dark Ages**) from the fall of Rome to about the tenth century, was a chaotic, unstable, and unsafe time. What protection and stability existed were represented and maintained by the Catholic Church and the feudal system.

Society and economics were characterized by decentralized, local governance, or **feudalism**, a hierarchy where land and protection were offered in exchange for loyalty. Feudalism was the dominant social, economic, and political hierarchy of the European middle ages from the time of Charlemagne (discussed further below).

In exchange for protection, **VASSALS** would pledge **FEALTY**, or **PAY HOMAGE** to **LORDS**, landowners who would reward their vassals' loyalty with land, or **FIEFS**. Economic and social organization consisted of **MANORS**, self-sustaining areas possessed by lords but worked by peasants. The peasants were **SERFS**, not slaves but entirely free. Tied to the land, they worked for the lord in exchange for protection; however they were not obligated to fight. Usually they were also granted some land for their own use. While not true slaves, their lives were effectively controlled by the lord.

DID YOU KNOW?
There were limits on sovereign power, however. In 1215, long before the revolution, English barons forced King John to sign the Magna Carta, which protected their property and rights from the king and was the basis for today's parliamentary system in that country.

Warriors who fought for lords, called **KNIGHTS**, were rewarded with land and could become minor lords in their own right. Lords themselves could be vassals of other lords; that hierarchy extended upward to kings or the Catholic Church. The Catholic Church itself was a major landowner and political power. In a Europe not yet dominated by sovereign states, the Pope was not only a religious leader, but also a military and political one.

Small kingdoms and alliances extended throughout Europe, and stable trade was difficult to maintain. The **CELTS** controlled Britain and Ireland until the invasion of the **SAXONS**; around 600 CE, the Saxons conquered Britain while the Celts were pushed to Ireland, Scotland, and Brittany in northwest France. While the Church was gaining power, it was insecure in Italy as the **GERMANIC TRIBES** vied for control in Germany and France. Monasteries in Ireland and England retained and protected classical documentation in the wake of the fall of Rome and insecurity in Italy. The Germanic tribes themselves were threatened by Asian invaders like the **HUNS**, increasing instability in central and eastern parts of Europe, where **SLAVS** also fought for supremacy north of Byzantium.

One exception to the chaos was the Scandinavian **VIKING** civilization. From the end of the eighth century until around 1100, the Vikings expanded their influence from Scandinavia, ranging from the Baltic Sea to the East to the North Sea through the North Atlantic, thanks to their extraordinary seafaring skills and technology. The Vikings traded with the Byzantine Empire and European powers; Byzantine and Middle Eastern artifacts have been found among Viking excavations in Scandinavia. They traveled to and sometimes raided parts of Britain, Ireland, France, and Russia.

The Icelandic **ERIK THE RED** established a settlement in Greenland, and his son **LEIF ERIKSON** may have traveled as far as North America. In addition to military prowess and advanced shipbuilding technology, the Vikings had a complex religion with a pantheon of gods and well-developed mythology; they also developed a literary canon of **SAGAS** in Old Norse, the basis of some Scandinavian languages today. Viking achievements have been documented in literature from other European cultures like the Anglo-Saxons, as well as the Arab historian Ibn Fadlan.

Meanwhile, by the eighth century the North African **MOORS**, part of the expanding Islamic civilization, had penetrated Iberia and were a threat to Christian Europe.

Charles Martel, leader of the **Franks** in what is today France, defeated the Moors at the **Battle of Tours (or Poitiers)** in 732 CE, effectively stopping any further Islamic incursion into Europe. The Christian Martel had previously consolidated his control of France, leading the Franks in victory over the Bavarians, Frisians, and other tribes and supporting their conversion to Christianity. Instability followed Charles Martel's death, however, and **Charlemagne**, the son of a court official, eventually took over the Merovingian kingdom following disputes over succession, complicated by the Merovingian traditions.

Charlemagne was able to maintain Frankish unity and consolidate his rule, extending Frankish control into Central Europe and defending the **Papal States** in central Italy. In what is considered the reemergence of centralized power in Europe, parts of Western and Central Europe were organized under Charlemagne, who was crowned emperor of the Roman Empire by Pope Leo III in 800 CE. While in retrospect this seems long after the end of Rome, at the time many Europeans still perceived themselves as somehow still part of a Roman Empire. Today Charlemagne's rule is referred to as the **Carolingian Empire**.

Charlemagne brought stability to Western and Central Europe during a period when two powerful, non-Christian, organized civilizations—the Vikings in the north and the Islamic powers in the south—threatened what was left of western Christendom, and when insecurity was growing to the east with the decline of the Byzantines and the emergence of the Umayyad Caliphate based in Damascus. His reign strengthened the Roman Catholic Church and enabled the reemergence of Roman and Christian scholarship that had been hidden in English and Irish monasteries.

It was also under Charlemagne that the feudal system became truly organized, bringing more stability to Western Europe. The Catholic Church would dominate Europe from Ireland towards Eastern Europe—an area of locally controlled duchies, kingdoms, and alliances. In 962 CE, **Otto I** became emperor of the **Holy Roman Empire** in Central Europe, a confederation of small states which remained an important European power until its dissolution in 1806.

While the Holy Roman Empire remained intact, the Carolingian Empire did not. While Spain and Portugal remained under Muslim control, France dissolved into small fiefdoms and territories. Meanwhile, England and Scotland were controlled by Norsemen (Vikings), especially Danish settlers, and various local Anglo-Saxon rulers, the remnants of the Germanic tribes that had come to rule Europe and led to the fall of Rome.

In 1066, **William the Conqueror** left Normandy in northwest France. The **Normans** established organization in England, including a more consolidated economy and kingdom supported by feudalism. They also consolidated Christianity as the local religion. English possessions included parts of France, nominally a kingdom but consisting of smaller territories with some level of independence. Intermarriage and conquest resulted in English control of Anjou and Bordeaux in France; William had brought control of French Brittany with him when he arrived on the island of Britain. Conflict between Britain and France would continue for several centuries, while rulers in Scandinavia and Northwest Europe consolidated power.

The Islamic World

Meanwhile, in the wake of the decline of the Byzantine Empire, **Arab-Islamic empires** characterized by brisk commerce, advancements in technology and learning, and urban development arose in the Middle East.

Before the rise of Islam in the seventh century, the Arabian Peninsula was located at the intersection of the Byzantine Empire, a diverse collection of ethnicities, ruled by Greek Orthodox Christians, and the **Sasanians** (Persians), who practiced **Zoroastrianism**. Both of these empires sought to control trade with Central and eastern Asia along the Silk Road; they also sought to establish trade ties with Christian **Axum** (Ethiopia).

In Arabia itself, Judaism, Christianity, and animist religions were practiced by the Arab majority. The Prophet **Muhammad** was born in Mecca around 570; he began receiving messages from God (Allah), preaching them around 613 as the last affirmations of the monotheistic religions and writing them as the **Qur'an**, the Islamic holy book. Driven from **Mecca** to Medina in 622, Muhammad and his followers were able to recapture the city and other major Arabian towns by the time of his death, establishing Islam and Arab rule in the region.

DID YOU KNOW?
A caliph was considered both a political and a religious leader.

After Muhammad's death in 632 CE, his followers, led by the first caliph **Abu Bakr**, went on to conquer land beyond Arabia north into the weakening Byzantine Empire. The well-organized Muslim Arabs, based in Arabia, led incursions into Syria, the Levant, and Mesopotamia, taking over these territories. Thanks to military, bureaucratic, and organizational skill as well as their ability to win over dissatisfied minorities, the Arabs eventually isolated the Byzantines to parts of Anatolia and Constantinople and crushed the Persian Sasanians.

Muhammad's cousin and son-in-law **Ali**, his wife **Fatima** (Muhammad's eldest daughter), and their followers, had always believed that the leader of the Muslim Arabs should be a blood relative of Muhammad. Since Muhammad had no sons, the logical choice was Ali. However, the Meccan elites had felt differently, and the popular Abu Bakr was chosen as the first caliph.

DID YOU KNOW?
The first four caliphs are known as the *Rashidun,* or rightly-guided ones.

Abu Bakr was succeeded by the second caliph Umar; upon his death the third caliph Uthman took over. Widely accused of corruption, Uthman was murdered in 656. The Islamic leadership finally settled on Ali to take over as the fourth caliph. However, others in power felt differently. **Muawiya**, based in Damascus, led the opposition to Ali; this conflict is at the heart of the **Sunni-Shi'a Schism**.

Ali and Fatima established their base in Kufa, in Mesopotamia. Unable to come to an agreement, the Arabs became embroiled in the First Civil War (656 – 661) over leadership; the conflict ended when Ali was murdered in 661. Unrest continued, and the bloody massacre of Ali's son Hussein and his family in 680 in Karbala triggered the Second Civil War (680 – 692).

DID YOU KNOW?
Ali's followers called themselves the *party of Ali* or, in Arabic, the *shiat Ali*, which is the origin of the word *Shia* or *Shi'ite Muslims*.

The violence of these years cemented divisions in Islam, and **SHI'ITE ISLAM** emerged in Mesopotamia. The Shi'ites believed that Ali was the rightful heir to Muhammad's early Islamic empire, and maintained a focus on martyrdom, especially that of Ali and Hussein. The followers of the Meccan elites became known as **SUNNIS**, "orthodox" Muslims with a focus on community rather than genealogy. Over the centuries, other differences in theology and history would develop.

Muawiya is considered the first caliph of the **UMAYYAD CALIPHATE** (empire), named for the leading Meccan tribe that had supported Muhammad from the beginning. The Arabs already controlled Arabia; by 750, they would control parts of Iberia, North Africa, Egypt, Arabia, the Levant, Mesopotamia, Persia, Armenia, and parts of Central Asia into Transoxiana (Uzbekistan) and the Indus River Valley (parts of Pakistan). Spain, or **AL-ANDALUS**, was settled as early as 711.

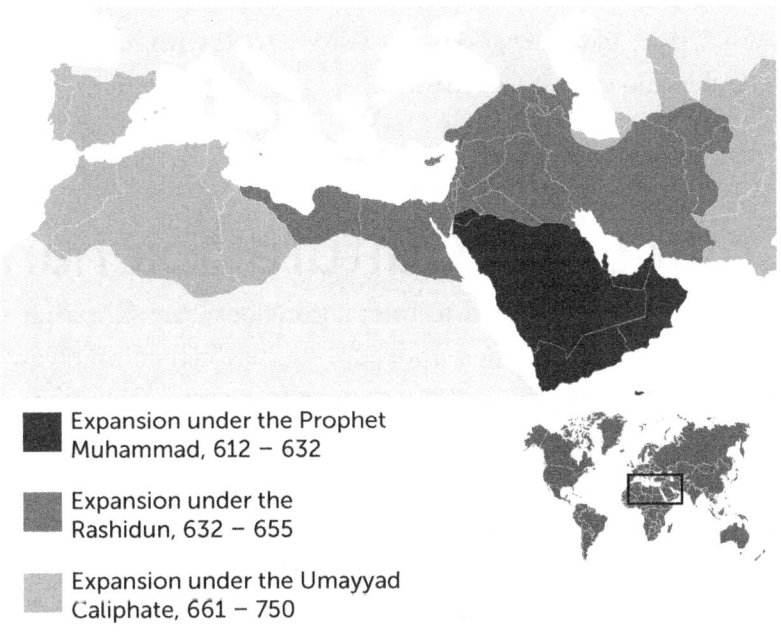

Figure 3.1. Islamic Expansion

Ongoing conflict among Arab elites resulted in the **ABBASID CALIPHATE** in 750 CE, based in Baghdad. The Umayyad were overthrown by the Arab-Muslim Abbasid family, which established a new capital in Baghdad. The caliph **AL-MUTASIM** professionalized the military, creating professional soldiers called **MAMLUKS**, freed slaves usually of Turkish origin. It was thought they would be more loyal with no family or national ties. The mamluks helped al-Mutasim consolidate imperial control and improve tax collection. Abbasid administration was also highly organized, allowing efficient taxation.

The administration and stability provided by the caliphates fostered an Arabic literary culture. Stability permitted open trade routes, economic development, and cultural interaction throughout Asia, the Middle East, North Africa, and parts of Europe. Furthermore, the Abbasid ruler **AL-MAMUN** fostered cultural and scientific study.

Thanks to the universality of the Arabic language, scientific and medical texts from varying civilizations—Greek, Persian, Indian—could be translated into Arabic and shared throughout the Islamic world. Arab thinkers studied Greek and Persian astronomy and engaged in further research. Arabs studied mathematics from around the world and developed algebra, enabling engineering, technological, and architectural achievements. Finally, Islamic art is well known for its geometric designs.

Around this time, the **SONG DYNASTY** (960 – 1276) controlled most of China. Under the Song, China experienced tremendous development and economic growth. Characterized by increasing urbanization, the Song featured complex administrative rule, including the difficult competitive written examinations required to obtain prestigious bureaucratic positions in government. Most traditions recognized as Chinese emerged under the Song, including the consumption of tea and rice and common Chinese architecture. The Song engaged not only in overland trade along the Silk Road, exporting silk, tea, ceramics, jade, and other goods, but also sea trade with Korea, Japan, Southeast Asia, India, Arabia and even East Africa.

Conflict and Cultural Exchange

Cultural exchange was not limited to interactions between Christian Europeans, Egyptians, and Levantine Muslims. Indeed, international commerce was vigorous along the **SILK ROAD**, trading routes which stretched from the Arab-controlled Eastern Mediterranean to Song Dynasty China, where science and learning also blossomed. The Silk Road reflected the transnational nature of Central Asia: the nomadic culture of Central Asia lent itself to trade between the major civilizations of China, Persia, the Near East, and Europe. Buddhism and Islam spread into China. Chinese, Islamic, and European art, pottery, and goods were interchanged between the three civilizations—early globalization. The Islamic tradition of the **HAJJ**, or the pilgrimage to Mecca, also spurred cultural interaction. Islam had spread from Spain throughout North Africa, the Sahel, the Middle East, Persia, Central Asia, India, and China; peoples from all these regions traveled and met in Arabia as part of their religious pilgrimage.

QUICK REVIEW
How did the Silk Road and Islam both contribute to global cultural exchange?

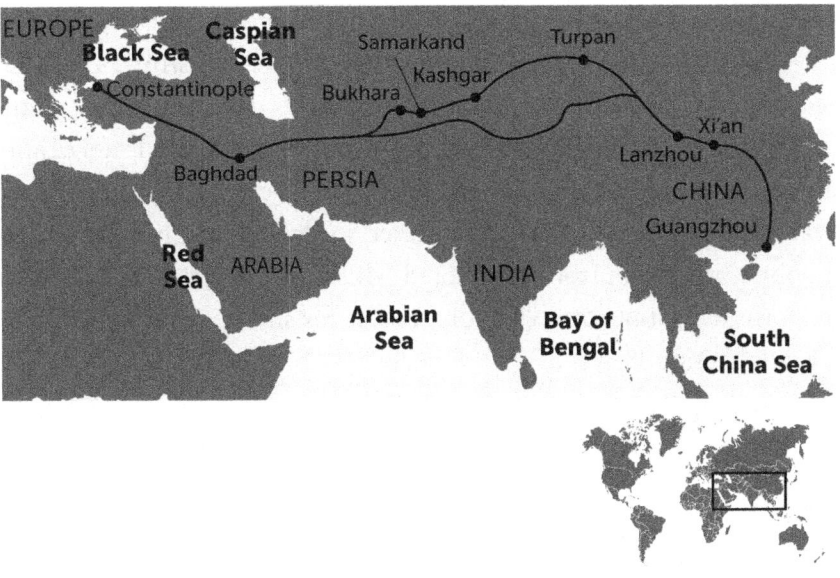

Figure 3.2. The Silk Road

Islam also spread along trans-Saharan trade routes into West Africa and the Sahel. Brisk trade between the gold-rich **Kingdom of Ghana** and Muslim traders based in Morocco brought Islam to the region around the eleventh century. The Islamic **Mali Empire** (1235 – 1500), based farther south in **Timbuktu**, eventually extended beyond the original Ghanaian boundaries all the way to the West African coast, and controlled the valuable gold and salt trades. It became a center of learning and commerce. At the empire's peak, the ruler **Mansa Musa** made a pilgrimage to Mecca in 1324. However, by 1500, the **Songhai Empire** had overcome Mali and eventually dominated the Niger River area.

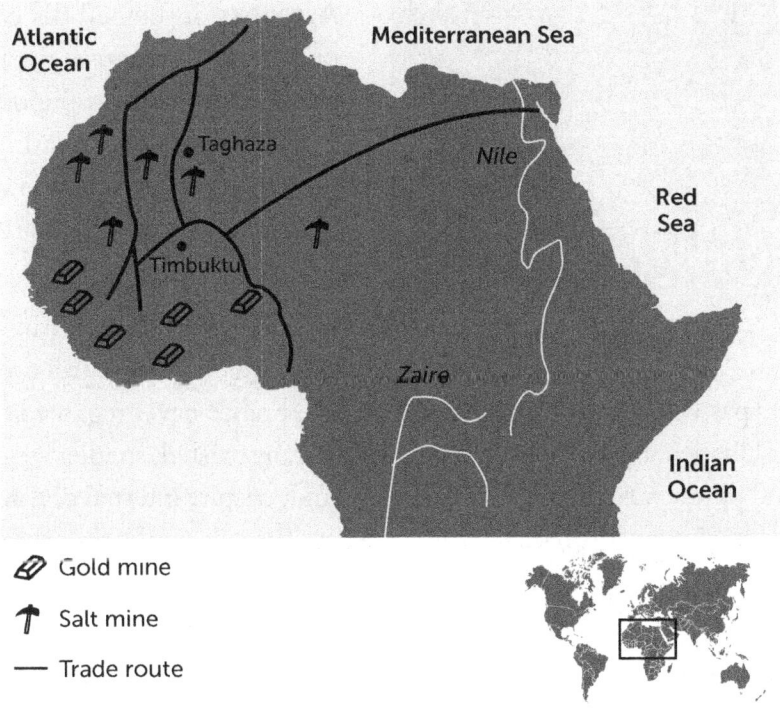

Figure 3.3. Trans-Saharan Trade Routes

Feudalism through the Era of Expansion

Loss of Byzantine territory to the Islamic empires meant loss of Christian lands in the Levant—including Jerusalem and Bethlehem—to Muslims. In 1095 CE, the Byzantine Emperor asked **Pope Urban II** for help to defend Jerusalem and protect Christians. With a history of Muslim incursions into Spain and France, anti-Muslim sentiment was strong in Europe and Christians there were easily inspired to fight them in the Levant, or **Holy Land**; the Pope offered lords and knights the chance to keep lands and bounty they won from conquered Muslims (and Jews) in this **Crusade**. He also offered Crusaders **indulgences** – forgiveness for sins committed in war and guarantees they would enter heaven.

Figure 3.4. The Great Mosque Cordoba

Meanwhile, towards the end of the tenth century, the Abbasid Caliphate was in decline. The Shi'ite **Fatimids** took control of Syria and Egypt, addressing the Shi'ite claim to the caliphate. Other groups took control of provinces in Mesopotamia, Arabia, and Central Asia. In Spain, **Abd al-Rahman III** (891 – 961) had defied the Abbasids and the Fatimids, taking over **al-Andalus** (Spain) himself and fostering a unique Hispano-Arabic culture where intellectual pursuits bloomed. Based in Cordoba, Rahman was responsible for the Great Mosque. In Muslim Spain, the famous Muslim philosopher **Averroes** developed his commentary on Aristotle; likewise, the Jewish **Maimonides** developed religious and philosophical thought. Conflict persisted with the Carolingians and with smaller Christian kingdoms in northern Spain, however.

In Western Europe, instability had been ongoing as control over continental territories passed between England and France. France never regained the strength it had under Charlemagne; while the French monarchy existed, smaller states remained powerful and power was decentralized. In England, despite internal divisions, organization accelerated upon William's 1066 conquest. The two civilizations were at odds.

Despite conflict in Europe, Christians found they had more in common with each other than with Muslims, and were able to unite to follow the Pope's call to arms to fight in the Middle East. The decline of the Abbasids had left the Levant vulnerable, and

Christian Crusaders were able to establish settlements and small kingdoms in Syria and on the Eastern Mediterranean coast, conquering major cities and capturing Jerusalem by 1099 in the **First Crusade** as called for by Pope Urban II (see above).

The Crusades continued over several centuries. In 1171, The Kurdish military leader **Salah al-Din** (Saladin) abolished the Fatimid Caliphate; in 1187 he reconquered Jerusalem, driving European Christians out for good. Following Salah al-Din's death and a succession of rulers, elite slave troops took power. The **Mamluks** (1250 – 1517), whose roots traced back to Abbasid Caliph al-Mutasim's fighting force, controlled Egypt; later they would defeat the Mongols in 1260, protecting Egypt and North Africa from the Mongol invasions.

While the ongoing Crusades never resulted in permanent European control over the Holy Land, they did open up trade routes between Europe and the Middle East, stretching all the way along the Silk Road to China. This increasing interdependence led to the European Renaissance.

Ongoing interactions between Europeans and Muslims exposed Europeans, who could now afford them thanks to international trade, to improved education and goods. However, the **Bubonic (Black) Plague** also spread to Europe as a result of global exchange, killing off a third of its population from 1347-1351. The plague had a worldwide impact: empires fell in its wake.

DID YOU KNOW?
During the Hundred Years' War, Joan of Arc led the French in the 1429 Battle of Orléans, reinvigorating French resistance to English incursions.

Back in Europe, conflict reached its height throughout the thirteenth and fourteenth centuries known as the **Hundred Years' War** (1337 – 1453). France was in political chaos during the mid-fourteenth century, decentralized and at times without a king; suffering the effects of the Black Plague; vulnerable to English attack; and periodically under English rule. While conflict would continue, England lost its last territory in France, Bordeaux, in 1453 to the French **King Charles VII**.

In **al-Andalus** (Spain), despite some coexistence between Christians and Muslims under Muslim rule, raids and conflict were ongoing during the lengthy period of the **Reconquista**, which did not end until 1492 when Christian powers took Grenada. From the zenith of Muslim rule under **Abd al-Rahman**, Christian raids continued, as did shifting alliances between the small kingdoms of Christian Spain and Portugal. By the second half of the thirteenth century, the only remaining Muslim power in Iberia was Grenada. By the fifteenth century, small Christian Spanish kingdoms were vying for dominance. The marriage of **Ferdinand** of Castilla and **Isabella** of Aragon in 1479 connected those two kingdoms, and the monarchs were able to complete the Reconquista by taking Grenada and uniting Spain.

DID YOU KNOW?
Ferdinand and Isabella launched the Inquisition, an extended persecution of Jews and Jewish converts to Christianity who continued to practice Judaism in secret. Jews were tortured, killed, and exiled; their belongings and property were confiscated. Muslims were also persecuted and forced to convert to Christianity or exiled.

Feudalism through the Era of Expansion

Empires in Transition

Beyond Egypt and the Levant, the collapse of the Abbasid Caliphate led to instability and decentralization of power in Mesopotamia, Persia, and Central Asia; smaller sultanates (territories ruled by sultans, regional leaders) emerged, and production and economic development declined. **TANG DYNASTY CHINA** closed its borders and trade on the Silk Road declined. In the eleventh century, the nomadic **SELJUKS**, Turks from Central Asia, nominally took over the region from Central Asia through parts of the Levant. However, the Seljuks lacked effective administration or central authority.

DID YOU KNOW?
During this period, Persian-influenced Sufi (mystical) Islam and poetry developed; Shi'ite theology and jurisprudence also developed as part of a strengthening independent Shi'ite identity.

Despite the lack of political cohesion, Islam remained a unifying force throughout the region, and political instability and decentralization paradoxically allowed local culture to develop, particularly Persian art and literature. Furthermore, Islam was able to thrive during this period: local religious leaders (**ULAMA**) had taken up community leadership positions following the loss of any powerful central authority, and Islam became a guiding force in law, justice, and social organization throughout the region. Yet political decentralization ultimately left the region vulnerable to the Mongol invasions of the twelfth and thirteenth centuries.

In the Near East, the **MONGOL INVASIONS** destroyed agriculture, city life and planning, economic patterns and trade routes, and social stability. After some time, new patterns of trade emerged, new cities rose to prominence, and stability allowed for prosperity, but the Mongol invasions dealt a blow to the concept that Islam was inherently favored by God.

The **MONGOL EMPIRE** was based in Central Asia; led by **GENGHIS KHAN**, the Mongols expanded throughout Asia thanks to their abilities in horsemanship and archery. Despite the rich history of transnational activity across Asia, the continent was vulnerable. Central Asia lacked one dominant culture or imperial power; Southwest Asia was fragmented following the decline of the Abbasids. These weaknesses, along with the disorganization of the Seljuks and the remnants of the Byzantines, allowed the Mongols to take over most of Eurasia—ultimately they controlled Pannonia (Hungary) through the Middle East, Persia, Central Asia, Northern and Western China, and Southeast Asia.

Likewise, in China, the Mongols destroyed local infrastructure, including the foundation of Chinese society and administration—the civil service examinations. However, in order to govern the vast territory effectively, the Mongols in China took a different approach. Genghis Khan's grandson **KUBLAI KHAN** conquered China and founded the Mongol **YUAN DYNASTY** in 1271.

Despite abolishing the examinations until 1315, the Yuan Dynasty maintained most of the administrative policy of the preceding Song Dynasty, including the Six Ministries, the Secretariat, and provincial administrative structure. Additionally, in spite of

Mongol distrust of Confucianism and Confucian administrator-scholars, Kublai Khan educated his son in the Confucian tradition. The Yuan did, however, upend Chinese social hierarchy; placing Mongols at the top, followed by non-ethnic Han Chinese and then Han Chinese.

Mongol attempts at imperial expansion in China into Japan and Southeast Asia, coupled with threats from the Black Plague, financial problems, and flooding, led to the decline of the Yuan Dynasty and the rise of the native Chinese **Ming Dynasty** in 1368. **Zhu Yuanzhang** led the Chinese to victory and ruled as the first Ming emperor from Nanjing; the capital later moved to Beijing in 1421. Ming China controlled land throughout Asia, accepting tribute from rulers in Burma, Siam (Thailand), Annam (Vietnam), Mongolia, Korea, and Central Asia.

The Ming reasserted Chinese control and continued traditional methods of administration; however the construction of the **Forbidden City**, the home of the Emperor in Beijing, helped consolidate imperial rule. The Ming also emphasized international trade; demand for ceramics in particular, in addition to silk and tea, was high abroad, and contact with seafaring traders like the Portuguese and Dutch in the sixteenth century was strong. The Ming also encouraged trade and exploration by sea; the Chinese explorer **Zheng He** traveled to India, Sri Lanka, and Asia.

Despite some decline in Mongol hegemony throughout Asia, the military leader **Timur** (also known as **Tamerlane**), a Mongol descendant from Transoxania (now Uzbekistan) began conquering land in the area around 1364. By 1383, he occupied Moscow and turned toward Persia. Up to the turn of the century he had conquered Persia, Mesopotamia, much of the Caucasus, and Delhi. In the early fifteenth century, Timur took Syria, invaded Anatolia, and extracted tribute from Egypt. He died in 1405 on an expedition to China.

While rarely spending too much time in one place, Timur had contributed to the development of the capital of his empire, **Samarkand**, enriching Central Asia culturally.

Mongol decline was not only isolated to China; in Russia, **Ivan the Great** brought Moscow from Mongol under Slavic Russian control. In the late fifteenth century, Ivan had consolidated Russian power over neighboring Slavic regions. Despite Muscovy's status as a vassal state, Ivan, through both military force and diplomacy, achieved Moscow's independence in 1480. Turning Russian attention toward Europe, he set out to bring other neighboring Slavic and Baltic lands, including Poland-Lithuania and later, parts of Ukraine, under Russian rule. Ivan achieved a centralized, consolidated Russia that was the foundation for empire and a sovereign nation that sought diplomatic status with Europe.

A century later, **Ivan the Terrible** set out to expand Russia further, to integrate it into Europe, and to strengthen Russian Orthodox Christianity. Named the first **tsar**, or emperor, Ivan reformed government further, strengthening centralization and administrative bureaucracy and disempowering the nobility. He led the affirmation of orthodox Christianity, calling councils to organize the church and to canonize Russian saints. Ivan also reorganized the military, including promoting officials based on merit rather than status. However, overextension of resources and his oppressive entourage, the **OPRICHNINA**, depopulated the state and gave him the reputation as a despotic ruler. However, despite his weaknesses, Ivan's reforms strengthened the apparatus of the Russian state; he also expanded and improved foreign policy and relations, and developed Russian culture and religion.

Farther south in Central Asia, one of Timur's descendents, **BABUR**, laid claim to Timur's dominions and would found the **MUGHAL EMPIRE** of India. Despite his Mongol roots, Babur identified as Turkic due to his tribal origins, and enjoyed support from the powerful Ottoman Empire in Turkey (see below). In 1525, Babur set out for India. By 1529, he had secured land from Kandahar in the west to Bengal in the east; his grandson, **AKBAR**, would consolidate the empire, which at the time consisted of small kingdoms. The Mughals would rule India until the eighteenth century and nominally control parts of the country until British takeover in the nineteenth century.

> **DID YOU KNOW?**
> The Mughal emperor Shah Jahan built the Taj Mahal in 1631.

During Mughal rule in India, the Ming Dynasty fell in China and the Qing took over. In 1644, the Ming fell to a peasant revolt; the **MANCHU**, a non-Han group from the north, took the opportunity to seize Beijing and take the country. Despite their status as non-Han Chinese, the Manchu were accepted; thus began the **QING DYNASTY**. They would also be China's last imperial rulers, losing power in 1911.

The first Qing emperor, the **KANGXI EMPEROR**, promoted the arts and education. Under the reign of the **QIANLONG EMPEROR** (1736 – 1796), China grew to its largest size, including Tibet, Mongolia, Xinjiang, and parts of Russia. It became the dominant power in East Asia and a successful multi-ethnic state. Like the Kangxi Emperor, the Qianlong Emperor was a patron of the arts.

Meanwhile, in Persia, the **SAFAVIDS** emerged in 1501 in the wake of the Timurid Empire. This dynasty would rule from Azerbaijan in the west through to modern-day Pakistan and Afghanistan. A major rival of the Ottoman Empire, the Safavids were a stabilizing force in Asia. Following Sufism, the Safavids supported art, literature, architecture, and other learning. Their organized administration brought order and stability to Persia throughout their rule, which lasted until 1736, when the **QAJAR DYNASTY** took over.

Despite the instability inland, Indian Ocean trade routes had continued to function since at least the seventh century. These oceanic routes connected the Horn of Africa, the East African Coast, the Arabian Peninsula, Southern Persia, India, Southeast Asia, and China. The ocean acted as a unifying force throughout the region, and the **MONSOON WINDS** permitted Arab, Persian, Indian, and Chinese merchants to travel to East Africa in search of goods such as ivory and gold—and slaves.

Despite the civilizational achievements of the Islamic empires, Tang and later Ming Dynasty China, and the Central Asian and Indian empires that would emerge from the Mongols, the **EAST AFRICAN SLAVE TRADE** remained vigorous until the nineteenth century. Arabs, Asians and other Africans kidnapped African people and sent them to lives of slavery throughout the Arab world and South Asia. Later, Europeans would take part in the trade, forcing Africans into slavery in colonies throughout South and Southeast Asia, and on plantations in Indian Ocean islands such as Madagascar.

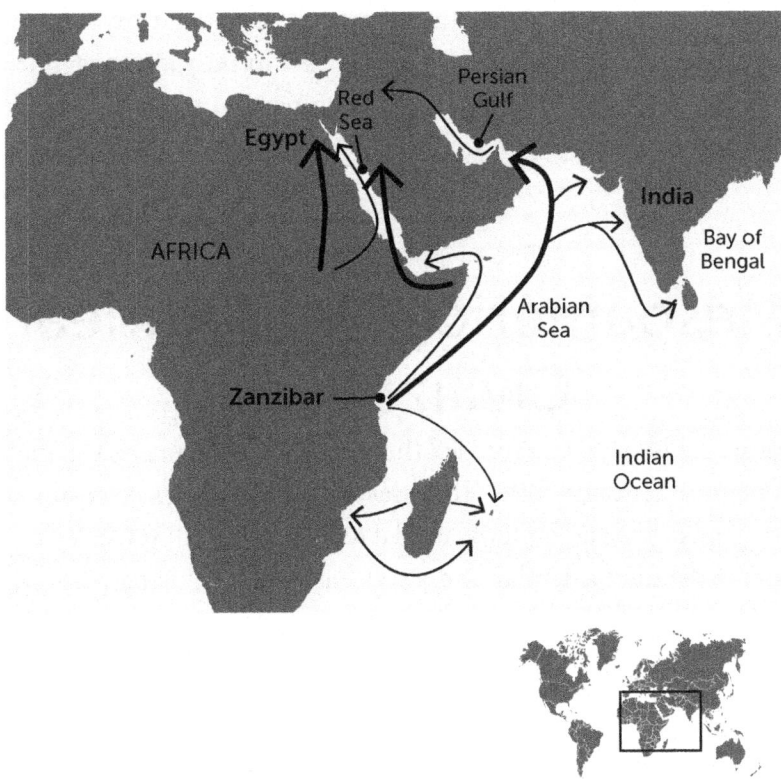

Figure 3.5. Indian Ocean Slave Trade

The major East African port was **ZANZIBAR**, from which slaves, gold, coconut oil, ivory, and other African exports made their way to Asia and the Middle East. However, enslaved persons from Sub-Saharan Africa were also forced north overland to markets in **CAIRO**, where they were sold and dispersed throughout the Arab-Islamic, Fatimid, and Ottoman empires.

Islam also spread throughout the African coast and inland; given the cosmopolitan nature of the coastline, the **SWAHILI** language adopted aspects of Arabic and other Asian languages.

Further north, the Ottoman Turks represented a threat to Central Europe. Controlling most of Anatolia from the late thirteenth century, the Ottomans spread west into the Balkans, consolidating their rule in 1389 at the **BATTLE OF KOSOVO**. In 1453 they captured Istanbul, from which the **OTTOMAN EMPIRE** would come to rule much of the Mediterranean world.

Under the leadership of **MEHMED THE CONQUEROR** in the fifteenth century and his successors, the Ottomans would conquer Pannonia (Hungary), North Africa, the

Caucasus, the Levant and Mesopotamian regions, western Arabia, and Egypt. Under **Suleiman the Magnificent** (1520-1566), the Ottoman Empire consolidated control over the Balkans, the Middle East, and North Africa and would hold that land until the nineteenth century.

The capture of Istanbul (Constantinople) had represented the true end of the Byzantine Empire; the remaining Christian Byzantines, mainly isolated to coastal Anatolia, Constantinople, and parts of Greece, fled to Italy, bringing Greek, Middle Eastern and Asian learning with them and enriching the emerging European Renaissance.

Mesoamerican and Andean Civilizations

In the Americas, the **Maya**, who preceded the Aztecs in Mesoamerica, came to dominate the Yucatan peninsula around 300. They developed a complex spiritual belief system accompanied by relief art, and built pyramidal temples that still stand today. In addition, they developed a detailed calendar and a written language using pictographs similar to Egyptian hieroglyphs; they studied astronomy and mathematics. Maya political administration was organized under monarchial city-states from around 300 until around 900, when the civilization began to decline.

Throughout Mayan history there is evidence of interaction with the Mesoamerican city-state of **Teotihuacan**, a major city likely comprised of various Mesoamerican peoples such as Toltecs, Mixtecs, Zapotecs, some Mayans, and other peoples. By around 1400, two major empires dominated Central and South America: the Incas and the Aztecs. These two empires would be the last indigenous civilizations to dominate the Americas before European colonization of the Western Hemisphere.

As smaller Mesoamerican civilizations had weakened and collapsed, the **Aztecs** had come to dominate Mexico and much of Mesoamerica. Their military power and militaristic culture allowed the Aztecs to dominate the region and regional trade in precious objects like quetzal bird feathers. The main city of the Aztec empire, **Tenochtitlan**, was founded in 1325 and, at its height, was a major world city home to several million people.

Aztec civilization was militaristic in nature and divided on a class basis: it included slaves, indentured servants, serfs, an independent priestly class, military, and ruling classes. However, it did allow for upward mobility, especially for those

Figure 3.6. Statue of Quetzalcoatl

who had proven themselves in battle. The Aztecs shared many beliefs with the Mayans; throughout Mesoamerica the same calendar was used. Central in the Aztec religion was worship of the god **Quetzalcoatl**, a feathered snake.

Meanwhile, in the Andes, the **Incas** had emerged. Based in **Cuzco**, the Incas had consolidated their power and strengthened in the area, likely due to a surplus of their staple crop maize, around 1300. They were able to conquer local lords and, later, peoples further south, thanks in part to domesticated llamas and alpacas which allowed the military to transport supplies through the mountains.

Inca engineers built the citadel of **Machu Picchu** and imperial infrastructure, including roads throughout the Andes. Thanks to highly developed mountain agriculture, they were able to grow crops at high altitudes and maintain waystations on the highways stocked with supplies, keeping track of them through a system called *QUIPUS*, knotted cords. In order to subdue local peoples, they moved conquered groups elsewhere in the empire and repopulated conquered areas with Incas.

EXAMPLES

1. Despite the violence of the Crusades, they were also beneficial for Europe in that they
   - A) resulted in substantial, long-term land gains for European leaders in the Middle East.
   - B) introduced European powers to the concept of nation-states, the dominant form of political organization in the Middle East.
   - C) exposed Europe to Islamic and Asian science, technology, and medicine.
   - D) enhanced tolerance of Islam throughout Europe.

2. Which of the following was a result of the rise of the Ottoman Turks?
   - A) Christian Byzantines left Constantinople for Western Europe, bringing classical learning with them.
   - B) The Ottomans were able to conquer the Balkans, the Levant and eventually North Africa and the Middle East, establishing a large Islamic empire.
   - C) The Ottomans represented an Islamic threat to European Christendom, given their grip on the Balkan Peninsula.
   - D) all of the above

Answer Key

1. A) is incorrect. While Europeans retained some territory in the Middle East, this was temporary.

   B) is incorrect. Nation-states did not become a form of governance in Europe for several centuries; furthermore, they were not a form of political organization in the Middle East.

   C) is correct. Europeans who traveled to the Levant to fight returned home with beneficial knowledge and technology.

   D) is incorrect. Christian Europe was not tolerant of Islam.

2. A) is incorrect. Byzantine scholars did leave Constantinople and bring classical learning to Europe, especially Rome; this reintroduction of the classics would go on to influence the Renaissance. However, the other answer choices also apply, so this answer is incomplete.

   B) is incorrect. At its height under Suleiman the Magnificent, the Ottoman Empire stretched from Morocco through Anatolia and the Levant to Persia. However, the other answer choices also apply, so this answer is incomplete.

   C) is incorrect. The Ottomans represented a serious threat to Europe for centuries, as they controlled the Balkans and much of Pannonia; they even besieged Vienna twice. However, the other answer choices also apply, so this answer is incomplete.

   D) is correct. All of the answer choices apply.

CHAPTER FOUR
Globalization
~1450 to 1750

The European Renaissance

The **Renaissance**, or *rebirth*, included the revival of ancient Greek and Roman learning, art, and architecture. However, the roots of the Renaissance stretched farther back to earlier interactions between Christendom, the Islamic World, and even China, during the Crusades and through Silk Road trade. Not only did the Renaissance inspire new learning and prosperity in Europe, enabling exploration, colonization, profit, and later imperialism, but it also led to scientific and religious questioning and rebellion against the Catholic Church and, later, monarchical governments.

It is important to note that Russia would not experience these cultural changes until the eighteenth century, when **Peter the Great** and **Catherine the Great** copied modern European culture, modernized the military, and updated technology, including building the new capital city of **St. Petersburg**, a cultural center.

Reinvigoration of classical knowledge was triggered in part by Byzantine refugees from the Ottoman conquest of Constantinople, including scholars who brought Greek and Roman texts to Italy and Western Europe. The fall of Constantinople precipitated the development of **humanism** in Europe, a mode of thought emphasizing human nature, creativity, and an overarching concept of truth in all philosophical systems (the concept of **syncretism**). Emerging in Italy, the seat of the Catholic Church, humanism was supported by some popes, including Leo X. However in the long term it represented a threat to religious, especially Catholic, orthodoxy, as it allowed for the questioning of religious teaching. Figures associated with humanism included Dante, Petrarch, and Erasmus. Ultimately humanism would be at the root of the Reformation of the sixteenth century.

Art, considered not just a form of expression but also a science in itself, flourished in fifteenth century Italy, particularly in **Florence**. Major figures who explored anatomy in sculpture, design and perspective, and innovation in architecture included Leonardo da

Vinci, Bramante, Michelangelo, Rafael, and Donatello. Leonardo is particularly known for his scientific pursuits in addition to artistic achievement. While artists worked throughout Italy and found patrons in the Vatican among other places, the Florentine **Medici family** funded extensive civic projects, construction, décor, and public sculpture throughout Florence, supporting Renaissance art in that city.

Meanwhile, scholars like Galileo, Isaac Newton, and Copernicus made discoveries in what became known as the **Scientific Revolution**, rooted in the scientific knowledge of the Islamic empires, which had been imported through economic and social contact initiated centuries prior in the Crusades. Scientific study and discovery threatened the power of the Church, whose theological teachings were often at odds with scientific findings and logical reasoning.

> **QUICK REVIEW**
> The Scientific Revolution changed European thinking. What was the impact of using reason and scientific methodology rather than religion to understand the world?

Also in the mid-fifteenth century, in Northern Europe, **Johann Gutenberg** invented the printing press; the first book to be published would be the Bible. With the advent of printing, texts could be more widely and rapidly distributed, and people had more access to information beyond what their leaders told them. Combined with humanism and increased emphasis on secular thought, the power of the Church and of monarchs who ruled by divine right was under threat. Here lay the roots of the **Enlightenment**, the basis for reinvigorated European culture and political thought that would drive its development for the next several centuries—and inspire revolution.

Transnational cultural exchange had also resulted in the transmission of technology to Europe. During the sixteenth century, European seafaring knowledge, navigation, and technology benefitted from Islamic and Asian expertise; European explorers and traders could now venture beyond the Mediterranean. Portuguese and Dutch sailors eventually reached India and China, where they established ties with the Ming Dynasty. Trade was no longer dependent on the Silk Road. Improved technology also empowered Europeans to explore overseas, eventually landing in the Western Hemisphere, heretofore unknown to the peoples of Eurasia and Africa.

Colonization of the Western Hemisphere

Interest in exploration grew in Europe during the Renaissance period. Technological advancements made complex navigation and long-term sea voyages possible, and economic growth resulting from international trade drove interest in market expansion. Global interdependence got a big push from Spain when King Ferdinand and Queen Isabella agreed to sponsor **Christopher Columbus'** exploratory voyage in 1492 to find a sea route to Asia, in order to speed up commercial trade there. Instead, he stumbled upon the Western Hemisphere, which was unknown to Europeans, Asians, and Africans to this point.

Columbus landed in the Caribbean; he and later explorers would claim the Caribbean islands and eventually Central and South America for Spain and Portugal. However, those areas were already populated by the major American civilizations.

The Aztec ruler **Montezuma II** led the Aztecs during their first encounter with Spain; explorer **Hernan Cortés** met with him in Tenochtitlan after invading other areas of Mexico in 1519. Due to Spanish superiority in military technology, Montezuma attempted to compromise with Cortes; however, Cortés, seeking wealth and prestige in Mexico, had unlawfully left the Spanish stronghold of Cuba, disobeying Spanish colonial authorities. Thus in no position to compromise with the Aztecs, a few days later Cortés arrested Montezuma and took over the city. Spain was especially interested in subduing the Aztec religion, which included ceremonies with human blood and human sacrifice, and in controlling Mexican and Mesoamerican gold. Spain then began the process of colonizing Mexico and Central America, and the Aztec Empire collapsed.

In South America, as in Mexico and Central America, the Spanish were interested in economic exploitation and spreading Christianity, accessing the continent in the early sixteenth century. In 1533, the Spanish conquistador **Francisco Pizzaro** defeated the Inca king **Atahuallpa** and installed a puppet ruler, marking the decline of the Inca Empire. While the empire remained nominally intact for several years, the Spanish desecrated important religious artefacts—like mummies important for ancestor worship—installed Christianity, and took economic and political control of the region.

Spain took over the silver- and gold-rich Mesoamerican and Andean territories, and the Caribbean islands where sugar became an important cash crop. Thus developed **mercantilism**, whereby the colonizing or **mother country** took raw materials from the territories they controlled for the colonizers' own benefit. Governments amassed wealth through protectionism and increasing exports at the expense of other rising colonial powers. This eventually involved developing goods and then selling them back to those colonized lands at an inflated price. The **encomienda** system granted European landowners the "right" to hold lands in the Americas and demand labor and tribute from the local inhabitants. Spreading Christianity was another important reason for European expansion. Local civilizations and resources were exploited and destroyed.

> **QUICK REVIEW**
> What was destructive about the encomienda system?

The **Columbian Exchange** enabled mercantilism to flourish. Conflict and illness brought by the Europeans—especially **smallpox**—decimated the Native Americans, and the Europeans were left without labor to mine the silver and gold or to work the land. **African slavery** was their solution.

Slavery was an ancient institution in many societies worldwide; however, with the Columbian Exchange slavery came to be practiced on a mass scale the likes of which the world had never seen. Throughout Africa and especially on the West African coast,

Europeans traded for slaves with some African kingdoms and also raided the land, kidnapping people. European slavers took captured Africans in horrific conditions to the Americas; those who survived were enslaved and forced to work in mining or agriculture for the benefit of expanding European imperial powers.

The Columbian Exchange described the **TRIANGULAR TRADE** across the Atlantic: European slavers took kidnapped African people from Africa to the Americas, sold them at auction and exchanged them for sugar and raw materials; these materials were traded in Europe for consumer goods, which were then exchanged in Africa for slaves, and so on.

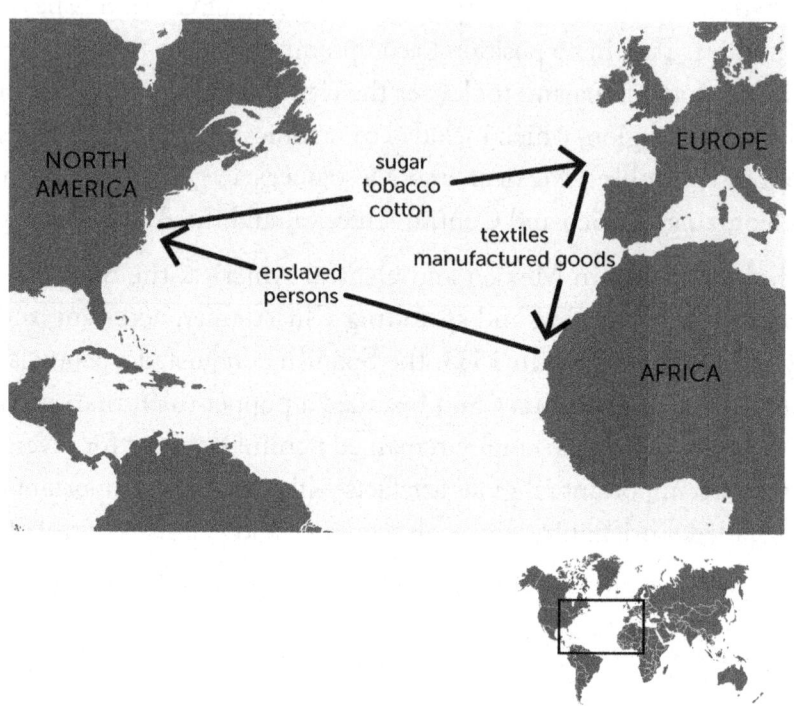

Figure 4.1. Triangular Trade

Enslaved Africans suffered greatly, forced to endure ocean voyages crammed on unsafe, unhygienic ships, sometimes among the dead bodies of other kidnapped people, only to arrive in the Americas to a life of slavery in mines or on plantations. Throughout this period, Africans did resist both on ships and later, in the Americas; **MAROON COMMUNITIES** of escaped slaves formed throughout the Western Hemisphere, the **UNDERGROUND RAILROAD** in the nineteenth-century United States helped enslaved persons escape the South, and **TOUSSAINT L'OUVERTURE** led a successful slave rebellion in Haiti, winning independence from the French for that country in 1791.

However, the slave trade continued for centuries. The colonies and later independent countries of the Western Hemisphere continued to practice slavery until the nineteenth century; oppressive legal and social restrictions based on race continue to affect the descendants of slaves to this day throughout the hemisphere.

During the eighteenth century, Spain and Portugal were preeminent powers in global trade thanks to colonization and **IMPERIALISM**, the possession and exploitation of land overseas. However, Great Britain became an important presence on the seas; it would later dominate the oceans throughout the nineteenth century.

Though Britain would lose its territories in North America after the American Revolution, it maintained control over the resource-rich West Indies. The kingdom went on to dominate strategic areas in South Africa, New South Wales in Australia, Mauritius in the Indian Ocean, and Madras and Bengal in the Indian Subcontinent, among other places. Later, in the nineteenth century, Britain would expand its empire further. Likewise, France gained territory in North America and in the West Indies; despite losses to Britain in the eighteenth century, that country would also expand its own global empire in the nineteenth century.

Armed Conflicts
REFORMATION and NEW EUROPE

While Spain and Portugal consolidated their hold over territories in the Americas, conflict ensued in Europe. With the cultural changes of the Renaissance, the power of the Catholic Church was threatened; new scientific discoveries and secular Renaissance thought were at odds with many teachings of the Church. The Catholic monk **MARTIN LUTHER** wrote a letter of protest to the Pope in 1517 known as the **NINETY-FIVE THESES**, outlining ways he believed the Church should reform; his ideas gained support, especially among rulers who wanted more power from the Church. Triggering the **REFORMATION**, or movement for reform of the Church, Luther's ideas led to offshoots of new versions of Christianity in Western Europe, separate from the Orthodox Churches in Russia and Greece. Protestant thinkers like Luther and **JOHN CALVIN** addressed particular grievances, condemning the **INFALLIBILITY** of the Pope (its teaching that the Pope was without fault) and the selling of **INDULGENCES**, or guarantees of entry into heaven.

The English **KING HENRY VIII** developed the Protestant **CHURCH OF ENGLAND**, further consolidating his own power, famously allowing divorce and marrying several times himself. The reign of Henry VIII, of the **HOUSE OF TUDOR**, initiated a chain of events leading to the consolidation of Protestantism in England, and eventually civil war and the empowerment of Parliament.

In Britain, religious and ethnic diversity between Protestant England and Scotland, and Catholic Ireland, made the kingdom unstable. The Catholic **MARY QUEEN OF SCOTS**, who was the daughter of the Scottish King James V and half French, had been betrothed to Henry VIII's son Edward. However her guardians canceled the arrangement, causing conflict with England. She temporarily married Francis of France, uniting Scotland with that Catholic country; however he quickly died from illness. Mary then married her Protestant cousin the Earl of Darnley, with whom she had a son, **JAMES**. Darnley forced her to abdicate the Scottish throne in 1567 and she fled to England, seeking safety with her Protestant cousin **Elizabeth I**, daughter of Henry VIII and queen of England. Her son, still a baby, became **King James VI** of Scotland.

The Tudor Queen Elizabeth imprisoned the Catholic Mary in England as she—and her son—represented a threat to her power. Not only was James' male sex a liability for Elizabeth's inheritance to the throne, but their religious identities as Catholics threatened Elizabeth's hold over the Catholics of England and Scotland, as well as her tenuous grip on Catholic Ireland. In 1587, Elizabeth had Mary executed following revelations of a Catholic plot to overthrow Elizabeth. Yet on Elizabeth's death in 1603, James succeeded Elizabeth as **King James I** of England and Ireland, ushering in the **House of Stuart**.

> **DID YOU KNOW?**
> The Gunpowder Plot to blow up the House of Lords and execute King James in the process was planned by Catholic fighters for the fifth of November, 1605. This plot was conceived by a group including the famous Guy Fawkes, who represents rebellion to this day; the saying "Remember, remember the fifth of November" comes from this plan.

James I attempted to balance the diverse ethnic and religious groups in England, Scotland, and Ireland, including the Catholic majority in Ireland and the Calvinist Scots, who disagreed on many points with the more liberal Church of England (Anglicans). Despite his efforts at maintaining a delicate political balance, instability grew. In fact, despite James' roots in Catholicism, his mother having been the Catholic Mary, oppression of Catholics continued.

Furthermore, James' daughter married into the Bohemian royal family, forcing English involvement in the Thirty Years' War as that family lost power to Catholics in Central Europe—foreign involvement James was loath to initiate. His son **Charles I** continued the anti-Catholic conflict in 1625 upon his succession to the throne; however, upon his withdrawal in 1630, conservative Protestants in England and Scotland (**Puritans**) began to suspect a royal movement to weaken Protestantism and even restore Catholicism in the kingdom. Many began moving to North America as a result.

Conflict between Protestants and Catholics was fierce on the Continent as well. The **Thirty Years' War** (1618 – 1648) began in Central Europe between Protestant nobles in the Holy Roman Empire who disagreed with the strict Catholic **Ferdinand II**, king of Bohemia and eventually archduke of Austria and king of Hungary (what was not under Ottoman domination). Elected Holy Roman Emperor in 1619, Ferdinand II was a leader of the **Counter-Reformation**, attempts at reinforcing Catholic dominance throughout Europe during and after the Reformation in the wake of the Renaissance and related social change. Ferdinand was also closely allied with the Catholic **Hapsburg** Dynasty, which ruled Austria and Spain.

Later interference in 1625 by Protestant Denmark and Sweden in Poland and Germany stirred further anti-Catholic discontent among local nobles in Germany, who yearned for independence from the imperial Holy Roman Empire. Despite Danish, Dutch, Swedish, and British support, the imperial military leader **Albrecht von Wallenstein** took control of most Protestant German states and Denmark. Ferdinand II issued the **EDICT OF RESTITUTION**, restoring rebellious Protestant German territory to imperial, Catholic control. 1629 also marked the defeat of Denmark as an important European power at that point in history.

Protestant Sweden engaged in further conflict with Catholic Poland. Polish political ambition drove it to take advantage of instability throughout the region, venturing east into Russia until the 1634 **PEACE OF POLYANOV**; it then battled Sweden for control over Baltic territory.

Meanwhile, farther west, Sweden had quickly reemerged in 1630 to reignite the Protestant cause. Allied with the Netherlands, Sweden reestablished a Protestant revival throughout Germany, driving imperial forces south. Ferdinand sought aid from the Catholic Spanish Hapsburgs and the Papacy; Sweden was defeated at **NORDLINGEN** in 1634 and Catholicism was reestablished in the south.

At the same time, despite France's status as a Catholic country, it came into conflict with its neighbors—Hapsburg-ruled Spain and Austria. Spain's victory in Central Europe in 1634 cemented its power in the region; Hapsburg dominance to France's south and east represented a threat to that country, which was now surrounded by a strong military power. As a result, despite their religious commonalities, France declared war on Spain in 1635 and shortly after on the Hapsburg-supported Holy Roman Empire. This political tactic represented a break from the prioritization of religious alliances and a movement toward emphasis on state sovereignty.

The tangled alliances between European powers resulted in war between not only France and Spain, but also Sweden and Austria, with the small states of the weakening Holy Roman Empire caught in the middle. The war had been centered on alliances and concerns about the nature of Christianity within different European countries. However, upon signing the 1648 **TREATY OF WESTPHALIA**, the European powers agreed to recognize **STATE SOVEREIGNTY** and practice **NON-INTERFERENCE** in each other's matters—at the expense of family and religious allegiance. 1648 marked a transition into modern international relations when politics and religion would no longer be inexorably intertwined.

The end of the Thirty Years' War represented the end of the notion of the domination of the Catholic Church over Europe and the concept of religious regional dominance, rather than ethnic state divisions. Over the next several centuries, the Church and—religious empires like the Ottomans—would eventually lose control over ethnic groups and their lands, later giving way to smaller **NATION-STATES**.

As state sovereignty became entrenched in European notions of politics, so too did conflict between states. Upon the death of the Hapsburg Holy Roman Emperor **CHARLES VI** in 1740, the **WAR OF THE AUSTRIAN SUCCESSION** began, a series of Continental wars over who would take over control of the Hapsburg territories. These conflicts would lead to the Seven Years' War.

Nominally, there was dispute over whether a woman, Charles' daughter **Maria Theresa**, could inherit the Austrian throne; however, it is more likely that **Frederick II** (or **Frederick the Great**) of Prussia took advantage of the instability in 1740 following Charles' death to capture the resource-rich province of Silesia from Hapsburg Austria. Prussia allied with France, Bavaria, and Spain; Maria Theresa sought help from Britain, which would be threatened by French dominance of Europe. Britain and Spain had been in conflict over territory beyond Europe for decades; Britain and France were rivals on the North American continent, in Asia, and in the West Indies. Thus conflict in Europe reflected overseas competition.

Fighting dragged on; forced by dwindling finances to the negotiating table, the European powers signed the Treaty of Aix la Chappelle in 1748, which granted Maria Theresa most Austrian possessions and gave Silesia to Prussia.

However, it was clear that Austria intended to regain Silesia. In an effort to protect its allies in Hannover during Continental instability, Britain formed a pragmatic alliance with Prussia, despite its traditional friendship with Austria. As a result, Austria allied with its former enemy France, in a development known as the *Diplomatic Revolution*.

In 1756, Austria was set to attack Prussia, but Frederick the Great attacked first, launching the **Seven Years' War**. In Europe, this war further cemented concepts of state sovereignty and delineated rivalries between European powers engaged in colonial adventure and overseas imperialism—especially Britain and France. It would kick-start British dominance in Asia and also lead to Britain's loss of its North American colonies, nearly bankrupting the Crown (as discussed below).

On the European front, Frederick the Great invaded Silesia and then Bohemia in 1787; however he was repelled by Austria. Meanwhile, while the English led a Hannoverian army against the French in the west, they too were defeated and the French marched on Prussia. Sweden attacked from the north, and Russia attacked from the east. So Frederick called on Britain for more support. **William Pitt the Elder**, the British political leader (essentially Prime Minister) authorized enormous financial contributions to Prussia; he also began focusing the war overseas against France in imperial possessions in the Western Hemisphere and Asia.

Fortunately for the Anglo-Prussian alliance in Europe, changes in Russian leadership led to Catherine the Great's takeover; she ended hostilities with Prussia and focused on development in Russia instead. Hostilities died down in Europe, but the conflict overseas set the stage for the building of empire (see below).

This time of change in Europe would affect Asia. European concepts of social and political organization became constructed around national sovereignty and nation-states. European economies had become dependent upon colonies and were starting to industrialize, enriching Europe at the expense of its imperial possessions in the Americas, in Africa, and increasingly in Asia.

Industrialization and political organization allowed improved militaries, which put Asian governments at a disadvantage. The major Asian powers—Mughal India, Qing China, the Ottoman Empire, and Safavid (and later, Qajar) Persia—would eventually succumb to European influence or come under direct European control.

EXAMPLES

1. Which of the following best explains the Atlantic Triangular Trade?
   A) American raw materials were transported to Africa, where they were exchanged for enslaved persons; enslaved persons were taken to the Americas, where they turned raw materials to consumer goods for sale in Europe.
   B) European consumer goods were sold in the Americas at a profit; these goods were also sold in Africa in exchange for raw materials and for enslaved persons, who were taken to the Americas.
   C) European raw materials were sent to the Americas to be transformed into consumer goods by people who had been kidnapped from Africa and enslaved. These consumer goods were then traded in Africa for more slaves.
   D) Enslaved African people were traded in the Americas for raw materials; raw materials harvested by slaves went to Europe where they were utilized and turned to consumer goods; European consumer goods were exchanged in Africa for enslaved people.

2. The Treaty of Westphalia
   A) laid out the final borders of Europe, setting the stage for modern foreign policy.
   B) established the notion of state sovereignty, in which states recognized each other as independent and agreed not to interfere in each other's affairs.
   C) gave the Catholic Church more power in the affairs of Catholic-majority countries.
   D) established the notion of the nation-state, in which culturally and ethnically similar groups would control their own territory as sovereign countries.

Answer Key

1. A) is incorrect. American raw materials were transported to Europe where they were turned to consumer goods, not to Africa. Furthermore, American raw materials were converted into consumer goods in Europe.

    B) is incorrect. European consumer goods were sold in Africa (and within Europe); the Americas were initially a source of raw materials, though this would later change. Furthermore, Africa was not a major source of raw materials for Europe until the nineteenth century.

    C) is incorrect. Raw materials in the Triangular Trade came from the Americas; they were converted to consumer goods in Europe.

    D) is correct. American raw materials (like sugar and tobacco) were used in Europe and also turned into consumer goods there. European goods (as well as gold extracted from the Americas) were exchanged in Africa for enslaved persons, who were forced to harvest the raw materials in the Americas.

2. A) is incorrect. Europe's modern borders have only very recently been drawn, and they may continue to change over the course of history.

    B) is correct. The Treaty of Westphalia was based on state sovereignty and non-interference, the core principles of modern international relations.

    C) is incorrect. The political power of the Church had been weakening; the principles of state sovereignty weakened it further.

    D) is incorrect. The notion of the nation-state would more fully develop in the nineteenth century and was not established by a treaty.

CHAPTER FIVE
The Age of Revolutions
~1750 to 1900

Revolution

Monarchies in Europe had been weakened by the conflicts between Catholicism and Protestant faiths; despite European presence and increasing power overseas, as well as its dominance in the Americas, instability on the continent and in the British Isles made the old order vulnerable. Enlightenment ideals like democracy and republicanism, coupled with political instability, would trigger revolution against **ABSOLUTE MONARCHY**. Revolutionary actors drew on the philosophies of enlightenment thinkers like John Locke, Jean-Jacques Rousseau, and Montesquieu, whose beliefs, such as **REPUBLICANISM**, the **SOCIAL CONTRACT**, the **SEPARATION OF POWERS**, and the **RIGHTS OF MAN** would drive the Age of Revolutions.

In England, Puritans and Separatists—strict, conservative Protestants—were suspicious of King Charles I, believing he was weakening Protestantism and even possibly supporting Catholic plots. At the same time, more moderate Protestant leaders, including the weak Parliament and aristocratic class, were upset by Charles' dictatorial reign.

The period marked the early days of the **AGE OF REVOLUTIONS**, influenced especially by Enlightenment thinkers like Locke and Rousseau, who believed in the natural rights of man and the social contract between the people and government. Charles I was despotic and sidelined Parliament, causing political and military unrest. Conflict between England and Scotland in the late 1630s and an Irish uprising in 1641 weakened Charles further, as disgruntled English aristocracy, who felt that Charles had become a tyrannical ruler, withdrew support and began consolidating their own power. In 1642, the **ENGLISH CIVIL WAR** broke out between the **ROYALISTS**, who supported the monarchy, and the **PARLIAMENTARIANS**, who wanted a republic.

Eventually, the Royalists succumbed to the Parliamentarians, and Charles was executed in 1649. Meanwhile, England had lost control over Ireland, and the Parliamentarian military leader **OLIVER CROMWELL** was sent to reestablish control over the island. Charles II, son of Charles I, had established control as king of Scotland; Cromwell defeated him and England took back control of Scotland in 1651. By 1653, England once again controlled Britain and Ireland; Cromwell was installed as Lord Protector.

Following Cromwell's death, Charles II restored the Stuart monarchy. However, stability was short lived once his Catholic brother James II succeeded him in 1685. By 1688, English Protestants asked the Dutch William of Orange, husband of James II's daughter Mary, to help restore Protestantism in Britain. **WILLIAM AND MARY** defeated James and consolidated Protestant control over England, Scotland, and Ireland under a Protestant constitutional monarchy in the **GLORIOUS REVOLUTION**. The **1689 ENGLISH BILL OF RIGHTS** established constitutional monarchy, in the spirit of the Magna Carta.

The French Revolution was the precursor to the end of the feudal order in most of Europe. **KING LOUIS XIV**, the *Sun King* (1643–1715), had consolidated the monarchy in France, taking true political and military power from the nobility. Meanwhile, French Enlightenment thinkers like **JEAN-JACQUES ROUSSEAU**, **MONTESQUIEU**, and **VOLTAIRE** criticized absolute monarchy and the repression of freedom of speech and thought; in 1789, the French Revolution broke out.

DID YOU KNOW?
Louis XIV built the palace of Versailles, to centralize the monarchy—and also to contain and monitor the nobility.

The power of the Catholic Church had weakened and the Scientific Revolution and the Enlightenment had fostered social and intellectual change. Colonialism and mercantilism were fueling the growth of an early middle class: people who were not traditionally nobility or landowners under the feudal system were becoming wealthier and more powerful thanks to early capitalism. This class, the **BOURGEOISIE**, chafed under the rule of the nobility, which had generally inherited land and wealth (while the bourgeoisie earned their wealth in business).

In France, the problem was most acute as France had the largest population in Europe at the time. At the same time, France had one of the most centralized monarchies in Europe and entrenched nobilities. With a growing bourgeoisie and peasant class paying increasingly higher taxes to the nobility, resentment was brewing.

Louis XIV had strengthened the monarchy by weakening the nobility's control over their land and centralizing power under the king. However, his successors had failed to govern effectively or win the loyalty of the people; both the nobility and the monarch were widely resented. Furthermore, the bourgeoisie resented their lack of standing in government and society. Moreover, advances in medicine had permitted unprecedented population growth, further empowering the peasantry and bourgeoisie.

The French government was struggling financially, having supported the American Revolution; in desperation, the controller-general of finances suggested reforms that would tax the nobility. An unwilling council of nobles instead called for the

ESTATES-GENERAL to be convened in 1787; this toothless body had not come together since 1614.

The Estates-General, a weak representative assembly, reflected French society: the clergy, the nobility, and the **THIRD ESTATE**—the middle class and the poor peasants, or *commoners*. The burden of taxation traditionally fell on the Third Estate. In fact, peasants had to **TITHE**, paying ten percent of their earnings to the nobles.

After a poor harvest in 1788, unrest spread throughout the country. King Louis XVI permitted elections to the Estates-General and some free speech; momentum against the elites grew. Once the Estates-General convened at Versailles in 1789, disagreement between the nobility and the elite clergy, on the one hand, and the Third Estate and lower-level parish priests, on the other, erupted. The two sides came to terms and formed the **NATIONAL CONSTITUENT ASSEMBLY**; still, the king and nobility were suspicious of the other side and Louis XVI planned to dissolve it.

At the same time, panic over dwindling food supplies and suspicion over a conspiracy against the Third Estate triggered the **GREAT FEAR** among the peasants in July 1789. Suspicion turned to action when the king sent troops to Paris, and on July 16 the people stormed the **BASTILLE** prison in an event still celebrated in France symbolic of the overthrow of tyranny. The peasantry then revolted in the countryside; consequently the National Constituent Assembly officially abolished the feudal system and tithing. Furthermore, the Assembly issued the **DECLARATION OF THE RIGHTS OF MAN AND THE CITIZEN**, the precursor to the French constitution assuring liberty and equality, in the model of Enlightenment thought.

> **DID YOU KNOW?**
> Charles Dickens' *A Tale of Two Cities* features a fictional account of the storming of the Bastille. Contrary to popular belief, Victor Hugo's *Les Misérables* takes place several decades after the French Revolution.

Louis XVI refused to accept these developments; as a result, the people marched on Versailles and brought the royals back to Paris, effectively putting the Assembly in charge. Members of the **JACOBINS**, revolutionary political clubs, became members of the Assembly; the more extreme of these political figures would play key roles in the immediate future of the country.

The Assembly continued reforms, including nationalizing the lands of the Catholic Church to pay off debt, disempowering the Church. It also reorganized the administration of the **ANCIEN RÉGIME** (the old government) including allowing the election of judges. When Louis XVI attempted to escape France, he was detained.

The French Revolution inspired revolutionary movements throughout Europe and beyond; indeed, the revolutionary principle of self-determination drove revolutionary France to support its ideals abroad. The country declared war on Austria in 1792, but following severe defeats by joint Austrian-Prussian forces, the people became suspicious of the unpopular queen **MARIE ANTOINETTE**. Marie Antoinette was originally from Austria

> **DID YOU KNOW?**
> An important tenet of the revolutionary ethos in France was the concept of self-determination, or the right of a people to rule themselves, which threatened rulers fearing revolution in their own countries.

and had, in fact, encouraged an invasion, hoping to suppress the revolution. The people imprisoned the royal family; the Jacobins abolished the monarchy, establishing the republic later that year.

War in Europe dragged on into 1793, with considerable French losses against an alliance between Austria, Prussia, and Great Britain. Within France, the Jacobins—essentially, the government of the Republic—were breaking into two main factions: the more moderate **Girondins**, who favored concentrating power in the hands of the bourgeoisie, and the more extreme **Montagnards**, led by **Robespierre**, who favored radical social policy empowering the poor.

Fearful of counterrevolutionaries in France and instability abroad, the republican government created the **Committee of Public Safety** in 1793. Robespierre led the Committee and the **Reign of Terror** began in France, during which time thousands of people were executed by **guillotine**, including Louis XVI and Marie Antoinette. Robespierre himself was executed a year later.

Ongoing war in Europe and tensions in France between republicans and royalists continued to weaken the revolution, but France had military successes in Europe. France had continued its effort to spread the revolution throughout the continent, led by **Napoleon Bonaparte**, who even occupied Egypt in an attempt to threaten British power abroad. In 1799, Napoleon took power in France: the revolution was over.

In 1804 Napoleon Bonaparte emerged as emperor of France, and proceeded to conquer much of Europe throughout the **Napoleonic Wars**, changing the face of Europe. French occupation of Spain weakened that country enough that revolutionary movements in its colonies strengthened; eventually Latin American colonies, inspired by the Enlightenment and revolution in Europe, won their freedom.

Napoleon's movement eastward also triggered the collapse of the Holy Roman Empire. However, the powerful state of **Prussia** emerged in its wake, and a strong sense of militarism and Germanic nationalism took root in the face of opposition to seemingly unstoppable France. (Prussia would later go on to unify the small kingdoms of Central Europe that had made up the Holy Roman Empire, forming Germany, as discussed below.)

Napoleon was finally defeated in Russia in 1812 and was forced by the European powers to abdicate in 1813. He escaped from prison on the Mediterranean island of Elba and raised an army again, overthrowing the restored monarch Louis XVIII. Defeated at Waterloo by the British, he was once again exiled, this time to St. Helena in the southern Atlantic Ocean.

By 1815, other European powers had managed to halt his expansion; at the **Congress of Vienna** in 1815, European powers including the unified Prussia, the **Austro-Hungarian Empire**, **Russia**, and **Britain** agreed on a **balance of power** in Europe. Despite Napoleon's brief reemergence, the Congress of Vienna was the first real international peace conference and set the precedent for European political organization.

Latin American countries joined Haiti and the United States in revolution against colonial European powers. Inspired by the American and French Revolutions, **SIMÓN BOLIVAR** led or influenced independence movements in **VENEZUELA**, **COLOMBIA** (including what is today **PANAMA**), **ECUADOR**, **PERU** and **BOLIVIA** in the early part of the nineteenth century.

European Division

The nineteenth century was a period of change and conflict, and the roots of the major twentieth century conflicts – world war and decolonization – are found in it. Modern European social and political structure and norms, including **NATIONALISM** and the **NATION-STATE**, would begin to emerge. Economic theories based in the Industrial Revolution like socialism and eventually **COMMUNISM** gained traction with the stark class divisions brought on by urbanization and industry.

Following the Napoleonic Wars, Prussia had come to dominate the German-speaking states that once comprised the Holy Roman Empire. Prussia, a distinct kingdom within the Holy Roman Empire since the thirteenth century, had become a powerful Central European state by the eighteenth century. It had become main rival of Austria for influence in the Germanic lands of Central Europe. By the nineteenth century and due in part to emphasis on military prowess, Prussia became an important military power and a key ally in the efforts against Napoleon.

Prussia had a particular rivalry with France, having lost several key territories during the Napoleonic Wars. In 1870, the militarily powerful kingdom went to war against France in the **FRANCO-PRUSSIAN WAR**, during which Prussia took control of **ALSACE-LORRAINE**, mineral rich and later essential for industrial development.

Following the Franco-Prussian War, **OTTO VON BISMARCK** unified those linguistically and culturally German states of Central Europe. Prussian power had been growing, fueled by nationalism and the nation-state, or the idea that individuals with shared experience (including ethnicity, language, religion, and cultural practices) should be unified under one government. In 1871, the **GERMAN EMPIRE** became a united state. Bismarck encouraged economic cooperation, instituted army reforms and, perhaps most importantly, created an image of Prussia as a defender of German culture and nationhood, portraying other European states in opposition to that.

Nationalism also led to **ITALIAN UNIFICATION**. As a region of small independent states, toward the end of the eighteenth century Italy was occupied by France and then Austria. Later invaded and occupied by Napoleon, the Italian peninsula was divided into three regions. Napoleonic concepts of nationalism, freedom, equality, and justice under the law spread throughout the peninsula, and what was left of feudalism faded.

Despite re-fragmentation throughout the nineteenth century following the fall of Napoleon, a secret movement for reorganization—the **RISORGIMENTO**—began working toward Italian unification. Following the 1859 Franco-Austrian War, Austria's loss of territorial control in northern Italy allowed Italian states to unite via elections. **Giuseppe Garibaldi** led the Northern Italian overthrow of Southern Italian monarchies, uniting the Peninsula with the exception of Rome and Venice. The Kingdom of Italy was declared in 1861, under **Victor Emmanuel II**. Thanks to an Italian alliance with Prussia during the **Austro-Prussian War** in 1866, in which Austria lost even more territory, Italy took control of Venice. Finally, the Kingdom of Italy entered Rome and incorporated that city and the Papal States during the Franco-Prussian War.

Conflict in the Balkans

Farther east, as European kingdoms and empires consolidated their power, the Ottoman Empire was in decline. The Ottoman Empire had long been a major force in Europe, controlling the bulk of the Balkans. However, the empire had lost land in Europe to the Austrians and in Africa to British and French imperialists. In the Balkans, rebellion among small nations supported by European puppet masters would put an end to Ottoman power in Europe for good.

Despite previous conflict between some of these powers, deeper rivalries throughout the continent inspired Russia, Germany and Austria-Hungary to form the **Three Emperors' League in 1873**. If one country went to war, the others would remain neutral, and the powers would consult each other on matters of war. However, the First Balkan Crisis in 1874 would put an end to this alliance.

In 1874, Bosnia Herzegovina rebelled against Ottoman rule. Christian peasants in Herzegovina were unwilling to submit to Muslim landlords; neither regional Christians nor Bosnian Muslims were willing any longer to submit to rule by the ethnically-different Turks. Thus began the **First Balkan Crisis**.

Two years later, the Ottoman autonomous principality of Serbia, joined by Montenegro, rebelled in support of Bosnia. Having come under Russian influence thanks to **pan-Slavism**—the concept that Slavic ethnic groups throughout Eastern and Southeastern Europe should embrace their Slavic heritage and turn toward Russia for support—Serbian rebellion attracted Russian attention. When the Ottoman **Sultan Hamid II** refused to institute reforms to protect Balkan Christians, Russia declared war.

The **Russo-Turkish War** ended in 1878 with the **Treaty of San Stefano**, which favored Russian territorial gains. However, Austro-Hungarian and British objections to the treaty, which threatened their influence in the region, led to the **1878 Congress of Berlin**, hosted by Otto von Bismarck. Unfortunately for Russia, which was the militarily and financially weaker power, Britain and Austria-Hungary changed the outcome of the war with the **Treaty of Berlin**. While the independence of Serbia and Montenegro was decided, Russia lost influence in Bulgaria as well as territorial gains in Asia. These insults would not be forgotten.

Germany and Austria-Hungary secretly formed the Dual Alliance to respond to fears of pan-Slavism, given developments in the Balkans. In 1882, Italy asked these countries for assistance against France, which had upset Italian imperial ambition in North Africa; thus formed the **Triple Alliance**, a secret political and military alliance. The 1885 **Second Balkan Crisis**, in which Bulgaria declared unification and independence, violating the Treaty of Berlin and Russian interests, further threatened stability in the Balkans and among the great powers. Serbia went to war against Bulgaria, requiring Austro-Hungarian support.

Eventually tension between Russia and Austria-Hungary—which was supported by Germany—led to the breakdown of Russian relationships with those countries, and improvement in Russian relations with Great Britain and France. In 1894, Russia and France became allies. This alliance would culminate in the 1907 **Triple Entente**, setting the stage for the system of alliances at the heart of the First World War.

Continued European involvement in the Balkans accelerated the ongoing loss of Ottoman influence there due to phenomena like nationalism, ethnocentrism (Pan-Slavism), military and political power, and religious influence. The small Balkan nations were empowered to continue rebellion against Ottoman rule, and European powers proceeded into the area.

In 1908, Austria-Hungary annexed Bosnia-Herzegovina, disregarding Russian objections. Russia helped form the **Balkan League**, comprised of Serbia, Montenegro, Greece, and Bulgaria, which went to war with the Ottomans in the 1912 **First Balkan War**. The Ottomans were defeated and lost nearly all their European possessions; however, disagreement over the division of land led to the **Second Balkan War** the following year between the Bulgaria and a Serbian-Greek alliance. Serbia wanted to keep Albanian territory, which Austria-Hungary insisted remain independent; Bulgaria wanted control over more land in Macedonia (which had come mainly under Greek and Serbian rule). Eventually, this instability would lead to the First World War which was triggered by the assassination of the Austro-Hungarian Archduke Franz Ferdinand by the Serbian nationalist Gavrilo Princip in Bosnia-Herzegovina in 1914.

Imperialism

As colonialism in the fifteenth and sixteenth centuries had been driven by mercantilism, conquest, and Christian conversion, so was seventeenth, eighteenth and nineteenth century imperialism driven by capitalism, European competition, and conceptions of racial superiority.

Britain and France, historic rivals on the European continent, were also at odds colonizing North America and in overseas trade. During the **Seven Years' War** (1756 – 1763), considered by many historians to be the first truly global conflict, these two powers fought in Europe and in overseas colonies and interests in North America and Asia.

As discussed above, while the Seven Years' War in Europe was the result of tangled alliances between Britain, Prussia, and Hanover on one side, and France, Austria, Sweden, and Russia on the other, that war's extension into the imperial realm made it a global conflict.

In North America, Britain and France had explored the region and controlled tremendous amounts of territory in what later would become Canada and the United States. Britain controlled the wealthy **Thirteen Colonies** on the Atlantic coast, which were rich in tobacco, rice, vegetables, and other crops. It also controlled major ports like Boston, New York, and Philadelphia.

Meanwhile, the French controlled **Quebec** and northeastern territories rich in natural resources like beaver pelts, valuable in Europe for their water-repellant properties. They also controlled the ports of Montreal and Quebec City, on the St. Lawrence River (leading to the Atlantic Ocean). France also controlled considerable strategic territory in the Midwestern portions of the continent, which allowed products from the interior to reach the oceans. These routes included much of the **Great Lakes** region including the Detroit River (leading to the St. Lawrence and the Atlantic Ocean), and the Mississippi River and the Port of New Orleans (leading to the Gulf of Mexico).

The **French and Indian War**, as the Seven Years' War is called in North America, resulted in net gains for Britain. France formed an important alliance with the powerful Algonquin in the northeast, while Britain was allied with the Iroquois. Thanks to strong military leaders like **George Washington**, Britain eventually took control of French Canada. However, financially exhausted from the costly conflict in Europe, Britain ceded control of the Northwest Territories (Michigan, Ohio, Indiana) to various tribes in the **Treaty of Paris in 1763** (agreements later not honored by the United States). In addition, the financial and military strain suffered by Britain in the Seven Years' War made it particularly vulnerable to later rebellion in the Colonies, helping the Americans win the Revolutionary War there.

According to Pitt the Elder's plan, Britain went to war with France in Asia as well. In India, with the decline of the Mughal Empire and the rising power of colonial companies specializing in exporting valuable resources like spices and tea, smaller Indian kingdoms were forming alliances with those increasingly influential corporations.

DID YOU KNOW?
The Netherlands was already coming to dominate Indonesia (at the time, the Dutch East Indies) thanks to similar actions by the Dutch East India Company.

By the mid eighteenth century, violence broke out between the **British East India Company** and the **French East India Company** and their allies among the small Indian states in a series of wars known as the **Carnatic Wars** (1746 – 1763). With the end of the Seven Years' War, the Treaty of Paris established British dominance in the Subcontinent as France was allowed some trading posts in the region, but forced to recognize British power there. By 1803, British interests effectively took control of the Subcontinent and the Mughals were pushed to the north.

Despite its loss of the Thirteen Colonies, at the dawn of the nineteenth century Britain retained control of Canada, rich in natural resources like beaver pelts and timber. In addition, it controlled the resource-rich and strategically important Indian Subcontinent. Britain would become the strongest naval power in the world and continue to expand its empire, especially in the search for new markets for its manufactured goods to support its industrial economy.

In 1837, **QUEEN VICTORIA** ascended to the throne. During her reign (1837–1901) the British Empire would expand to heretofore unseen lengths. In 1788, Britain had begun sending convicts to the penal colony of **AUSTRALIA**; however in 1851, when gold was discovered there British subjects began to voluntarily settle Australia and the Pacific. In 1857, the **INDIAN MUTINY** against private British troops controlled by the East India Company caused the British government to intervene, sending in military and eventually resulting in Victoria taking the title of **EMPRESS OF INDIA**, cementing the imperial nature of government and the **RAJ** (imperial administration).

In 1877, the British annexed **SOUTH AFRICA**; following the Boer Wars, Britain would retain control of diamond- and gold-rich South Africa (see below). The imperialist **CECIL RHODES** and his company, the British South Africa Company (BSAC), were chartered by Victoria to explore north from South Africa to mine the land. This was despite of conflicting European claims to the land, despite claims by the **AFRIKAANERS**, and despite the residence of the **MATABELE**, who had lived there for centuries. Rhodes and the BSAC forcefully took over Northern Rhodesia (**ZAMBIA**), Rhodesia (**ZIMBABWE**), Nyasaland (**MALAWI**) and Bechuanaland (**BOTSWANA**) using treaties, diplomacy, and violence. These territories were under English rule.

In East Africa, the British explorer **DAVID LIVINGSTONE** had been working in Kenya; the government had influence over the Sultan of Zanzibar. However, secret German agreements with coastal leaders and the establishment of the German colony of **TANGANYIKA** forced the British into more activity in the region. In an agreement with the Germans, the British took control over what would become **KENYA** and **UGANDA**, while Germany maintained Tanganyika. Borders were drawn without regard for the **KIKUYU**, **MASAI**, **LUO**, and other tribes living in the area.

The concept of the **WHITE MAN'S BURDEN**, wherein white Europeans were "obligated" to bring their "superior" culture to other civilizations around the globe, also drove imperialist adventure, popularizing it at home in Britain and elsewhere in Europe.

Despite its small size, **BELGIUM** controlled the **CONGO**, along with its vast resources in Central Africa. Coming into conflict with Rhodes at its southern edges, the Belgian Congo, which reached its heights under **KING LEOPOLD II** was rich in rubber, timber, minerals, and diamonds. Furthermore, this territory was strategically important; controlling the Congo meant controlling

QUICK REVIEW
List some of the European powers' justifications for imperialism.

the Congo River basin, allowing the extraction of materials from the interior to the Atlantic Coast.

DID YOU KNOW?
The Boxers were so called because of their belief that physical exercises, like shadow boxing, would make them impervious to bullets. This rebellion was led by a secret society called the Yihequan, or the Society of Righteous and Harmonious Fists.

To gain access to closed Chinese markets, Britain forced China to buy Indian opium; the **OPIUM WARS** ended with the **TREATY OF NANKING** (1842), signed between the British and the increasingly impotent Qing government. As a consequence, China lost great power to Britain and later, other European countries, which gained **SPHERES OF INFLUENCE**, or areas of China they effectively controlled, and **EXTRATERRITORIALITY**, or privileges in which their citizens were not subject to Chinese law.

Discontent with the Qing Dynasty was growing as Chinese people perceived that their country was coming under control of European imperialists, even though nominally Chinese leadership still governed. Coupled with economic hardship and huge casualties in the Opium Wars and in the **SINO-JAPANESE WAR OF 1896**, a violent uprising was inevitable. In 1900, the **BOXER REBELLION**, an uprising led by a Chinese society against the Emperor, was only put down with Western (including American) help. The Qing were humiliated further by being forced to pay the West enormous reparations for their assistance; meanwhile, living conditions for Chinese people continued to deteriorate.

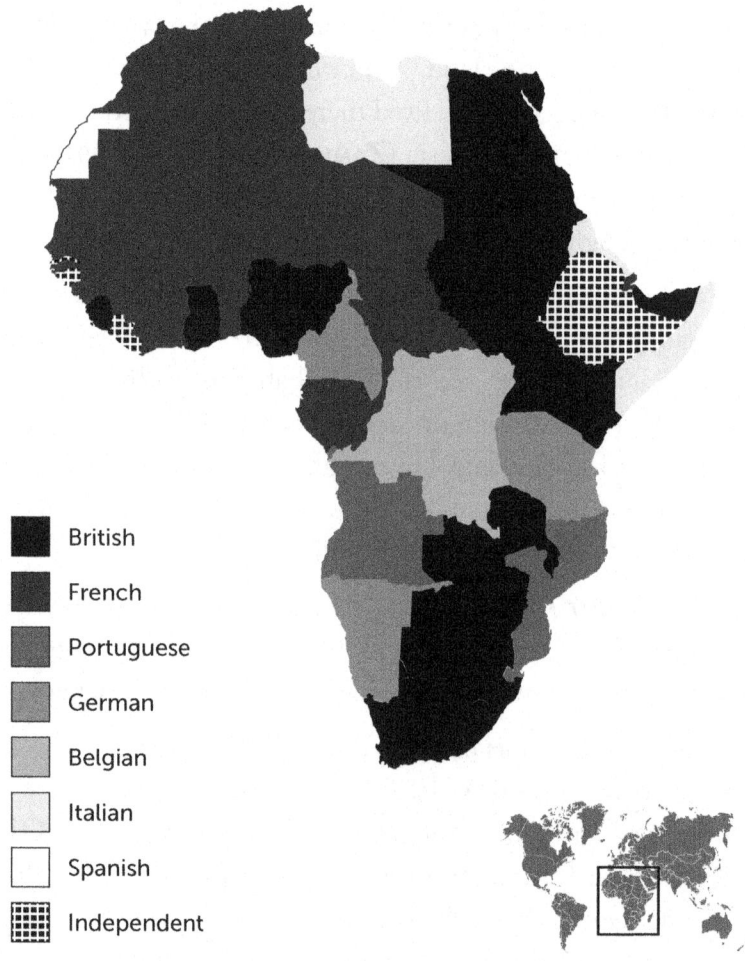

Figure 5.1. Imperial Africa

The European powers were immersed in became known as the **Scramble for Africa**; the industrial economies of Europe would profit from the natural resources abundant in that continent, and the white man's burden continued to fuel colonization. At the **1884 Berlin Conference**, control over Africa was divided among European powers (Africans were not consulted in this process). Following the **Boer War** (1899-1902) between Afrikaaners of Dutch origin and the English, Britain officially gained control of South Africa, and whites would rule the country until the end of **Apartheid** in the early 1990s. France controlled West Africa and eventually North Africa, especially Algeria, Mali, Niger, Chad, Cameroon and what has become the Republic of the Congo (not to be confused with Belgian Congo, now the Democratic Republic of the Congo).

However, not all non-European countries fell to European imperialism. During the **Meiji Restoration** in Japan in 1868, the Emperor Meiji promoted modernization of technology, especially the military. Japan proved itself a world power when it defeated Russia in the Russo-Japanese War in 1905, and would play a central role in twentieth century conflict.

Industrial Revolution

Throughout this entire period, raw goods from the Americas fueled European economic growth and development, leading to the **Industrial Revolution** in the nineteenth century. This economic revolution began with textile production in Britain, fueled by cotton from its overseas territories in North America, and later India and Egypt. The first factories were in Manchester, where **urbanization** began as poor people from rural areas flocked to cities in search of higher-paying unskilled jobs in factories.

Early industrial technology sped up the harvesting and transport of crops and their conversion to textiles. This accelerated manufacturing was based on **capitalism**, the **laissez-faire** (or **free market**) theory developed by **Adam Smith**, who believed that an *invisible hand* should guide the marketplace—that government should stay out of the economy regardless of abuses, as the economy would eventually automatically correct for inequalities, price problems, and any other problematic issues.

Technology like the **spinning jenny** and **flying shuttle** exponentially increased the amount of cotton that workers could process into yarn and thread. The **steam engine** efficiently powered mills and ironworks; factories no longer had to be built near running water to access power. Advances in **iron** technology allowed for stronger machinery and would support the later **Second Industrial Revolution** in the late nineteenth and early twentieth century, which was based on **heavy industry**, railroads, and weapons.

To access the raw materials needed to produce manufactured goods, Britain and other industrializing countries in Western Europe needed resources—hence the drive for imperialism as discussed above. Cotton was harvested in India and Egypt for textile mills; minerals mined in South Africa and the Congo to power metallurgy. Furthermore, as industrialization and urbanization led to the development of early middle classes in Europe and North America, imports of luxury goods like tea, spices, silk, precious metals, and other items from Asia increased to meet consumer demand. Colonial powers also gained by selling manufactured goods back to the colonies from which they had harvested raw materials in the first place, for considerable profit.

Largely unbridled capitalism had led to the conditions of the early Industrial Revolution; workers suffered from abusive treatment, overly long hours, low wages or none at all, and unsafe conditions, including pollution. The German philosophers **KARL MARX** and **FRIEDRICH ENGELS**, horrified by conditions suffered by industrial workers, developed **SOCIALISM**, the philosophy that workers, or the **PROLETARIAT**, should own the means of production and reap the profits, rather than the bourgeoisie, who had no interest in the rights of the workers at the expense of profit and who did not experience the same conditions.

In his work ***DAS KAPITAL***, Marx argued for the abolition of the class system, wages, and private property. He argued instead for collective ownership of both the means of production and products, with equal distribution of income to satisfy the needs of all. Later, Marx and Engels wrote the ***COMMUNIST MANIFESTO***, a pamphlet laying out their ideas and calling for revolution. It inspired the formation of socialist groups worldwide.

> **DID YOU KNOW?**
> The *Communist Manifesto* contained the famous words *Workers of the world, unite!*

A different version of socialism would later help Russia become a major world power. The Russian intellectuals **VLADIMIR LENIN** and **LEON TROTSKY** would take Marx and Engels' theories further, developing **MARXISM-LENINISM**. They embraced socialist ideals and believed in revolution; however they felt that communism could not be maintained under a democratic governing structure. Lenin supported dictatorship, more precisely the **DICTATORSHIP OF THE PROLETARIAT**, paving the way for the political and economic organization of the Soviet Union.

EXAMPLES

1. Which of the following was an important factor leading to the French Revolution?
    A) the corruption of Louis XIV
    B) the strong organization of the Estates-General
    C) support from the United States of America
    D) the anti-monarchical philosophies of Enlightenment thinkers like Rousseau and Voltaire

2. How did Pan-Slavism affect the crises in the Balkans?

   A) Pan-Slavism led Russia to directly intervene militarily throughout the nineteenth century in the Balkans, leading to violent conflict.

   B) Pan-Slavism generally ensured Russian support for Slavic ethnic groups in the Balkans, which contributed to ongoing tensions there already fueled by competing European and Ottoman interests and diverse nationalities.

   C) Russian interests in Slavic groups in the Balkans strengthened its alliance with Turkey.

   D) Pan-Slavism did not have a major effect on the Balkans, as the major Slavic cultures are located farther north in Europe.

3. Which of the following is NOT a way that the racist concept of *the white man's burden* influenced imperialism?

   A) It inspired Europeans to settle overseas in order to improve what they believed to be "backward" places.

   B) Europeans believed in imperialism as in the best interest of native people, who would benefit from adopting European languages and cultural practices.

   C) Europeans believed it burdensome to be forced to tutor non-Europeans in their languages and customs.

   D) Many Europeans supported the construction of schools for colonial subjects and even the development of scholarships for them to study in Europe.

4. What did Marx and Engels believe?

   A) The proletariat must control the means of production to ensure a wageless, classless society to meet the needs of all equitably.

   B) The dictatorship of the proletariat would enable workers to control the means of production in a non-democratic society.

   C) An organized revolution directed by a small group of leaders was necessary to bring about social change and a socialist society.

   D) The bourgeoisie would willingly give up control of the means of production to the proletariat.

Answer Key

1. A) is incorrect. Louis XIV strengthened the monarchy several decades before the revolution.

    B) is incorrect. The Estates-General was weak and poorly organized, actually facilitating revolution.

    C) is incorrect. While there was support for the revolutionaries, the United States maintained a cautious stance on the revolution given its hesitance to become embroiled in European conflict.

    D) is correct. Enlightenment thinking fueled the Age of Revolutions, and revolutionary French thinkers and writers like Rousseau, Voltaire, and others influenced revolutionary French leaders.

2. A) is incorrect. While Russia was very much involved in the Balkans (and continues to be), it was not always necessarily involved in a military capacity.

    B) is correct. Russian support for Slavic ethnic groups in the Balkans—especially Serbia—helped fuel nineteenth century tensions in the region (and continued to do so throughout the twentieth century).

    C) is incorrect. Russia and Ottoman Turkey were not allies; in fact they went to war in the Russo-Turkish War after the First Balkan Crisis.

    D) is incorrect. Pan-Slavism had a tremendous effect on the dynamics of the nineteenth century Balkans, as several Slavic ethnic groups live in Southeast Europe and had alliances with Russia.

3. A) is incorrect. White Europeans approved of settled colonies; part of the rationale of settlement was the idea that a white European presence was helping "civilize" the area.

    B) is incorrect. According to the idea of the white man's burden, the lives of non-Europeans would improve by adopting European customs and traditions.

    C) is correct. The idea of the white man's burden was not meant to suggest a literal burden; it was a racist, paternalistic concept of responsibility used to justify imperial dominance.

    D) is incorrect. Schools were built throughout many colonies (though not all were of high quality, nor were they accessible to all people); furthermore, many colonial subjects moved to England, France, Belgium, and elsewhere in Europe to study.

4. **A) is correct.** Marx and Engels believed in abolishing wages and the class structure in exchange for a socialist society where the means of production were commonly held and in which income was equally distributed.

    B) is incorrect. The dictatorship of the proletariat was a Leninist concept.

    C) is incorrect. While Marx and Engels believed in revolution, they believed that the workers would be able to bring it about; Lenin would later argue that the proletariat needed direction in revolution.

    D) is incorrect. Marx and Engels believed that a socialist society could only be achieved through revolution.

CHAPTER SIX
Global Conflict
~1900 to present

Pre-Revolutionary Russia

Russia had gone to war with Japan in 1904 to secure access to the Pacific and secure its interests in Asia. **Tsar Nicholas II**, unpopular at home, also believed that a victory would improve his security as a ruler. Japan, concerned about losing influence in Korea and seeking influence in China, attacked Russia; the **Russo-Japanese War** quickly ended in 1905 due to superior Japanese military technology, including naval technology, training, and leadership.

Russia's loss to Japan in the 1905 Russo-Japanese War was just another example of its difference from other European powers. While technically a European country, Russia had been slow to industrialize, due in part to its size and terrain. A largely agrarian country at the turn of the century, **serfdom**, the practice of "tying" peasants to the land and the last vestiges of feudalism, had only been abolished in 1861. Most Russians were still poor, rural farmers, and industrialization brought wretched conditions to workers in the cities. Russia also continued to have an absolute monarchy, unlike many European powers whose governments had shifted during the Age of Revolution.

Tsar Nicholas faced dissent at home due to the humiliating defeat by the Japanese; discontent was fueled by longer-term economic hardship in the face of a strengthening European industrial economy and limited freedoms in comparison to those enjoyed elsewhere in Europe. Unlawful trade unions appeared; workers began striking; and peasants rose up in protest of oppressive taxation.

Still, many Russians blamed the Tsar's advisors and minor officials for conditions, believing that the Tsar himself would act to improve conditions for Russians. These ideas were shattered in 1905 when a peaceful protest of working conditions in St. Petersburg ended in a bloody massacre of civilians by the Tsar's troops. **Bloody Sunday**, as the event came to be called, resulted in the **Revolution of 1905**, during which the Tsar temporarily lost control of Russia and was discredited.

Following the Revolution of 1905, the Tsar made some reforms in Russia, including the establishment of a **Duma**, or Parliament. However, economic hardship and social discontent continued in Russia.

While not directly involved with the failed Revolution of 1905, the Marxist Social Democrats, made up of the **Bolsheviks**, led by **Lenin**, and the **Mensheviks**, would gain power. They would eventually take over the country in 1917.

World War I

Instability in the Balkans and increasing tensions in Europe culminated with the assassination of the Austro-Hungarian **Archduke Franz Ferdinand** by the Serbian nationalist **Gavrilo Princip** in Sarajevo on June 28, 1914. In protest of continuing Austro-Hungarian control over Serbia, Princip's action kicked off the **system of alliances** that had been in place among European powers.

Austria-Hungary declared war on Serbia, and Russia came to Serbia's aid. As an ally of Austria-Hungary as part of the Triple Alliance, Germany declared war on Russia. Russia's ally France prepared for war; as Germany traversed Belgium to invade France, Belgium pleaded for aid from other European countries and so Britain declared war on Germany.

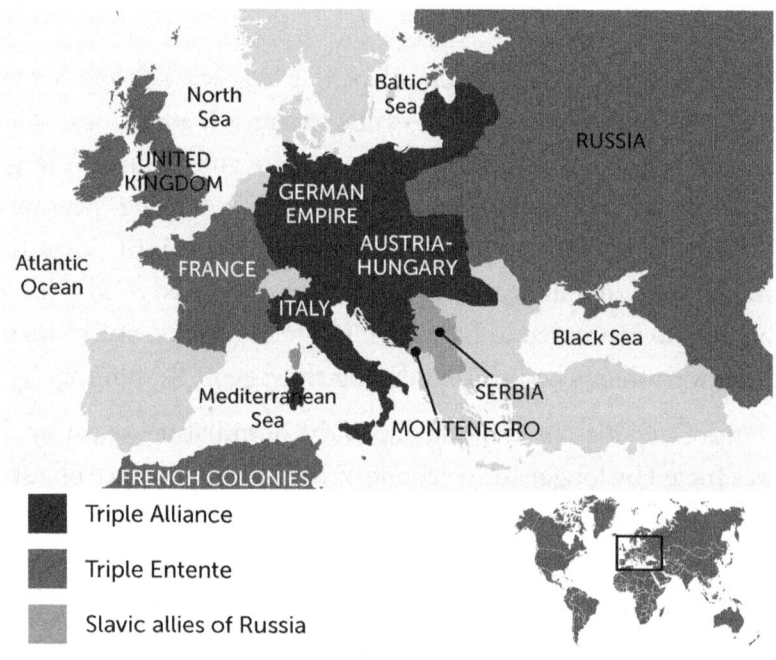

Figure 6.1. WWI Alliances

Germany had been emphasizing military growth since the consolidation and militarization of the empire under Bismarck in the mid-nineteenth century. Now, under

Kaiser Wilhelm II, who sought expanded territories in Europe and overseas for Germany (including the potential capture of overseas British and French colonies), Germany was a militarized state and important European power in its own right.

Wilhelm, the grandson of Frederick II on his father's side and of Queen Victoria, took over the German Empire in 1888. He had focused on improving naval power and expanding German territory overseas. Despite his connections to Britain, Germany's threat to British overseas power brought the war beyond Europe to Africa and Asia. In **Togo**, Britain and France took over an important German communications point. In China, Japan allied with Britain and France, taking control of the German settlement of Tsingtao and of German colonies in the **Pacific Islands**.

Britain's imperial power allowed it to call on troops from all over the globe—Indians, Canadians, Australians, South Africans, and New Zealanders all fought in Europe. France, too, imported colonial fighters from North Africa.

In Europe, the 1914 **Battle of the Marne** between Germany and French and British forces defending France resulted in trench warfare that would continue for years, marking the Western Front. At **Gallipoli** in 1915, Australian and New Zealander troops fought the **Ottoman Empire**, allies of Germany, near Istanbul. Later that year, a German submarine, or **U-boat**, sank the **Lusitania**, a passenger ship in the Atlantic, killing many American civilians. In 1916, the **Battle of Verdun**, the longest battle of the war, ended in the failure of the Germans to defeat the French army. In 1916, the British navy pushed back the German navy in the **Battle of Jutland**; despite heavy losses, Britain was able to ensure that German naval power was diminished for the rest of the war. On July 1, 1916, the **Battle of the Somme** became part of an allied effort to repel Germany using artillery to end the stalemate on the Western Front; after four months, however, the front moved only five miles.

DID YOU KNOW?
The first international war to use industrialized weaponry, WWI was called "the Great War" because battle on such a scale had never before been seen.

Finally, in 1917, the United States caught the **Zimmerman Telegram**, in which Germany secretly proposed an alliance with Mexico to attack the U.S. This finally spurred U.S. intervention in the war; despite Russian withdrawal after the Bolshevik Revolution in October 1917, Germany was forced to surrender in the face of invasion by the U.S.-supported allies.

According to the **Schlieffen Plan**, Germany had planned to fight a war on two fronts against both Russia and France. However, Russia's unexpectedly rapid mobilization stretched the German army too thin on the Eastern Front, while it became bogged down in **trench warfare** on the Western Front against the British, French, and later the Americans. Germany lost the war and was punished with the harsh **Treaty of Versailles**, which held it accountable for the entirety of the war. The Treaty brought economic hardship on the country by forcing it to pay **reparations**. Wilhelm was forced to abdicate and never again regained power in Germany. German military failure and consequent economic collapse due to the Treaty of Versailles and later worldwide economic depression set the stage for the rise of fascism and Adolf Hitler.

The Treaty also created the **League of Nations**, an international organization designed to prevent future outbreaks of international war; however, it was largely toothless, especially because the powerful United States did not join.

Change in the Middle East

The end of WWI also marked the end of the Ottoman Empire, which was officially dissolved in 1923. From the end of the nineteenth century, the British had been increasing their influence throughout Ottoman territory in Egypt and the Persian Gulf, seeking control over the Suez Canal and petroleum resources in the Gulf. The Ottomans had already lost their North African provinces to France in the mid-nineteenth century.

> **DID YOU KNOW?**
> In 1915, the Ottoman Empire launched a genocide against the Christian Armenian people, part of a campaign to control ethnic groups it believed threatened the Turkish nature of the empire. An estimated 1.5 million Armenians were forcibly removed from their homes and killed. To this day, the Turkish government denies the Armenian Genocide.

In 1908, the **Young Turks**, a military government, had effectively taken over the empire in an effort to modernize it. They were especially concerned with nationalism and promoting *Turkishness*, a focus on Turkish ethnicity and culture, throughout the diverse empire. An ally of Germany, the Ottoman Empire had been defeated in the war; tremendous losses led to the collapse of many Ottoman institutions. Poor organization and refugee movements led to starvation and chaos throughout the region.

In 1916, France and Britain concluded the **Sykes-Picot Agreement**, which secretly planned for the Middle East following the defeat of the Ottoman Empire. The Agreement divided up the region now considered the Middle East into spheres of influence to be controlled by each power; Palestine would be governed internationally. In 1917, the secret **Balfour Declaration** promised the Jews an independent state in Palestine, but Western powers did not honor this agreement; in fact it conflicted directly with the Sykes-Picot Agreement. The state of Israel was not established until 1948.

> **DID YOU KNOW?**
> The Zionist movement promoted the migration of European Jews to Palestine, where they settled, establishing a stronger Jewish presence in the area in addition to those Jews, Muslims, and Christians of Arab and other ethnicities already living in the region.

At the end of the war the area was indeed divided into **mandates**, areas nominally independent but effectively controlled by Britain and France. The borders drawn are essentially those national borders that divide the Middle East today. After the First World War, the nationalist **Mustafa Ataturk**, one of the Young Turks who pushed a secular, nationalist agenda, kept European powers out of Anatolia and abolished the Caliphate in 1924, establishing modern Turkey.

After the dissolution of the Ottoman Empire, the future of the Middle East was uncertain. Despite its weaknesses, the Ottoman

Empire had been the symbolic center of Islam, controlling Mecca and Medina. The Ottoman sultan held the title of Caliph, or the one entrusted with the leadership of those two holy cities. With the region broken up into European-controlled protectorates and an independent, nationalist, secular Turkey turned toward Europe, the social and political fabric of the region was becoming undone.

There was no more Caliph. Refugees and migrants had traveled throughout the Ottoman Empire over the course of the war, stopping in areas that were now suddenly restricted by international borders from their places of origin. People lacked identification papers. Ethnic and religious groups were divided by what would become the borders of the modern Middle East.

France and Britain backed different political factions in their mandates. While nominally autonomous, Egypt and its ruler, **KING FUAD**, were close allies of the British, having essentially been under their control. At the same time, **HUSAYN IBN ALI (KING HUSSEIN)** the Sherif of Mecca, claimed the title of Caliph, but was eventually driven out of Mecca and granted the title of king of Jordan by the British (his family controls the monarchy to this day). The rest of the Arabian Peninsula, where oil had not yet been discovered, was taken by the **SAUDIS**, a tribe from the desert which followed an extreme form of Islam, the **WAHHABI MOVEMENT**; King Saud would eventually conquer Mecca and Medina but never take the title of Caliph.

The roots of two competing ideologies, **PAN-ARABISM** and **ISLAMISM**, developed in this context. According to Pan-Arabism, Arabs and Arabic speakers should be aligned regardless of international borders. Similar to Pan-Slavism, Pan-Arabism eventually became an international movement espousing Arab unity in response to European and U.S. influence and presence later in the twentieth century.

Islamism began as a social and political movement. The **MUSLIM BROTHERHOOD** was established in Egypt in the 1920s, filling social roles that the state had abandoned or could not fill. Eventually taking a political role, the Muslim Brotherhood's model later inspired groups like Hamas and Hezbollah.

Russian Revolution

By 1917, Russia was suffering from widespread food shortages and economic crisis; morale was low due to conscription and as the military suffered enormous losses and humiliating defeats under the command of Nicholas II. During WWI, this combination of failures at home and on the front only added to widespread dissatisfaction with the rule of the Tsar. An enormous strike in Petrograd in January 1917 commemorating Bloody Sunday ended in revolt; soldiers refused to fire on protestors and the people formed the elected **PETROGRAD SOVIET** (Council) instead in the **FEBRUARY REVOLUTION**. The Tsar was forced to abdicate; the revolutionary movement resulted in the fall of his family, the Romanovs.

A weak provisional government was formed until elections could be held; however, it was widely regarded as working in the interests of the elite, making unpopular decisions like continuing to engage in WWI and putting off land reform. Meanwhile, other Soviets formed beyond Petrograd. The Provisional Government was ineffective in solving economic problems; however, the elected Soviets seemed to better represent the interests of the workers and peasants who suffered the most, and so they became more powerful. At the same time, the Soviets appealed to discontented soldiers fighting in the unpopular war.

The Bolsheviks, unlike the Mensheviks, believed that revolution must be planned and instigated at the right moment, not a phenomenon meant to occur naturally. The Bolsheviks, led by Lenin, consequently were not involved in the February Revolution. Lenin believed that revolution must be planned and that the proletariat needed direction in beginning and pursuing a revolution. However, later in 1917, the Bolsheviks had become a stronger force, and Lenin believed that the time was right to trigger revolution in Russia.

Lenin and the Bolsheviks proposed that power be concentrated in the Soviets, not in the Duma; that Russia would make peace and withdraw from European hostilities; that land would be redistributed among the peasants; and that economic crises in the cities would be solved. Lenin's plan was to take control of the Petrograd Soviet, of which **Leon Trotsky** had become chairman. In the **October Revolution** Lenin, Trotsky, and the Bolsheviks took control of Russia, defeating the Provisional Government in a coup.

In 1918, despite withdrawal from WWI, the **Russian Civil War** was underway; the **White Armies**, former supporters of the Tsar, were in conflict with the Bolshevik **Red Army**. During the war, the communists consolidated their power by nationalizing industry, developing and distributing propaganda portraying themselves as the defenders of Russia against imperialism, and forcefully eliminating dissent. For many, it was more appealing to fight for a new Russia with hope for an improved standard of living than to return to the old times under the Tsar; furthermore, many Russians feared the specter of imperialism or interference by foreign powers. By 1921, the Bolsheviks were victorious and formed the **Soviet Union** or **Union of Soviet Socialist Republics (U.S.S.R.)**.

Following Lenin's death in 1924, Trotsky and the Secretary of the Communist Party, **Josef Stalin**, struggled for power. Stalin ultimately outmaneuvered Trotsky, who was exiled and assassinated. Under Stalin's totalitarian dictatorship, the U.S.S.R. became socially and politically repressive; the Communist Party and the military underwent **purges** where any persons who were a potential threat to Stalin's power were imprisoned or executed. This paranoia and oppression extended to the general population: Russians suffered under the **Great Terror** throughout the 1920s. Any hint of dissent was to be reported to the secret police—the **NKVD**—and usually resulted in imprisonment for life.

DID YOU KNOW?
In the 1920s, around **twenty million Russians** were sent to the *gulags*, or prison labor camps, usually in Siberia, thousands of miles from their homes. Millions died.

Stalin also enforced **Russification** policies, persecuting ethnic groups. People throughout the U.S.S.R. were forced to speak Russian and limit or hide their own cultural practices. Religious practices were restricted or forbidden.

In 1931, Stalin enforced the **collectivization** of land and agriculture in an attempt to consolidate control over the countryside and improve food security. He had the **kulaks**, or landowning peasants, sent to the *gulags*, enabling the government to confiscate their land. By 1939, most farming and land was controlled by the government, and most peasants lived on collective land. Collectivizing the farms enabled Stalin to encourage more peasants to leave the city and become industrial workers, to produce agricultural surpluses to sell overseas, and to eliminate the *kulaks*. However, systemic disorganization in the 1920s and early 1930s did result in famine and food shortages.

As part of modernizing Russia, Stalin focused on accelerating industrial development. Targeting heavy industry, these **Five Year Plans** increased production in industrial materials and staples like electricity, petroleum, coal, and iron; they also resulted in the construction of major infrastructure throughout the country from 1929–1938. These developments provided opportunities for women, but conditions for the workers were dismal. The U.S.S.R. quickly became an industrial power, but at the expense of millions of Russians, Ukrainians and other groups who lost their lives in purges, forced labor camps, and famine.

Change in East Asia

Following its victory in the Russo-Japanese War, Japan had been more visible internationally in the early part of the twentieth century. That country had undergone rapid modernization after being closed off from 1600 until the mid-nineteenth century under the **Tokugawa Shogunate**; now, recognized as a military power for defeating Russia, Japan had joined a world focused on industry and imperialism.

Japan, having already embraced industrialization and modern militarization, turned towards imperialism throughout Asia. From 1894–1895, Japan had fought the **First Sino-Japanese War** with Qing Dynasty China, establishing trading rights there, gaining influence over China's vassal **Korea**, and controlling **Taiwan** in the **Treaty of Shimonoseki**. This conflict revealed Chinese military and organizational limitations and showed Japanese military superiority.

The Russo-Japanese War had been important not only to solidify Japanese influence in Korea and Manchuria, but also to confirm Japan's status in the eyes of European empires as a world power. In 1910, Japan annexed Korea. After WWI, Japan was granted Germany's **Pacific Islands** by the League of Nations.

Following the First World War, despite having provided assistance to the French and British in Asia, Japan began its own imperialist adventure in East and Southeast Asia not only to gain power and access to raw materials, but also to limit and eventually expel European rule in what Japan considered its *SPHERE OF INFLUENCE*. In 1931, Japan invaded **MANCHURIA**, creating the puppet state **MANCHUKUO**.

While Japan was building military and economic strength in Asia and its global reputation, China was undergoing political change. The **XINHAI REVOLUTION** broke out in 1911, resulting in the overthrow of the Qing and the end of dynastic Chinese rule, establishing the short-lived **REPUBLIC OF CHINA**. Led by **SUN YAT-SEN**, the revolutionaries not only had the support of the disaffected Chinese people; they also had the financial support of millions of Chinese living abroad.

However, despite Republican recognition by major international powers, the power vacuum left by the end of imperial China allowed the rise of warlords throughout the enormous country, and the government was unable to establish total control. The **KUOMINTANG (KMT)**, or Nationalist Party of the revolutionary government worked to consolidate government power; following Sun Yat-sen's death in 1925, the KMT leader **CHIANG KAI-SHEK** (or **JIANG JIESHI**) went on to take control of much of China back from the warlords.

At the same time, communism was emerging in China. The country felt betrayed by European powers, which had awarded German possessions in China to Japan in the Treaty of Versailles. China refused to sign the treaty, and communism became popular among some Chinese leaders; thus emerged the **CHINESE COMMUNIST PARTY**. Temporarily

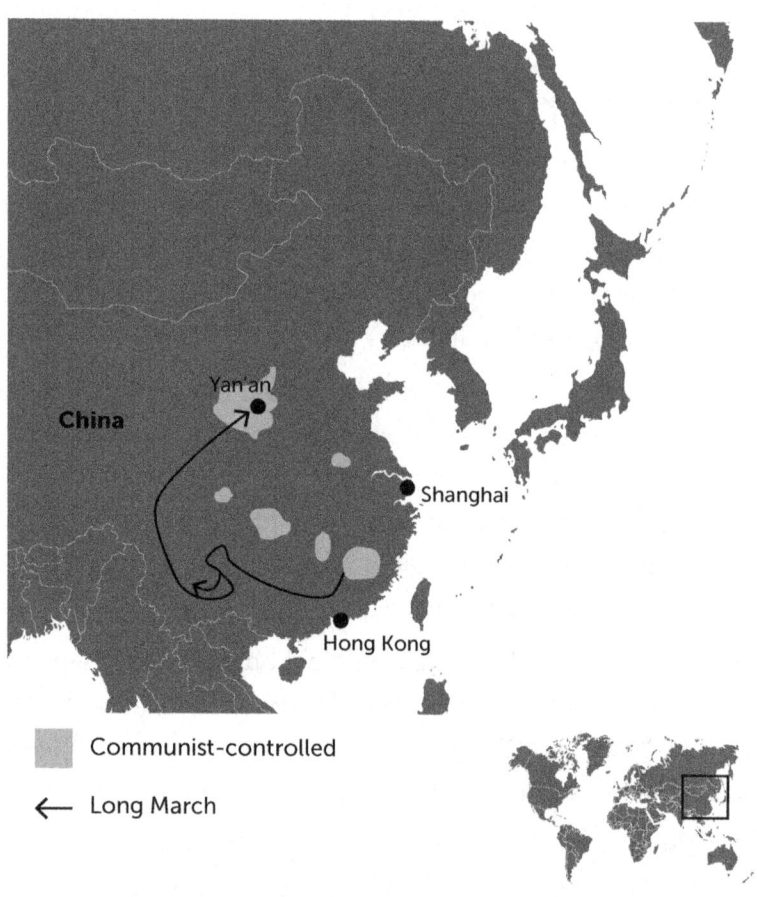

Figure 6.2. The Long March

working together, the KMT and CCP were able to bring Chinese territory back under Republican control. However, Chiang turned against the CCP in 1927, driving it south.

The CCP focused its organizing activities in the countryside on the peasants, becoming powerful in southern China. However, KMT attacks on the CCP in the south in 1934 forced the CCP to retreat on the **LONG MARCH** north. During this time of hardship, **MAO ZEDONG** emerged as the leader of the movement.

World War II

Meanwhile, Germany suffered under the provisions of the Treaty of Versailles. In 1919, a democratic government was established at Weimar—the **WEIMAR REPUBLIC**. Germany was in chaos; the Kaiser had fled and the country was torn apart by war. However, the new government could not bring stability.

Blamed for WWI, Germany owed huge **REPARATIONS** according to the treaty to pay for the cost of the war, setting off **HYPERINFLATION** and impoverishing the country and its people. The rise of communists and a workers' party that came to be known as the National Socialist Party, or **NAZI PARTY**, led to further political instability. Following the crash of the stock market in 1929, German unemployment reached six million; furthermore, the United States had called in its foreign loans. Consequently, unemployed workers began supporting communism. On the other hand, the Nazis, led by **ADOLF HITLER**, gained support from business interests, which feared communist power in government. Thus, the Nazis became an important force in the Weimar Republic at the beginning of the 1930s.

Hitler maneuvered into the role of chancellor by 1933. His charisma and popular platform—to cancel the Treaty of Versailles—allowed him to rise. Enjoying the support of the wealthy and big business, which feared communism (especially with the development of Soviet Russia), Nazi ideals appealed strongly to both industry and the workers in the face of global economic depression. Finally, the Nazi Minister of Propaganda **JOSEPH GOEBBELS** executed an effective propaganda campaign, and would do so throughout Hitler's rule, known as the **THIRD REICH**.

The following year, Hitler became the **FÜHRER**, or leader, of Germany. A series of chaotic events followed: a fire in the Reichstag (German Parliament), which allowed Hitler to arrest communist leaders; the rise of the **GESTAPO**, or secret police (which violently enforced Nazi rule among the people); and the banning of political parties and trade unions. As a result, Hitler and the Nazis consolidated total control. They also set into motion their agenda of racism and genocide against "non-Aryan" (non-Germanic) or "racially impure" people.

Jewish people were particularly targeted. Germany had a considerable Jewish population; so did the other Central and Eastern European countries that Germany would come to control. Throughout the 1930s, the Nazis passed a series of laws limiting Jewish rights, including jobs that Jewish people could hold, rights to citizenship, places they could go, public facilities they could use, whom they could marry, even the names they could have. **Kristallnacht** took place in 1938, an organized series of attacks on Jewish businesses, homes, and places of worship, so called because the windows of these places were smashed.

In 1939, Jews were forced from their homes into **ghettoes**, isolated and overcrowded urban neighborhoods; in 1941, they were forced to wear **yellow stars** identifying them as Jewish. Millions of Jewish people were sent to **concentration camps**; the Nazis decided on the **Final Solution** to the "Jewish Question": to murder Jewish people by systematically gassing them at death camps. At least six million European Jews were murdered by the Nazis in the **Holocaust**.

Roma, Slavic people, homosexuals, disabled people, people of color, prisoners of war, communists, and others not considered "Aryan" were also forced into slave labor in concentration camps and murdered there. Later, this concept of torturing and killing people based on their ethnicity in order to exterminate them would become defined as **genocide**.

Hitler was a **fascist**, believing in a mostly free market accompanied by a dictatorial government with a strong military. He sought to restore Germany's power and expand its reach by annexing **Austria** (the **Anschluss**, or *union*) and the **Sudetenland**, German-majority areas in part of what is today the Czech Republic.

With the collapse of the Weimar Republic and the League of Nations at its weakest state, France and Britain granted the Sudetenland to Hitler in 1938 in a policy called **appeasement** in an effort to maintain stability in Europe and avoid another war. In fact, given the threat posed by the new Soviet Union, Britain and France actually believed that a stronger Germany would be in their interests.

However, appeasement failed when Hitler invaded the rest of **Czechoslovakia** and formed an alliance with Italy the next year.

The Soviet Union made a pact with Germany in 1939: Germany would not invade the U.S.S.R., and the two countries would divide **Poland**. Germany then invaded Poland; its 1939 invasion is commonly considered the beginning of the **Second World War** (though some historians actually consider the Japanese invasion of Manchuria in 1931 to be the beginning of the war).

War exploded in Europe in 1939 as Hitler gained control of more land than any European power since Napoleon. In 1940, Germany had taken Paris. The **Battle of Britain** began in July of that year; however Germany suffered its first defeat and was unable to take Britain. Despite staying out of combat, in 1941 the United States enforced the **Lend-Lease Act** which provided support and military aid to Britain. The two also released the **Atlantic Charter**, outlining common goals.

When Japan joined the **Axis** powers of Germany and Italy, the **Second Sino-Japanese War** of 1937 would also be subsumed under the Second World War, ending in 1945. The CHINESE CIVIL WAR between communists led by Mao Zedong and nationalists led by Chiang Kai-shek was interrupted by the Second Sino-Japanese War, when Japan tried to extend its imperial reach deeper into China, resulting in atrocities like the RAPE OF NANKING (1937–1938).

At this time, Chiang was forced to form an alliance with Mao and the two forces worked together against Japan. By the end of the war, the CCP was stronger than ever, with widespread support from many sectors of Chinese society, while the KMT was demoralized and had little popular support.

In June of 1941, Japan, now part of the Axis along with Germany and Italy, attacked the United States at Pearl Harbor. Consequently, the U.S. joined the war in Europe and in the Pacific, deploying thousands of troops in both theaters.

DID YOU KNOW?
The Atlantic Charter described the "eight common principles" shared by the US and Britain, the most important of which were restoring self-governance in occupied Europe and the liberalization of international trade.

Meanwhile, in Asia, Japan continued its imperialist policies. In the early 1940s, it took advantage of chaos in Europe and the weakened European colonial powers to invade and occupy FRENCH INDOCHINA, INDONESIA, and BURMA; it also occupied the PHILIPPINES. Controlling these strategic areas meant the Axis was a direct threat to British India, Australia, and the eastern Soviet Union, not to mention European imperial and economic interests.

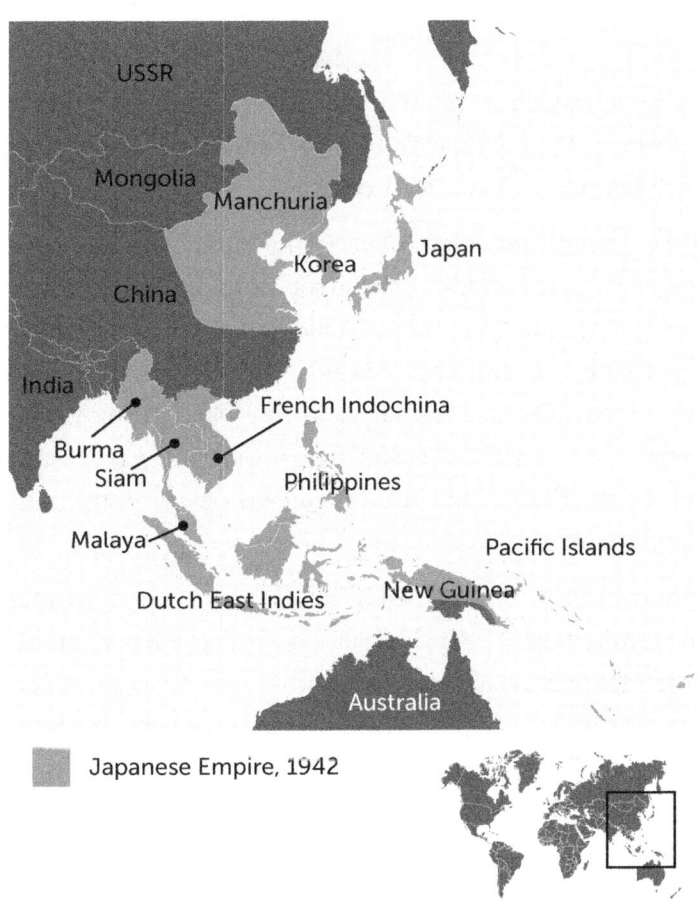

Figure 6.3. Japanese Expansion in Asia

Back in Europe, having broken his promise to the Soviet Union, Hitler invaded Russia. But in 1942, the U.S.S.R. defeated Germany at the **Battle of Stalingrad**, a turning point in the war during which the Nazis were forced to turn from the Eastern Front. In 1943, Churchill, Roosevelt, and Stalin all met in Teheran to discuss the invasion of Italy; the Allies took Rome later that year.

In 1944, the Allies invaded France on **D-Day**. While they liberated Paris in August, the costly **Battle of the Bulge** extended into 1945. Despite thousands of American casualties, Hitler's forces were pushed back. In the spring of 1945, the U.S. crossed the Rhine while the U.S.S.R. invaded Berlin; Hitler killed himself and the Allies accepted German surrender.

The war in the Pacific would continue, however. Strategic battles were fought in **Saipan** and **Iwo Jima** to secure landing strips for American B-52 bombers. At **Leyte**, the U.S. destroyed most of the Japanese Navy. Despite casualties of up to 400,000, Japan continued to fight the U.S. for territory in the Philippines. Finally, even after the war in Europe had ended, the U.S. and Japan fought over **Okinawa**, which the U.S. planned to use as a staging point for an invasion of Japan in order to force Japanese surrender.

An American invasion of Japan would have likely resulted in hundreds of thousands of casualties. **President Truman**, who had succeeded Roosevelt, elected to use the nuclear bomb on Japan instead to force surrender. In 1945, the U.S. bombed the Japanese cities of **Hiroshima** and **Nagasaki**. The tremendous civilian casualties did force the Emperor to surrender; at that point, the Second World War came to an end.

That year in China, the Chinese Civil War recommenced; by 1949 the communists had emerged victorious. The KMT withdrew to Taiwan, while Mao and the CCP took over China, which became a communist country.

WWII and the period immediately preceding it saw horrific violations of human rights in Europe and Asia, including the atrocities committed during the Japanese invasions of China, Korea and Southeast Asia, and the European Holocaust of Jews and other groups like Roma and homosexuals. The war finally ended with the U.S. atomic bombings of Hiroshima and Nagasaki in 1945, ending years of firebombing civilians in Germany and Japan; devastating ground and naval warfare throughout Europe, Asia, the South Pacific, and Africa; and the deaths of millions of soldiers and civilians all around the world.

The extreme horrors of WWII helped develop the concept of **genocide**, or the effort to extinguish an entire group of people because of their ethnicity, and the idea of **human rights**. The **United Nations** was formed, based on the League of Nations, as a body to champion human rights and uphold international security. Its **Security Council** is made up of permanent member states which can intervene militarily in the interests of international stability.

Allied forces took the lead in rebuilding efforts: the U.S. occupied areas in East Asia and Germany, while the Soviet Union remained in Eastern Europe. The Allies had planned to rebuild Europe according to the **Marshall Plan**; however, Stalin broke his promise made at the 1945 **Yalta Conference** to adhere to that plan and allow Eastern European countries to hold free elections. Instead, the U.S.S.R. occupied these countries and they came under communist control. The **Cold War** had begun.

The Cold War

At the Yalta Conference in February 1945, Stalin, Churchill, and Roosevelt had agreed upon the division of Germany, the free nature of government in Poland, and free elections in Eastern Europe. However, at the **Potsdam Conference** in July 1945, things had changed. Harry Truman had replaced Franklin D. Roosevelt, who had died in office, and Clement Atlee had replaced Winston Churchill. Stalin felt betrayed by the U.S. use of the nuclear bomb; likewise, the U.S. and the British felt that Stalin had violated the agreement at Yalta regarding democracy in Eastern Europe.

Stalin ensured that communists came to power in Eastern Europe, setting up satellite states at the Soviet perimeter in violation of the Yalta agreement. The Soviet rationale was to establish a buffer zone following its extraordinarily heavy casualties in WWII—around twenty million. With Stalin's betrayal of the Allies' agreement, in the words of the British Prime Minister **Winston Churchill**, an *iron curtain* had come down across Europe, dividing east from west.

Consequently, western states organized the North Atlantic Treaty Organization or **NATO**, an agreement wherein an attack on one was an attack on all; this treaty provided for collective security in the face of the Soviet expansionist threat. The United States adopted a policy of containment, the idea that communism should be *contained*, as part of the **Truman Doctrine** of foreign policy. The United States also sponsored the **Marshall Plan**, which provided aid to European countries in an effort to restart the European economy and rebuild the continent. Stalin did not permit Soviet-controlled countries to take Marshall aid.

In response, the Soviet Union created the **Warsaw Pact**, a similar organization consisting of Eastern European communist countries. **Nuclear weapons**, especially the development of the extremely powerful **hydrogen bomb**, raised the stakes of the conflict. The concept of **mutually-assured destruction**, or the understanding that a nuclear strike by one country would result in a response by the other, ultimately destroying the entire world, may have prevented the outbreak of active violence.

QUICK REVIEW
How did the Cold War erupt between the Allies and the Soviet Union?

Germany itself had been divided into four zones, controlled by Britain, France, the U.S., and the U.S.S.R. Berlin had been divided the same way. Once Britain, France, and the U.S. united their zones into West Germany in 1948 and introduced a new currency, the U.S.S.R. cut off West Berlin in the **Berlin Blockade**. Viewing this as an aggressive attempt to capture the entire city, for nearly a year western powers provided supplies to West Berlin by air in the **Berlin Airlift**.

Berlin continued to be a problem for the U.S.S.R. Until 1961, refugees from the Eastern Bloc came to West Berlin, seeking better living conditions in the West. Furthermore, West Berlin was a center for Western espionage. In 1961, the U.S.S.R., now led by **Nikita Khrushchev**, closed the border and constructed the **Berlin Wall**.

Following the Second World War, Korea had also been divided. In the northern part of the country, the communist **Kim il Sung** controlled territory. South of the **thirty-eighth parallel**, the non-communist Syngman Rhee controlled the rest of the country. In 1950, Kim il Sung invaded the south with Russian and Chinese support, intending to create a communist Korea.

According to the Truman Doctrine, communism needed to be contained. Furthermore, according to **Domino Theory**, if one country became communist, then more would, too, like a row of dominoes falling. Therefore, the United States, by way of the United Nations, became involved in the **Korean War** (1950–1953).

Figure 6.4. The Communist World

UN troops dominated and led by the U.S. came to the aid of the nearly defeated South Koreans, pushing back Kim il Sung's troops. China supported Kim il Sung, and war on the peninsula continued until 1953, when U.S. President Eisenhower threatened to use the nuclear bomb, ending the war in a stalemate.

Later, in **CUBA**, the revolutionary **FIDEL CASTRO** took over in 1959. Allied with the Soviet Union, he allowed missile bases to be constructed in Cuba, which threatened the United States. During the **CUBAN MISSILE CRISIS** in 1962, the world came closer than ever to nuclear war when the U.S.S.R. sent missiles to Cuba. Its ships facing an American blockade, tension grew as the U.S. considered invading Cuba. President Kennedy and Premier Khrushchev were able to come to an agreement in which the U.S.S.R. promised to dismantle its Cuban bases as long as the U.S. ended the blockade and secretly dismantled its own missile bases in Turkey. Nuclear war was averted.

Despite this success, the United States engaged in a lengthy violent conflict in Southeast Asia. Supporting anti-communist fighters in Vietnam in keeping with containment and Domino Theory, the United States pursued the **VIETNAM WAR** for almost a decade. The **GULF OF TONKIN RESOLUTION** authorized the U.S. president to manage the ongoing conflict without consulting Congress, so for a period of years troops continued to be deployed to the region, fueling the conflict.

The U.S. had become involved in the war after coming to the aid of Vietnam's old colonial master, France. **HO CHI MINH**, the revolutionary Vietnamese leader, had actually originally approached the Americans for assistance in asserting Vietnamese independence. He led the North Vietnamese forces (**VIET CONG**) in a guerrilla war for independence throughout the 1960s.

Despite being outnumbered, Viet Cong familiarity with the difficult terrain, support from Russia and China, and determination eventually resulted in victory. Bloody guerrilla warfare demoralized the American military, but the 1968 **TET OFFENSIVE** was a turning point. Despite enormous losses, the North Vietnamese won a strategic victory in this coordinated, surprise offensive. Extreme objection to the war within the United States, high casualties, and demoralization eventually resulted in U.S. withdrawal in 1975.

Toward the end of the 1960s and into the 1970s, the Cold War reached a period of **DÉTENTE**, or a warming of relations. The U.S. and U.S.S.R. signed the **NUCLEAR NON-PROLIFERATION TREATY**, in which they and other nuclear power signatories agreed not to further spread nuclear weapons technology. Later, the U.S.S.R. and the U.S. signed the **SALT I TREATY** (Strategic Arms Limitation Treaty), limiting strategic weaponry. Some cultural exchanges and partnerships in outer space took place.

At the same time, the United States began making diplomatic overtures toward communist China. This was however, part of a different Cold War strategy. Despite its status as a communist country, China and the U.S.S.R. had difficult relations due to their differing views on the nature of communism. While Khrushchev was taking a more moderate approach to world communism, Mao believed in more aggressive policies. Following the **SINO-SOVIET SPLIT** of the 1960s, China had lost much Soviet support for its modernization programs and despite advances in agriculture and some industrialization, Mao's programs like the **GREAT LEAP FORWARD** had taken a toll on the people.

In 1972, President Nixon visited China, establishing relations between the communist government and the United States. Communist China was permitted to join the UN (previously, China had been represented by the KMT, which was isolated to Taiwan).

The climate would change again, however, in the 1970s and 1980s. The U.S. and U.S.S.R. found themselves on opposite sides in proxy wars throughout the world (see below). In addition, and the ARMS RACE was underway. PRESIDENT RONALD REAGAN pursued a militaristic policy, prioritizing weapons development with the goal of outspending the U.S.S.R. on weapons technology.

DID YOU KNOW?
Perhaps the most famous proposal in weapons technology during this time was the Strategic Defense Initiative; popularly known as *Star Wars*, this outer-space based system would have intercepted Soviet intercontinental ballistic missiles.

Decolonization

Meanwhile, the former colonies of the fallen European colonial powers had won or were in the process of gaining their independence. One role of the United Nations was to help manage the DECOLONIZATION process. Already, the leader MOHANDAS GANDHI had led a peaceful independence movement in India against the British, winning Indian independence in 1949. His assassination by Hindu radicals led to conflict between HINDUS and MUSLIMS in the SUBCONTINENT, resulting in PARTITION, the bloody division

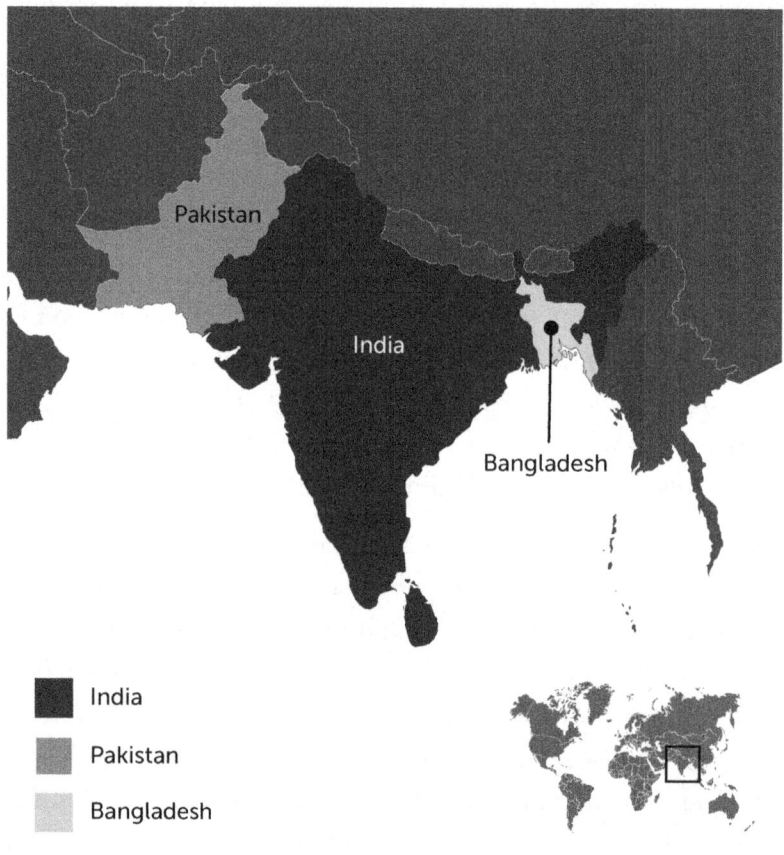

Figure 6.5. Partition

of India: Hindus fled into what is today India, while Muslims fled to **East Pakistan** (now **Bangladesh** and **West Pakistan**). Instability is ongoing on the Subcontinent.

Bloody conflict in Africa like the **Algerian War** against France (1954–1962), the **Mau Mau Rebellion** against the British in Kenya in the 1950s, and violent movements against Belgium in the Congo ultimately resulted in African independence for many countries in the 1950s, 1960s, and 1970s; likewise, so did strong leadership by African nationalist leaders and thinkers like **Jomo Kenyatta**, **Julius Nyerere** and **Kwame Nkrumah**. The apartheid regime in South Africa, where segregation between races was legal and people of color lived in oppressive conditions, was not lifted until the 1990s; **Nelson Mandela** led the country in a peaceful transition process.

In the Middle East, following the fall of the Ottoman Empire after WWI European powers had taken over much of the area; these **protectorates** became independent states with arbitrary borders drawn and rulers installed by the Europeans. The creation of the state of **Israel** was especially contentious: in the 1917 **Balfour Declaration**, the British had promised the **Zionist** movement of European Jews that they would be given a homeland in the British-controlled protectorate of Palestine; however, the U.S. assured the Arabs in 1945 that a Jewish state would not be founded there. Israel emerged from diplomatic confusion, chaos and tragedy after the murder of millions of Jews in Europe, and violence on the ground in Palestine carried out by both Jews and Arabs. This legacy of conflict lasts to this day in the Middle East.

While the Middle East had been divided into protectorates or into nominally independent states like Egypt that were still under strong European influence, these areas had become independent after the Second World War. Liberal activists against monarchical and dictatorial regimes and popular movements like Pan-Arabism and Islamism put pressure on Middle Eastern monarchies. Countries created by artificial borders based on the Sykes-Picot Agreement and comprised of divided and diverse ethnic and religious groups were already vulnerable to political instability; with added unrest, Middle Eastern governments fell. Furthermore, the Middle East became a Cold War battleground, with regimes courting the support of the Cold War powers.

In Egypt, **Gamal Abdul Nasser** led the Pan-Arabist movement in the region, which included creating an Arab alliance against Israel. In 1967, Arab allies launched a war against Israel; they were badly beaten, however, in the **Six Day War**, an embarrassing defeat for the Arab states and one from which Nasser never truly recovered. Furthermore, Israel took control of the Sinai Peninsula, the Golan Heights and the West Bank of the Jordan River.

During the 1973 **Yom Kippur War**, while the U.S. supported **Israel**, the U.S.S.R. supported **Syria** and **Egypt**. Syria and Egypt had launched a surprise attack on Israel on the holiest day of the Jewish year in an attempt to gain back territory lost years prior. However, Israel was able to maintain its defenses.

In 1978, the American president Jimmy Carter was able to broker a peace agreement between the Egyptian leader **Anwar Sadat** and the Israeli leader **Menachem Begin** known as the **Camp David Accords**. However, other Arab countries, aside from Jordan, did not make peace with Israel. By the 1970s, Pan-Arabism was no longer the popular, unifying movement it had once been.

The **Non-Aligned Movement** arose in response to the Cold War. Instead of the bipolar world of the Cold War (one democratic, led by the U.S., the other communist, led by the U.S.S.R.), the Non-Aligned Movement sought an alternative: the **Third World**. Non-Aligned or Third World countries wanted to avoid succumbing to the influence of either of the superpowers, and many found a forum in the United Nations in which to strengthen their international profiles.

However, throughout the Cold War, **proxy wars** between the U.S. and the U.S.S.R. were fought around the world. In the 1980s, the United States began supporting the anti-communist **Contras** in **Nicaragua**, who were fighting the communist **Sandinista** government. In 1979, the U.S.S.R. invaded **Afghanistan**, an event which would contribute to the Soviet collapse; in response, the U.S. began supporting anti-Soviet **Mujahideen** forces (some of whose patrons would later attack the U.S. as part of international terrorist groups). Other examples include the **Angolan Civil War**, the **Mozambican Civil War**; and the **Nicaraguan Revolution**.

In the **Horn of Africa**, Somalia was formed when the Italian-administered UN trust territory of Somalia united with the British protectorate of Somaliland in 1960. Initially supported by the U.S.S.R. for its socialist leanings, Somalia and its leader, Mohamed Siad Barre, initated a war against Ethiopia in 1977. Ultimately the U.S.S.R. supported Ethiopia, and the United States supported Somalia.

QUICK REVIEW
What is a proxy war? Why were proxy wars important in the context of the Cold War?

While never officially colonized, **Iran** had been under the oppressive regime of the western-supported **Shah Reza Pahlavi** for decades. During its imperial era, Britain had begun exploring petroleum interests in what was then Persia, and western oil companies had remained powerful in that country. The **Pahlavi Dynasty** had taken over Persia in 1920 from the Qajars, who had ruled since 1785, and who themselves had been important in administration under the Safavids since the sixteenth century.

By the 1970s, the Shah's corrupt, oppressive regime was extremely unpopular in Iran, but it was propped up by the West. Several underground movements worked against the Shah, including communists and Islamic revolutionaries inspired by the Islamism of the early twentieth century. In the 1979 **Iranian Revolution**, these forces overthrew the Shah; shortly afterward, Islamist revolutionaries took over the country. The new theocracy was led by a group of clerics led by the Supreme Leader **Ayatollah Khomeini**. The Ayatollah became Supreme Leader and instituted political and social reforms, including stricter interpretations of Islamic laws and traditions and enforcing those throughout the country as national and local law. Later that year, radical students

DID YOU KNOW?
The revolutionary Iranian government would go on to support Shi'a militants (the Hezbollah, or the Party of God) in the **Lebanese Civil War** throughout the 1980s; this group is also inspired by Islamism.

who supported the revolution stormed the U.S. Embassy and held a number of staff hostage for over a year; the **IRAN HOSTAGE CRISIS** would humiliate the United States.

Following the Iranian Revolution, the Iraqi leader **SADDAM HUSSEIN**, an ally of the United States, declared war against Iran. While governed by Sunnis, Iraq was actually a Shi'ite-majority country, and Saddam feared Iran would trigger a similar revolution there. Iraq also sought control over the strategic Shatt al-Arab waterway and some oil-rich territories inland. The war raged from 1980–1990.

EXAMPLES

1. Which of the following was a weakness of the Schlieffen Plan?
   A) It overstretched the German army.
   B) It failed to anticipate a stronger resistance in France.
   C) It underestimated Russia's ability to mobilize its troops.
   D) all of the above

2. According to the Sykes-Picot Agreement,
   A) Israel would become an independent state.
   B) Husayn ibn Ali would become Caliph.
   C) Ataturk would lead an independent Turkey.
   D) Palestine would be under international supervision.

3. Which of the following led to the rise of the Nazis in early 1930s Germany?
   A) the impact of reparations and the support of German industrialists
   B) the impact of the Great Depression and the support of the workers
   C) support from the international communist movement and the impact of reparations on the German economy
   D) support from German industrialists and strong backing from other political factions in the Reichstag

4. The Cold War was rooted in
   A) Stalin's unwillingness to cede control of East Berlin to the allies following the fall of the Nazis.
   B) the erection of the Berlin Wall.
   C) Stalin's failure to honor the agreement at Yalta, installing communist regimes in Eastern Europe rather than permitting free, democratic elections
   D) the Cuban Missile Crisis

5. Which of the following precipitated the end of the Cold War?
   A) the Iran Hostage Crisis
   B) the Soviet War in Afghanistan
   C) the Iran-Iraq War
   D) the Yom Kippur War

Post-Cold War World

In 1991, the Soviet Union fell when Soviet Premier **Mikhail Gorbachev**, who had implemented reforms like **glasnost** and **perestroika** (or *openness* and *transparency*) was nearly overthrown in a coup; a movement led by **Boris Yeltsin**, who had been elected president of Russia, stopped the coup. The U.S.S.R. was dissolved later that year and Yeltsin became president of the Russian Federation. The war in Afghanistan and military overspending in an effort to keep up with American military spending had weakened the U.S.S.R. to the point of collapse, and the Cold War ended.

COLD WAR CONSEQUENCES

That same year, Saddam Hussein, the leader of Iraq, invaded Kuwait and took over its oil reserves and production facilities. In response, the United States and other countries went to war—with a UN mandate—to expel Iraq from Kuwait and to defend Saudi Arabia in order to regain control of the world's petroleum reserves in the **Gulf War**. This event cemented the U.S. status as the sole world superpower; the global balance of power had changed.

Despite stability throughout most of Europe, the changes following the fall of the Iron Curtain led to instability in the Balkans. In 1992, Bosnia declared its independence from the collapsing state of Yugoslavia, following Croatia and Slovenia. Violence broke out in Bosnia between Bosnian Serbs on one side, and Bosnian Muslims (Bosniaks) and Croatians on the other. The **Bosnian War** raged from 1992 to 1995, resulting in the deaths of thousands of civilians and another European genocide—this time, of Bosnian Muslims.

Also following the Cold War, proxy wars throughout the world and instability in former colonies continued. In 1994, conflict in Central Africa resulted in the **Rwandan Genocide**. Hutus massacred Tutsis, and violence continued on both sides. In **Zaire**, the country descended into instability following the fall of **Mobutu Sese Seko**, the U.S.-supported dictator, in 1997. Renamed the **Democratic Republic of the Congo**, parts of this country and others in Central Africa would remain wracked by poverty and torn by violence for decades.

In the 1980s, drought in the Horn of Africa led to widespread famine; humanitarian affairs and issues came into the public eye and the general public, especially in wealthier families, became more concerned about providing foreign aid to the suffering.

The Somali leader Mohamed Siad Barre was overthrown in 1991 and Somalia was broken up under the control of various warlords and clans. The people suffered from starvation with the breakdown of social order. The United States intervened as part of a UN peacekeeping mission in an attempt to provide humanitarian aid; however, strong military resistance from the warlord Muhammad Aideed impacted U.S. public opinion and the effort failed. To this day there is no central government in Somalia, and much of the country is still dependent on aid; however, autonomous areas function independently.

COOPERATION and CONFLICT

Following the end of the Cold War and post-decolonization, the balance of economic and political power began to change. The **G-20**, the world's twenty most important economic and political powers, includes many former colonies and non-European countries. The **BRICS**—Brazil, Russia, India, China, and South Africa—are recognized as world economic and political leaders. With the exception of Russia, all these countries were only recently classified as developing countries. While still wrestling with considerable social, economic, and political challenges, the BRICS are world powers in their own right as independent nations—unthinkable developments a century ago.

Steps toward European unification had begun as early as the 1950s; the **European Union**, as it is known today, was formed after the **Maastricht Treaty** was signed in 1992. As the former Soviet satellite states moved from communism to more democratic societies and capitalistic economies, more countries partnered with the EU and eventually joined it; as of 2015, twenty-eight countries are members, with more on the path to membership.

European Union countries remain independent, but they cooperate in international affairs, justice, security and foreign policy, environmental matters, and economic policy. Many also share a common currency, the **euro**. According to the **Schengen Agreement**, some EU countries even have open borders.

Continental integration exists beyond Europe. In Africa, the **African Union**, originally the Organization of African Unity, has become a stronger political force in its own right, organizing peacekeeping missions throughout the continent. An organization similar to the EU, the AU is a forum for African countries to organize and align political, military, economic, and other policies.

In this era of globalization, international markets became increasingly open through free-trade agreements like **NAFTA** (the North American Free Trade Agreement), **Mercosur** (the South American free-trade zone), and the **Trans-Pacific Partnership**, a proposed free-trade zone between nine countries on the Pacific Ocean. The **World Trade Organization** oversees international trade. Technological advances like improvements in transportation infrastructure and the **internet** made international communication faster, easier and cheaper.

However, more open borders, reliable international transportation, and faster, easier worldwide communication brought risks, too. In the early twenty-first century, the United States was attacked by terrorists on **September 11, 2001**, resulting in

DID YOU KNOW?
While benefits of international trade include lower prices and more consumer choice, unemployment often increases in more developed countries and labor and environmental violations are more likely in developing countries.

thousands of civilian casualties. Consequently, the U.S. launched a major land war in Afghanistan and another later in Iraq.

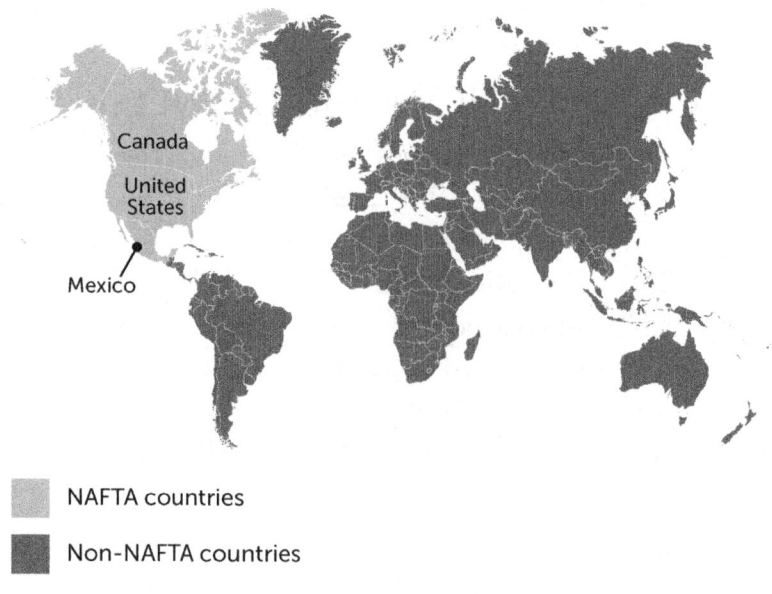

Figure 6.6. NAFTA Countries

Following the attacks on 9/11, the United States attacked Afghanistan as part of the **War on Terror**. Afghanistan's radical Islamist **Taliban** government was providing shelter to the group that took responsibility for the attacks, **al Qaeda**. Led by **Osama bin Laden**, al Qaeda was inspired by Islamism and also by the radical Wahhabism of the remote Arabian desert followed by the Saudis. Bin Laden had fought the Soviets with the U.S.-supported Afghan *mujahideen* during the 1980s; despite that alliance, bin Laden and his followers were angered by U.S. involvement in the Middle East throughout the 1990s and its support of Israel. While bin Laden was killed by the United States in 2011, and while control of Afghan security was turned over from the U.S. to the U.S. backed government in 2014, the U.S. still maintains a strong military presence in the country.

The Iraq War began in 2003 when the U.S. invaded that country under the faulty premises that Saddam Hussein's regime was involved with al Qaeda, supported international terrorism, and possessed weapons of mass destruction that it intended to use in pursuit of terrorism. Iraq descended into chaos, with thousands of civilian and military casualties, Iraqi and American alike. While the country technically and legally remains intact under a U.S.-supported government, the ethnically and religiously diverse country is de facto divided as a result of the disintegration of central power.

Elsewhere in the Middle East, reform movements began in the 2011 **Arab Spring** in Tunisia, Egypt, Bahrain, and Syria. Some dictatorial regimes have been replaced with democratic governments; other countries still enjoy limited freedoms or even civil unrest. In Syria, unrest erupted into civil war between **Bashar al Assad**, who inherited leadership from his father, and opposition fighters. One consequence has been enormous movements of refugees into Europe.

Today, a new group known as the Islamic State of Iraq and al Sham (**ISIS**) referring to Iraq and Syria (or Islamic State of Iraq and the Levant—ISIL) has filled the vacuum in parts of northern and western Iraq and eastern Syria. ISIS has established a de facto state in Iraq and Syria with extremist Islamist policies and presents a global terror threat.

Uprisings in Israeli-occupied West Bank and Gaza have continued sporadically. Israel passed control of **Gaza** to the Palestinian Authority in 2005; however following political divisions within Palestinian factions, Gaza is controlled by Hamas while the Palestinian Authority represents Palestinian interests abroad and in the **West Bank**. In 1999, U.S. President Clinton attempted to broker a final peace deal between the Israelis and Palestinians delineating borders as part of a two-state solution, but these efforts failed and conflict continues.

EXAMPLES

6. While immediately after the fall of the Soviet Union the U.S. emerged as the sole superpower, in the twenty-first century, which phenomenon has so far characterized global governance?
    - A) international terrorism
    - B) international economic and political organizations
    - C) international conflict
    - D) the European Union

7. What was one reason for the Bosnian War?
    - A) attacks by Bosniak Islamic extremists
    - B) the dissolution of Yugoslavia
    - C) the separation of Yugoslavia from the U.S.S.R.
    - D) attacks by Middle Eastern Islamic extremists

8. What is one major role that the African Union plays?
    - A) The AU is a free trade area.
    - B) The AU manages a single currency.
    - C) The AU manages several peacekeeping forces.
    - D) The AU represents individual African countries in international diplomacy.

9. Which of the following is NOT a reason that the Soviet Union collapsed?
    - A) *glasnost*
    - B) *perestroika*
    - C) the war in Afghanistan
    - D) the rise of the Taliban

10. Despite his alliance with the U.S.-supported mujahedeen in the war in Afghanistan against the Soviets, Osama bin Laden sponsored attacks against the United States because

- **A)** he opposed a U.S. military presence in Saudi Arabia.
- **B)** he opposed U.S. support of Israel.
- **C)** he wanted to establish a global Islamist regime in accordance with the extremist, unorthodox beliefs rooted in Wahhabism.
- **D)** all of the above

Answer Key

1. A) is incorrect. While the German army was stretched too thin, the answer is incomplete as the other answer choices are also true.

   B) is incorrect. While the Schlieffen Plan did indeed underestimate resistance on the Western Front, this answer choice is also incomplete as the other answer choices are also true.

   C) is incorrect. While the Schlieffen Plan did fail to anticipate rapid Russian mobilization, this answer choice is incomplete given the other options.

   D) is correct. All of the answer choices are true.

2. A) is incorrect. Sykes-Picot made no promises of an independent Jewish state.

   B) is incorrect. Husayn ibn Ali, while taken into account in the Agreement in determining positions of power, was never offered the title of Caliph.

   C) is incorrect. Ataturk himself took control of Turkey, having been part of its leadership for some time and having held off European interference.

   D) is correct. Sykes-Picot put Palestine under the supervision of various international powers.

3. **A) is correct.** The Nazis planned to cease paying reparations, so their nationalist approach appealed to many Germans suffering from the hyperinflation that reparations had triggered. Furthermore, the Nazis had the support of German industrialists, who feared the rise of communism among the working classes.

   B) is incorrect. While the economic suffering brought on by the Great Depression made the Nazis' promises appealing to many, they did not have the support of the majority of German workers, who mostly supported communists at the time.

   C) is incorrect. The Nazis were against communism.

   D) is incorrect. While they had support from German industrialists, the Nazis did not have widespread support in government: they were elected by popular vote.

4. A) is incorrect. There had never been a plan for the Soviet Union to immediately cede control of East Berlin following the fall of the Nazis; dividing Berlin among the four allied powers had been foreseen.

   B) is incorrect. The Berlin Wall was built in 1961, several years after the Cold War had begun.

   C) is correct. The Cold War was rooted in Stalin's creation of communist satellite states in Eastern and Central Europe.

   D) is incorrect. The Cuban Missile Crisis occurred in 1962, well into the Cold War.

5. A) is incorrect. While the Iran Hostage Crisis was an embarrassment for the United States, it did not significantly alter its role in the Cold War nor did it contribute to the collapse of the U.S.S.R.

B) is correct. The Soviet invasion of Afghanistan and the subsequent ten-year war sapped Soviet financial and military resources—and morale. This draining war, plus the high price of the arms race with the United States, contributed significantly to the fall of the Soviet Union.

C) is incorrect. While the Cold War powers had strong interests and some involvement in this war—particularly the United States, an enemy of the revolutionary Iranian government—it did not significantly affect the balance of power between the U.S. and the U.S.S.R. Furthermore, both superpowers supported Iraq.

D) is incorrect. Arguably, the Yom Kippur War was indeed a proxy war: the Soviet Union supported Syria and Egypt, so the United States came to Israel's aid. However this war did not significantly change the balance of power between the superpowers, although it did significantly affect the Middle East.

6. A) is incorrect. While international terrorism has been a major feature of the past fifteen years, it is not a form of governance or political order.

B) is correct. While the United States remains a leading world power, the emergence of international organizations like the BRICS, the EU, the G-20, and the AU has empowered other countries. Furthermore, international trade agreements are helping mold the international balance of power.

C) is incorrect. While international conflict has unfortunately been a major feature of the past fifteen years, there has been sufficient political global order to confidently state that the world has not fully descended into chaos.

D) is incorrect. The European Union is an important world power as an international organization, but is not the dominant global superpower.

7. A) is incorrect. Bosniak Muslims were primarily the victims of genocide during the Bosnian War. Furthermore, while some *mujahideen* from the Soviet war in Afghanistan did go to the Balkans to fight, Islamic extremism is not traditionally a feature of Balkan Islam.

B) is correct. One reason for the Bosnian War was the Yugoslav government's attempt to force the country to stay together; following the end of the Cold War and the collapse of communism, the formerly communist Yugoslavia had started to break up.

C) is incorrect. Yugoslavia was never part of the U.S.S.R.

D) is incorrect. No actors from the Middle East triggered the Bosnian War.

8. A) is incorrect. The AU is not a free trade zone; it is an organization of fifty-four African countries to convene and act in their common interests. While they may align trade policies, the entire continent is not a free trade zone.

B) is incorrect. There is no single African currency.

C) is correct. The AU organizes and manages peacekeeping forces in Africa; it also cooperates with the United Nations in peacekeeping.

D) is incorrect. Individual African countries are sovereign and manage their own international relations.

9. A) is incorrect. *Glasnost*, or openness, was one of Gorbachev's policies of reform, allowing for more free speech in the U.S.S.R.; this arguably helped weaken the regime.

    B) is incorrect. *Perestroika*, or transparency, was one of Gorbachev's policies of reform, providing a more transparent and democratic government under communism; this arguably helped weaken the regime.

    C) is incorrect. The Soviet war in Afghanistan was financially ruinous for the U.S.S.R. and cost the country much in morale.

    D) is correct. The Taliban did not emerge in Afghanistan until well after Soviet withdrawal from the country.

10. A) is incorrect. While this is true, it is incomplete as it is not the only correct answer choice.

    B) is incorrect. While bin Laden opposed the U.S.-Israeli alliance, this answer is incomplete as it is not the only correct answer choice.

    C) is incorrect. While bin Laden did indeed want to establish such a regime, this answer is incomplete as it is not the only correct answer choice.

    D) is correct. Bin Laden cited all of these reasons for his violent acts.

PART II
Test Your Knowledge

CHAPTER SEVEN
Practice Test One

Selected-Response Questions

Read the question, and then choose the most correct answer.

1. In which country did the Industrial Revolution begin?
    A) Russia
    B) Britain
    C) France
    D) the United States
    E) China

3. What is a *ziggurat*?
    A) a burial pyramid
    B) a Mesopotamian ruler
    C) a Mesopotamian stepped pyramid
    D) a temple
    E) a flat area used for Mesoamerican ball games

4. In which region were alpacas and llamas domesticated?
    A) Mesoamerica
    B) the Andes
    C) China
    D) Africa
    E) the Middle East

5. When did horses reach the Americas?
    A) with the first humans
    B) around 5000 years ago
    C) around 1000 years ago
    D) around 500 years ago
    E) around 8000 years ago

6. When did Germany unite to form an Empire?
    A) 1871
    B) 1914
    C) 1918
    D) 1891
    E) 1817

7. Work on the Great Wall of China began in which dynasty?
    A) Qin
    B) Tang
    C) Song
    D) Qing
    E) Ming

8. The Boer War took place on which continent?
   A) Australia
   B) Asia
   C) South America
   D) Europe
   E) Africa

9. Fascism is—
   A) an authoritarian system of government.
   B) a form of racism.
   C) a government driven by racism or anti-Semitism.
   D) the hatred of Jewish people.
   E) a government motivated by religion.

10. Which of the following is NOT associated with the Neolithic era?
    A) Mudbrick architecture
    B) the development of pottery
    C) the domestication of animals
    D) the domestication of plants
    E) the use of iron weapons

11. Who was Mao Zedong?
    A) the last emperor of China
    B) the leader of the Chinese communist party
    C) the last democratically elected leader of China
    D) the leader of the Chinese Nationalists
    E) the first emperor of China

12. Under the Roman Republic, who held power in the government?
    A) the Senate
    B) the Emperor
    C) the people
    D) the Vestal Virgins
    E) the military

2. The Red Army and the White Army are associated with what conflict?
   A) the Civil War in the United States
   B) the Russian Revolution
   C) the Boer War
   D) World War II
   E) World War I

13. Which ruler is commonly credited with Hellenism?
    A) Genghis Khan
    B) Julius Caesar
    C) Nero
    D) Alexander the Great
    E) Herodotus

14. Which of the following is most closely associated with ancient Greece?
    A) the sonnet
    B) drama
    C) Fresco painting
    D) aqueducts
    E) pyramids

15. Choose the best explanation for the fall of Rome.
    A) Rome fell to a superior military force.
    B) Rome fell due to the influence of the Christian church.
    C) Rome fell due to poor management, weak rulers, and an invading external force.
    D) Rome fell because it was morally depraved.
    E) Rome fell because of Caligula.

16. The Golden Horde was—
    A) the name given to trade caravans on the Silk Road.
    B) a famous inn on the Silk Road.
    C) a type of glass that was commonly traded.
    D) the name given to the Mongol army.
    E) the treasury of the Chinese emperor.

17. Which of the following was a prominent trading port in the Middle Ages and Renaissance in Europe?
    A) Paris
    B) London
    C) Rome
    D) Naples
    E) Venice

18. The building called *Hagia Sophia* has been both a Christian church and a Muslim mosque. It is located in what city?
    A) Rome
    B) Ravenna
    C) Istanbul
    D) Athens
    E) Barcelona

19. The Treaty of Versailles—
    A) divided Africa among the colonial powers.
    B) allowed Germany to unite and form an empire.
    C) ended World War I.
    D) created the Triple Entente.
    E) led to the declaration of war in World War II.

20. Choose the best description for the Russian strategy of empire-building.
    A) Russia opted to colonize other regions, building a trans-oceanic empire.
    B) Russia spread its empire eastward into Siberia and west into Eastern Europe.
    C) Russia attempted to gain control of Japan.
    D) Russia remained isolated and avoided expansion.
    E) Russia lacked the resources to build an empire.

21. Who first devised the League of Nations?
    A) Adolf Hitler
    B) Woodrow Wilson
    C) Winston Churchill
    D) Kaiser Wilhelm I
    E) Franklin Delano Roosevelt

22. Which of the following is an Enlightenment-era ruler?
    A) Napoleon
    B) King Louis XIV
    C) Catherine the Great
    D) Qin Shi Huang
    E) Queen Elizabeth I

23. The mandate of heaven is linked with the rule of what nation?
    A) Britain
    B) France
    C) China
    D) Russia
    E) Japan

24. Charlemagne was—
- A) the last Roman Emperor.
- B) the first Holy Roman Emperor.
- C) king of France.
- D) the first king of England.
- E) a Spanish knight.

25. Choose the best explanation for the origin of the Byzantine Empire.
- A) After the fall of Rome, the Eastern Roman Empire or Byzantine Empire became progressively more powerful.
- B) With Rome in danger, the Emperor moved the Roman Empire eastward.
- C) After the introduction of Christianity, Byzantium was founded as a Christian empire.
- D) Following the death of Muhammad, his followers created the Byzantine Empire.
- E) The Byzantine Empire began in Persia.

26. What is a Janissary?
- A) a Byzantine official
- B) an Ottoman soldier, born to a Christian family
- C) a diplomat from Persia
- D) a Venetian trader
- E) a merchant living in a community far from his home

27. Which of the following was first identified in the 18th century?
- A) vaccination
- B) antibiotics
- C) sterilization
- D) the true shape of the earth
- E) fertilizers

28. Select the best definition for diaspora.
- A) the dispersion of Muslims from Mecca
- B) the dispersion of any group from their homeland, commonly in reference to Jews
- C) trading communities of a particular ethnicity
- D) Roman communities set up on the borders of the Roman Empire
- E) towns along the Silk Road

29. What is social Darwinism?
- A) the belief in evolution
- B) the belief that survival of the fittest applies not only to creatures, but also communities of people, particularly identified by race
- C) a rejection of the theory of evolution
- D) the belief that evolution applies only to creatures and not social groups
- E) belief in the Big Bang Theory

30. Choose the factor that most significantly altered the food supply in Europe in the 16th and 17th centuries.
- A) the potato blight
- B) the introduction of new forms of rice
- C) the introduction of the potato and other new world foods
- D) the use of new crop rotation
- E) the use of fertilizers

31. What factor was most responsible for the decimation of native populations after the European conquest of the Americas?
    A) forced labor
    B) disease
    C) starvation
    D) war
    E) forced migration

32. Slaves were originally brought to the Americas to work—
    A) cotton plantations.
    B) sugar plantations.
    C) tobacco plantations.
    D) in colonists' homes.
    E) in all of the above.

33. What goods were commonly exported from China along the Silk Road?
    A) silk, porcelain, jade
    B) cotton and silk
    C) silk and glass
    D) silk, gunpowder, and porcelain
    E) silk

34. Choose the answer that best describes possible push factors for immigrants.
    A) access to jobs, land, economic improvement
    B) better climate, religious tolerance, stable government
    C) poor job market, lack of opportunity, war, religious intolerance
    D) communities of immigrants, family connections
    E) expense of immigration, legal difficulties of immigration

35. The city of Jerusalem is holy to what religions?
    A) Islam and Christianity
    B) Judaism and Christianity
    C) Christianity
    D) Islam and Judaism
    E) Islam, Judaism, and Christianity

36. Which of the following is the most ancient world religion?
    A) Islam
    B) Hinduism
    C) Buddhism
    D) Christianity
    E) Judaism

37. Traders visiting India brought what back to Europe?
    A) silk and porcelain
    B) slaves and camels
    C) horses and silk
    D) cotton and spices
    E) salt and cotton

38. Maroon societies were—
    A) social groups for immigrants.
    B) escaped slave communities.
    C) abolitionist groups.
    D) enlightenment philosophers.
    E) groups to educate slaves.

39. The Holodomor was—
    A) the mass killing of Russian Jews by the Einsatzgruppen.
    B) starvation in China at the time of the Great Leap Forward.
    C) starvation in the Ukraine under Stalin's rule.
    D) the Russian Revolution.
    E) *gulags* in Siberia for Soviet political prisoners.

40. The Thirty Years' War—
    A) ended with the Berlin Conference.
    B) led to a political alliance between Sweden and Russia.
    C) decimated the German landscape.
    D) eliminated Protestantism in Germany.
    E) ended with the Peace of Augsburg.

41. Who was Marco Polo?
    A) a Venetian explorer
    B) a Genoese trader
    C) a Spanish explorer
    D) a conquistador
    E) an Islamic explorer

42. Which of the following is associated with the French Revolution?
    A) the Declaration of Independence
    B) the Reign of Terror
    C) the Red Army
    D) Napoleon III
    E) the Battle of Verdun

43. Choose the best description for the agriculture of the Aztecs.
    A) The Aztecs farmed on terraced land.
    B) The Aztecs grew wheat and rice.
    C) The Aztecs grew corn and other crops on large reed mats in a lake.
    D) The Aztecs imported food to cities over a long distance.
    E) The Aztecs relied on large animals to plow their land.

44. Which country or region invented the following items: gunpowder, printing, and paper money?
    A) the Abbasid Caliphate
    B) Germany
    C) Britain
    D) India
    E) China

45. The Mauryan Emperor Asoka is associated with the spread of—
    A) Hinduism.
    B) technology.
    C) Buddhism.
    D) Islam.
    E) literacy.

46. Women played a significant role in trade in what region?
    A) Europe
    B) East Asia
    C) Southeast Asia
    D) Africa
    E) Mesoamerica

47. The astrolabe is—
    A) a type of compass.
    B) a device used to determine distance over water.
    C) a device used to determine latitude on water.
    D) a type of calendar.
    E) a mathematical tool.

48. Which African country or region remained predominantly Christian?
    A) Zimbabwe
    B) Ethiopia
    C) Nigeria
    D) Egypt
    E) Algeria

49. The Mughal Empire took its name from—
    A) a region of India.
    B) a Hindu deity.
    C) Indian tradition.
    D) a local river.
    E) the Mongol Empire.

50. The Netherlands was best known as—
    A) a political power.
    B) a military power.
    C) a trading power.
    D) a site of religious conflict.
    E) fabric production.

51. Select the best definition of *mit'a*.
    A) *Mit'a* is a system of rule by the religious elite.
    B) *Mit'a* is a form of feudalism.
    C) *Mit'a* is a type of Aztec agriculture.
    D) *Mit'a* is a ball game played in Mesoamerica.
    E) *Mit'a* is a system of involuntary labor among the Inca, exploited by the Spanish.

52. Which religious or philosophical beliefs are commonly associated with China?
    A) Buddhism
    B) Confucianism
    C) Daoism
    D) Islam
    E) all of the above EXCEPT Islam

53. Monasticism is associated with what religions?
    A) Christianity and Judaism
    B) Judaism and Islam
    C) Islam and Christianity
    D) Buddhism and Christianity
    E) Hinduism and Buddhism

54. The Abbasid Caliphate is closely associated with what city?
    A) Constantinople
    B) Mecca
    C) Medina
    D) Baghdad
    E) Jerusalem

55. Choose the best definition of Dar-al Islam.
    A) the desire to spread Islam throughout the world
    B) the ideal Islamic education
    C) the overall spread or influence of Islam
    D) Islamic holy war
    E) the totality of Islamic belief

56. Which best describes the difference between a serf and a slave?
    A) Serfs had families, slaves did not.
    B) Serfs were connected to the land, not an owner and could only be sold as part of a land exchange.
    C) Serfs were freed after some number of years of service.
    D) Serfs were paid for their labor, slaves were not.
    E) Serfs were native-born, slaves were forced migrants.

Practice Test One

57. Who was Zheng He?
    A) a Chinese Emperor
    B) a Chinese explorer
    C) a Chinese communist
    D) a Chinese philosopher
    E) a Chinese inventor

58. The city of Machu Pichu is associated with what group?
    A) the Maya
    B) the Aztecs
    C) the Olmec
    D) the Inca
    E) the Gupta

59. The Bantu language and its descendants are associated with what region?
    A) West Africa
    B) East Africa
    C) Southern Africa
    D) Southeast Asia
    E) East Asia

60. Choose the best explanation of the Meiji Restoration.
    A) The Meiji Restoration was an isolated, feudal government in Japan.
    B) The Meiji Restoration was an attempt at a nationalist government in China.
    C) The Meiji Restoration was an ancient Japanese government, influenced by Chinese tradition.
    D) The Meiji Restoration was the independent government of Korea.
    E) The Meiji Restoration was a modern, Westernized government in Japan, beginning in the middle of the 19th century.

61. Which of the following describes a common trait in most of the earliest agricultural communities?
    A) stone and mudbrick architecture
    B) a walled city center
    C) placement in a river valley
    D) the worship of nature deities
    E) the use of horses

62. Which of the following did not have a state-sponsored or supported religion?
    A) the Abbasid Caliphate
    B) the Byzantine Empire
    C) the Ottoman Empire
    D) the Song Dynasty
    E) the Maya people

63. Why did Mesoamerican civilizations fail to develop the wheel?
    A) They lacked the materials.
    B) They lacked the technology.
    C) They did not have large animals to pull plows or carriages.
    D) They did not have large scale agriculture.
    E) They did not have domesticated plants.

64. North and South Korea were divided—
    A) by the Chinese.
    B) after World War II.
    C) after World War I.
    D) after the Korean War.
    E) by the Japanese.

65. Which of the following materials is most closely associated with the second phase of the Industrial Revolution?
    A) cotton
    B) coal
    C) steel
    D) silk
    E) wool

66. Choose the best definition of the Green Revolution.
    A) The Green Revolution was marked by a new interest in environmental protections.
    B) The Green Revolution was marked by technological improvements in agriculture.
    C) The Green Revolution was marked by reduced industrial emissions.
    D) The Green Revolution is a name for global warming.
    E) The Green Revolution describes a global movement to protect animals and plants.

67. Which of the following statements describes both the French Revolution and the Russian Revolution?
    A) Both originated among the wealthiest elites.
    B) Both valued the rights of the citizens.
    C) Both valued agricultural workers over the middle class.
    D) Both began in the bourgeoisie or wealthier members of the middle class.
    E) Both sought a totally egalitarian society, with publicly owned means of production.

68. The first democracy was—
    A) Rome.
    B) Athens.
    C) Sparta.
    D) Constantinople.
    E) St. Petersburg.

69. Confucianism is defined by—
    A) respect for authority, both familial and political.
    B) a desire to reach Nirvana.
    C) respect for nature.
    D) a belief that Muhammad is the prophet of Allah.
    E) a personal desire for unity with the divine.

70. The Pax Mongolica protected—
    A) trade along the Silk Road.
    B) trade in the Indian Ocean.
    C) the boundaries of the Mongolian Empire.
    D) the boundaries of the Mughal Empire.
    E) the Mongolian Emperor.

Free-Response Questions

For questions 1 and 2, write a short essay based on your knowledge of World History. For question 3, write a short essay based on your knowledge and the accompanying historical texts.

1. Choosing one country for the subject of your essay, consider how colonialism altered the experience of native peoples over time. Depending upon the country you choose, the period of time may differ, but should begin with the introduction of colonialism and continue through the modern era.

2. How did trade develop on the Indian Ocean as compared to the Silk Road?

3. Historians have long argued over the origin of the Final Solution. Integrating what you know about Nazi Germany and the Holocaust, analyze whether or not the Final Solution was Hitler's original intention or a plan that developed due to the imminent loss of World War II.

SS HIMMLER: SPEECH in POSNAN, 1943

I mean the evacuation of the Jews, the extermination of the Jewish race. It's one of those things it is easy to talk about, "the Jewish race is being exterminated", says one party member, "that's quite clear, it's in our program, elimination of the Jews, and we're doing it, exterminating them". And then they come, 80 million worthy Germans, and each one has his decent Jew. Of course the others are vermin, but this one is an A-1 Jew. Not one of those who talk this way has watched it, not one of them has gone through it. Most of you know what it means when 100 corpses are lying side by side, or 500, or 1,000. To have stuck it out and at the same time - apart from exceptions caused by human weakness - to have remained decent fellows, that is what has made us hard. This is a page of glory in our history which has never been written and is never to be written.

I ask of you that what I say in this circle you really only hear and never speak of. We come to the question: how is it with the women and the children? I have resolved even here on a completely clear solution. That is to say I do not consider myself justified in eradicating the men - so to speak killing or ordering them killed - and allowing the avengers in the shape of the children to grow up for our sons and grandsons. The difficult decision has to be taken, to cause this Volk [people] to disappear from the earth.

GOEBBELS: DIARIES, 1942

Beginning with Lublin, the Jews in the General Government [Nazi occupied Poland] are now being evacuated eastward. The procedure is a pretty barbaric one and not to be described here more definitely. Not much will remain of the Jews. On the whole it can be said that about 60 percent of them will have to be liquidated whereas only 40 percent can be used for forced labor.

THE WANNSEE CONFERENCE, 1942

The Chief of the Security Police and the SD then gave a short report of the struggle which has been carried on thus far against this enemy, the essential points being the following:

1. the expulsion of the Jews from every sphere of life of the German people,
2. the expulsion of the Jews from the living space of the German people.

In carrying out these efforts, an increased and planned acceleration of the emigration of the Jews from Reich territory was started, as the only possible present solution.

LETTER from CHIEF of INSTITUTION for FEEBLE-MINDED in STETTEN to REICH MINISTER of JUSTICE DR. FRANK, SEPTEMBER 6, 1940.

Dear Reich Minister,

The measure being taken at present with mental patients of all kinds have caused a complete lack of confidence in justice among large groups of people. Without the consent of relatives and guardians, such patients are being transferred to different institutions. After a short time they are notified that the person concerned has died of some disease...

If the state really wants to carry out the extermination of these or at least of some mental patients, shouldn't a law be promulgated, which can be justified before the people - a law that would give everyone the assurance of careful examination as to whether he is due to die or entitled to live and which would also give the relatives a chance to be heard, in a similar way, as provided by the law for the prevention of Hereditarily affected Progeny?

TESTIMONY of SS PRIVATE BOECK.

Extracted from "Der Auschwitz Prozess", by Hermann Langbein, Vol. I, quoted in "Auschwitz: Technique and operation of the gas chambers – J.C Pressac, the Beate Klarsfeld Foundation, NY, 1989, p. 181:

ROBERT JACKSON, OPENING REMARKS, NUREMBERG TRIAL

What these men stand for we will patiently and temperately disclose. We will give you undeniable proofs of incredible events. The catalogue of crimes will omit nothing that could be conceived by a pathological pride, cruelty, and lust for power. These men created in Germany, under the Fuehrerprinzip, a National Socialist despotism equalled only by the dynasties of the ancient East. They took from the German people all those dignities and freedoms that we hold natural and inalienable rights in every human being. The people were compensated by inflaming and gratifying hatreds toward those who were marked as "scape-goats." Against their opponents, including Jews, Catholics, and free labor the Nazis directed such a campaign of arrogance, brutality, and annihilation as the world has not witnessed since the pre-Christian ages. They excited the German ambition to be a "master race," which of course implies serfdom for others. They led their people on a mad amble for domination. They diverted social energies and resources to the creation of what they thought to be an invincible war machine. They overran their neighbors. To sustain the "master race " in its war making, they enslaved millions of human beings and brought them into Germany, where these hapless creatures. now wander as "displaced persons". At length bestiality and bad faith reached such excess that they aroused the sleeping strength of imperiled civilization. Its united efforts have ground the German war machine to fragments. But the struggle has left Europe a liberated yet prostrate land where a demoralized society struggles to survive. These are the fruits of the sinister forces that sit with these defendants in the prisoners' dock.

GOVERNMENT DECREES against JEWS, 1933–1936

When the Nazi Party gained control of the German State, the conspirators used the means of official decrees as a weapon against the Jews. In this way the force of the state was applied against them.

- Jewish immigrants were denaturalized (1933 Reichsgesetzblatt, Part I, page 480, signed by Frick and Neurath).
- Native Jews were precluded from citizenship (1935 Reichsgesetzblatt, Part I, page 1146, signed by Frick).
- Jews were forbidden to live in marriage or to have extramarital relations with persons of German blood (1935 Reichsgesetzblatt, Part I, page 1146, signed by Frick and Hess).
- Jews were denied the right to vote (1936 Reichsgesetzblatt, Part I, page 133, signed by Frick).
- Jews were denied the right to hold public office or civil service positions (1933 Reichsgesetzblatt, Part I, page 277, signed by Frick) .

RESETTLEMENT of the JEWS, 1943, PREPARED for SS-HIMMLER

The Auschwitz camp plays a special role in the resolution of the Jewish question. The most advanced methods permit the execution of the Fuhrer-order in the shortest possible time and without arousing much attention. The so-called "resettlement action" runs the following course: The Jews arrive in special trains (freight cars) toward evening and are driven on special tracks to areas of the camp specifically set aside for this purpose. There the Jews are unloaded and examined for their fitness to work by a team of doctors, in the presence of the camp commandant and several SS officers. At this point anyone who can somehow be incorporated into the work program is put in a special camp. The curably ill are sent straight to a medical camp and are restored to health through a special diet. The basic principle behind everything is: conserve all manpower for work. The previous type of "resettlement action" has been thoroughly rejected, since it is too costly to destroy precious work energy on a continual basis.

Practice Test One Answer Key
SELECTED-RESPONSE QUESTIONS

1. B)
2. C)
3. B)
4. D)
5. A)
6. A)
7. E)
8. A)
9. E)
10. B)
11. A)
12. B)
13. D)
14. B)
15. C)
16. D)
17. E)
18. C)
19. C)
20. B)
21. B)
22. C)
23. C)
24. B)
25. A)
26. B)
27. A)
28. B)
29. B)
30. C)
31. B)
32. B)
33. A)
34. C)
35. E)
36. B)
37. D)
38. B)
39. C)
40. C)
41. A)
42. B)
43. C)
44. E)
45. C)
46. C)
47. C)
48. B)
49. E)
50. C)
51. E)
52. E)
53. D)
54. D)
55. C)
56. B)
57. B)
58. D)
59. C)
60. E)
61. C)
62. D)
63. C)
64. B)
65. C)
66. B)
67. D)
68. B)
69. A)
70. A)

FREE-RESPONSE QUESTIONS

1. Choosing one country for the subject of your essay, consider how colonialism altered the experience of native peoples over time. Depending upon the country you choose, the period of time may differ, but should begin with the introduction of colonialism and continue through the modern era.

In 1490, the native peoples of Mesoamerica, including the Aztec, were strong, technologically developed civilizations. They built monumental architecture, fought, lived, farmed, and thrived in the lush climate, from the city of Tenochtitlan to the smaller towns. Their cultures, both that of the Aztecs and those of their enemies, were old, strong and well-developed, but they fell and fell quickly to the guns, horses and diseases brought by Spanish conquistadors and their native allies in Mesoamerica.

The invasion in 1519 led to the capture of the leader of the Aztecs and eventually their defeat. While there were a number of battles, the Spanish conquistadors had another distinct advantage. Smallpox had reached the Aztec communities around the same time, killing as much as 50 percent of the population. With the defeat of the Aztecs, the most powerful warriors in the region, the Spanish conquistadors had secured their control of modern-day Mexico. After the fall of the Aztecs, the Spanish renamed the region New Spain.

While many of the Aztec nobility were killed by conquistadors, those that remained held a relatively high social status, continuing their traditional role to a lesser extent. They were referred to by Spanish noble titles, including don and dona. Some learned Spanish, and many converted to Christianity, after regular interactions with Jesuit missionaries. While Aztec nobles retained some status, the Spanish implemented the encomienda system, a forced labor system resembling feudalism. This was based in both South American and European traditions, but adapted for the colonial world. In Europe, feudalism had disappeared, altering the face of Europe.

Conditions for forced laborers were quite poor, both those working in agriculture and those in the mines. Spanish men who settled in New Spain frequently married native women or took native concubines, creating the new class known as mestizos. While the mestizos were, by blood, both Spanish and Aztec, the culture and traditions of the Aztecs were largely rejected and were, in many cases, illegal. While the mestizos lacked the social status of the creoles or new settlers, they could attain a high social status and role.

For the Spanish, the Aztecs were less than, but were not subhuman. Mendicant friars, including the Dominicans and Franciscans, believed that they could be converted and could benefit the Catholic Church. The introduction of smallpox was unintentional, but certainly advantageous, helping the Spanish to secure their victory. While forced laborers were not well-treated and were often abused, they were not slaves and there was no intentional attempt to destroy the Aztec population; however, the actions of the Spanish destroyed the Aztec way of life and culture.

2. HOW DID TRADE DEVELOP ON THE INDIAN OCEAN AS COMPARED TO THE SILK ROAD?

The Silk Road and Indian Ocean Trade Network were both critical to international trade, with the Silk Road dominating trade in an earlier period and the Indian Ocean Trade Network somewhat later. The two overlap and interrelate with one another and both illustrate the importance of political stability and traders in maintaining trade, as well as the impact of trade on various communities.

The Silk Road ran East to West across much of the known world. It relied upon ancient roads, many put in place in the Persian Empire as early as 475 BCE. These routes expanded under Alexander the Great in the 4th century BCE. By the 2nd century BCE, this network of roads extended into China, and under the Romans, a more extensive trade network developed. The land-based trade network continued to grow, expand and develop, even as new cultures did. There were several different routes, one to the north, one to the south, and one to the southwest.

Following a brief interruption during the Mongolian Conquest, the Silk Road was reestablished under the Pax Mongolica or Mongolian Peace. The roads were stable and protected, allowing traders to easily move caravans of goods from place to place. From China, porcelain and silk moved into other parts of Asia, North Africa and Europe. Spices and cotton traveled from India and glass and furs from other parts of the world. The most commonly traded goods were small, luxury items that were relatively easy to transport from place to place. Languages, information, culture and religion also travelled along the Silk Road.

Throughout its existence, the Silk Road was impacted by political conditions. When political conditions were stable and the state supported trade, for instance, the Chinese ruling dynasty, it resulted in improved trade along the Silk Road. When conditions were less safe, there was less trade along the Silk Road. Eventually, the Silk Road was largely abandoned as shipbuilding technology, including the Portuguese caravel and the Arabic dhow, improved.

The Indian Ocean Trade Network was somewhat less significant than the Silk Road, but was significantly more stable and less likely to be affected by the actions of local governments. While the Chinese administration was frequently involved in the management of portions of the Silk Road, trade on the Indian Ocean was self-regulated by traders. Local ports could set their own regulations; however, conditions were, on the whole, designed to be favorable for free and profitable trade.

Sea-based trade was typically faster and more efficient than trade over land routes, enabling more extensive trade. The Indian Ocean also offered opportunities for exploration, with both the Chinese and Portuguese expressing interest in that exploration; however, Chinese explorations, led by Zhang He, were terminated by the Ming Dynasty. Eventually, the Portuguese were granted access to West Africa by the Catholic Church. Other noted powers in the region included the Venetians and Ottomans. Later, the British and Dutch controlled trade in the Indian Ocean.

Several differences marked trade between these regions. Often, the same goods were traded by land and sea; however, trade by sea required more investment and was, eventually, largely controlled by a few countries. The Silk Road and land-based trade was less easily managed by large governments and more suited to small-scale trade. It was significantly slower and could move less goods.

3. Historians have long argued over the origin of the Final Solution. Integrating what you know about Nazi Germany and the Holocaust, analyze whether or not the Final Solution was Hitler's original intention or a plan that developed due to the imminent loss of World War II.

The "Final Solution" is the name the Nazi party gave to their plan to exterminate the Jews, killing the entire Jewish population of Europe. Today, we commonly refer to this as the Holocaust, the genocide that resulted in approximately 11 million deaths. Identifying the origins of the "Final Solution" poses a number of problems, as, unsurprisingly, the Nazis attempted to hide their intentions, disguised them with euphemisms like "special treatment" and destroyed records wherever possible.

If we begin early in Nazi party history, we find that the Nazis blamed the Jews or a conflation of Jews and communists for the conditions in post-World War I Germany. The anti-Semitic rhetoric of the early days of the party, both before the Munich Beer Hall Putsch and in the early 1930s suggests that there was already, even at this time, a strong desire to eliminate the Jews from Germany and purify the country.

Once the Nazis gained political power in 1933, they had the ability to initiate laws limiting the rights of Jews. Early laws banned Jews from civil service, banned intermarriage, reduced the rights of Jews, including property rights and limited their ability to travel freely, as indicated by the decrees from 1933-1936. Not long after, sterilization laws were initiated. These, while not specifically anti-Semitic, were also intended to purify the German people by eliminating unwanted individuals, including the Roma and the disabled. Not long after, before 1940 as evidenced by the letter from the Reich Minister, euthanasia programs begin, killing disabled children, the mentally ill and even the elderly. The people of Germany did not approve of these programs and the party eventually restructured them to hide their actions. While they hid their plan to kill the unwanted in Germany to avoid negative public opinion, the gas chambers developed in the euthanasia program would be used on a much larger scale in Poland.

While the Wannsee Conference may have defined the "Final Solution" and organized plans for it, this does not, with research, suggest that this was the first plan to destroy the Jewish people. Not long after the invasion of Poland, the Nazis began to move Jewish people into ghettos, limiting not only their right to move freely, but also working to kill them through starvation and disease. It is also clear, in the Goebbels diary, that the "Final Solution" was relatively well-known and not, by all appearances, a shocking revelation to the Nazi administration. Himmler's speech, in fact, suggests that this was not only a public secret among the Nazis, but something he spoke of with great pride.

The implementation of the "Final Solution" relied upon the technology developed during the euthanasia program, gas chambers. They had used gassing vans, first during Operation Barbarossa and later at Chelmno, but this was not adequate for the numbers killed during Operation Reinhard and later in Nazi-occupied Poland. Large-scale gas chambers were built for this purpose. There is one key difference between Auschwitz-Birkenau and the camps of Operation Reinhard. Auschwitz did include a labor camp, and as reflected in the Resettlement document, some individuals were spared immediate execution. Goebbels' letter suggests the use of forced labor as well; however, it would be inaccurate to assume this reflects an intent to spare Jews. Rather, it is more likely an intent to simply work some to death, taking whatever they could before killing them, through deplorable conditions, murder or exhaustion.

Attempts were made, as the war progressed and failure seemed imminent, to hide the evidence of the killing. The opening statements by Robert Jackson at the war crimes trial reflect that fact, as well as the massive amount of evidence collected by the prosecution.

From the first days of the Nazi Party, there was a desire to create a pure German state, free of any sort of racial impurity. The worst of that impurity was, in the eyes of the Nazis, the Jewish people. It is possible that there was some initial intent to simply remove the Jews from Germany, as Jews were free to leave early on, albeit without their property; however, plans to actively deport Jews, like the ghettos of Poland, seem to have been designed to result in the end of the Jewish people, regardless of the factory-style death camps. Those camps made the German plan more practical and efficient, eliminating any need to give space over to the Jews even temporarily.

CHAPTER EIGHT
Practice Test Two

Selected-Response Questions
Read the question, and then choose the most correct answer.

1. Who were the citizens of the Roman Empire?
   A) anyone born in Rome
   B) anyone who served in the Roman military
   C) all free men in the Roman Empire
   D) all men in the Roman Empire
   E) all free people in the Roman Empire

2. Who was responsible for the conversion of the Saxon peoples to Christianity in the Middle Ages?
   A) Constantine
   B) Augustine of Canterbury
   C) Benedict
   D) Charlemagne
   E) Boniface

3. Vikings built a permanent settlement in—
   A) Greenland.
   B) Ireland.
   C) Scotland.
   D) Iceland.
   E) North America.

4. A *caravanserai* was—
   A) a camel saddle.
   B) a guard for caravans.
   C) an inn designed to meet the needs of caravans.
   D) a type of carriage pulled by camels.
   E) a trading post.

5. The first inoculation or vaccination prevented what illness?
   A) Polio
   B) Bubonic plague
   C) Smallpox
   D) Measles
   E) Mumps

6. Trench warfare was first used during—
   A) the Thirty Years' War.
   B) the American Revolutionary War.
   C) the Napoleonic Wars.
   D) World War I.
   E) World War II.

7. The Crusades provided the west with one significant, positive, and lasting consequence. What was it?
   A) land in Jerusalem
   B) improved hygiene
   C) wealth
   D) access to lost classical learning
   E) a new understanding of medicine

8. The elaborate examinations and qualifications associated with bureaucracy in imperial China are known as—
   A) the Mandate of Heaven.
   B) the Imperial System.
   C) Confucianism.
   D) Neo-Confucianism.
   E) the Civil Service System.

9. Which emperor's actions led to the widespread conversion of the Roman Empire to Christianity?
   A) Constantine
   B) Charlemagne
   C) Nero
   D) Justinian
   E) Augustus

10. Where did monasticism continue to thrive during the period after the fall of Rome in Western Europe?
    A) France
    B) Italy
    C) Greece
    D) Britain
    E) Germany

11. Foot-binding was a custom associated with what country or region?
    A) Africa
    B) The Middle East
    C) Southeast Asia
    D) India
    E) China

12. The battles between Rome and what city are particularly famous?
    A) Athens
    B) Sparta
    C) Persia
    D) Phoenicia
    E) Carthage

13. Who was the first Roman Emperor?
    A) Julius Caesar
    B) Caligula
    C) Nero
    D) Tiberius
    E) Augustus

14. The Ottoman Empire was defeated by—
    A) the Byzantines.
    B) the Abbasid Caliphate.
    C) the Crusades.
    D) World War I.
    E) the Germans.

15. Which of the following statements best explains the status of women in Tang Dynasty China?
    A) Women were highly limited in their activities.
    B) Women had bound feet and could barely walk.
    C) Women had a relatively high status and more freedom than later Chinese women.
    D) Women were elevated in the courtly love tradition.
    E) Women were relegated to closed spaces and not seen in public at all.

16. Choose the best definition for the Columbian Exchange.
    A) The Columbian Exchange describes trading relations between Europe and the Americas.
    B) The Columbian Exchange describes the slave trade to the Americas.
    C) The Columbian Exchange describes the exchange of foods, people, diseases and goods between Europe and the Americas.
    D) The Columbian Exchange describes the trade in colonial properties.
    E) The Columbian Exchange describes the migrations to the Americas.

17. A *mestizo* was—
    A) a Spanish colonist in South America.
    B) an individual with Spanish and Native American blood.
    C) a slave.
    D) an indentured servant.
    E) a conquistador.

18. What was the First Five Year Plan?
    A) a plan to create a communist state in Russia
    B) a plan to modernize the young Soviet Union
    C) a plan to industrialize Chinese agriculture
    D) a plan to stamp out western influences in communism
    E) a plan to expand the Russian Empire

19. In what way did the Chinese and Russian Revolutions differ?
    A) The Russian Revolution focused on industrialization, the Chinese on agriculture.
    B) The Chinese employed starvation as a control technique, the Soviets did not.
    C) The Soviets used prison camps, the Chinese did not.
    D) The Chinese tolerated cultural difference. The Soviets imprisoned those who refused to accept their ideology.
    E) The Russian Revolution was peaceful, the Chinese was not.

20. The Umayyad Dynasty held control of a portion of Spain until—
    A) the 12th century.
    B) the 13th century.
    C) the 15th century.
    D) the 19th century.
    E) the 20th century.

Practice Test Two 115

21. Which of the following best describes the Counter-Reformation?
    A) The Counter-Reformation was a response to corruption in the Church that divided the Catholic Church.
    B) The Counter-Reformation was a response to the Protestant Reformation.
    C) The Counter-Reformation occurred in response to the discovery of the Americas.
    D) The Counter-Reformation occurred in response to growing secularism in society.
    E) The Counter-Reformation addressed the needs of the Catholic Church in the 20th century.

22. The first university operated in—
    A) Paris.
    B) Bologna.
    C) Baghdad.
    D) Granada.
    E) North Africa.

23. The capital of the Tang Dynasty was—
    A) Beijing.
    B) Shanghai.
    C) Chang'an.
    D) Nanjing.
    E) Hangzhou.

24. Islam was founded around—
    A) 600 BCE.
    B) 600 CE.
    C) 700 CE.
    D) 800 CE.
    E) 900 CE.

25. Tobacco and chocolate were—
    A) Silk Road trade goods.
    B) Indian Ocean trade goods.
    C) part of the Columbian Exchange.
    D) part of the Sub-Saharan trade network.
    E) rarely traded.

26. Coffee was a common trade good, frequently imported by—
    A) Europeans.
    B) Islamic regions.
    C) India.
    D) China.
    E) Africa.

27. Human or blood sacrifice is commonly associated with—
    A) Andean cultures.
    B) African cultures.
    C) Neolithic cultures.
    D) Ancient China.
    E) Mesoamerica.

28. The Louisiana Purchase, Mexican-American War, and purchase of Alaska are examples of—
    A) Imperialism.
    B) Colonialism.
    C) Aggression.
    D) Isolationism.
    E) Exceptionalism.

29. India was originally conquered by—
    A) the British military.
    B) the British navy.
    C) the British East India Company.
    D) the Dutch East India Company.
    E) the Netherlands.

30. Which of the following best describes the consequences of the Opium Wars?
   A) British occupation of China
   B) Chinese victory over Britain
   C) Unequal trade treaties favoring China
   D) Unequal trade treaties favoring Britain
   E) The British gained control of Korea

31. The Raj refers to—
   A) the government of Mughal India.
   B) the British government of India.
   C) the Indian Ocean trade network.
   D) Queen Victoria.
   E) the partition of India.

32. Mahatma Gandhi advocated—
   A) the partition of India.
   B) Indian dependence on Britain.
   C) the creation of Pakistan.
   D) nonviolence.
   E) violent resistance.

33. Conscription is—
   A) voluntary military service.
   B) forced labor.
   C) coerced labor.
   D) forced migration.
   E) involuntary military service.

34. The invasion of what country marked the beginning of WWII?
   A) Czechoslovakia
   B) The Soviet Union
   C) France
   D) Poland
   E) Austria

35. The Central Powers initially included—
   A) Austria-Hungary and Italy.
   B) Germany, Austria-Hungary, and Italy.
   C) Germany, Austria-Hungary, and the Ottoman Empire.
   D) Germany and Austria-Hungary.
   E) Germany, Russia, and Austria-Hungary.

36. The Warsaw Pact was—
   A) a defense organization composed of the Soviet Union and Eastern Bloc.
   B) a Polish anti-Nazi organization.
   C) a Soviet alliance with Poland.
   D) Soviet control over Eastern Europe.
   E) the division of Eastern Europe after WWII.

37. Choose the best explanation for the blockade of Berlin.
   A) The Americans were attempting to gain control of East Germany.
   B) The Soviets hoped to gain control of all of Berlin.
   C) The Soviets were trying to starve the Nazi administration.
   D) The Western Allies were hoping to capture Hitler.
   E) The Allies hoped to retake Berlin from the Soviets.

38. What was the goal of the Gallipoli campaign in World War I?
    A) the destruction of the Central Powers
    B) the defeat of the Ottoman Empire
    C) capturing the city of Istanbul
    D) capturing Greece
    E) regaining control of North Africa

39. Which of the following countries claimed independence based on a slave revolt?
    A) Cuba
    B) Brazil
    C) Haiti
    D) Mexico
    E) Jamaica

40. Widespread civilian deaths in World War II, outside of the Holocaust, were largely the result of—
    A) machine guns.
    B) famine.
    C) air bombing.
    D) poison gas.
    E) trench warfare.

41. In the Holocaust, *ghettos* were—
    A) protected neighborhoods.
    B) traditionally Jewish neighborhoods.
    C) closed, overcrowded neighborhoods used to house Jews by the Nazis.
    D) concentration camps.
    E) death camps.

42. Select the best definition of the Caste system.
    A) a defined, unchangeable social and religious hierarchy, determined by birth
    B) a changeable social hierarchy
    C) a religious hierarchy in Hinduism
    D) hierarchy determined by skills and education
    E) a social hierarchy, determined by birth

43. Siddharta Gautama was—
    A) an Indian Emperor responsible for the spread of Buddhism.
    B) a Buddhist monk.
    C) the Buddha.
    D) a Hindu author.
    E) an Indian political figure supporting independence.

44. The Borobudur Temple is a religious site. What religion produced this monument?
    A) Hinduism
    B) Buddhism
    C) Christianity
    D) Islam
    E) Jainism

45. Choose the best definition of syncretism.
    A) Syncretism is the blending of different artistic elements.
    B) Syncretism is the blending of different linguistic elements.
    C) Syncretism is the blending of different religious elements.
    D) Syncretism is the blending of different historical periods.
    E) Syncretism is a cultural blending that occurs through trade.

46. Arabic numerals developed in what country?
    A) Iraq
    B) India
    C) Saudi Arabia
    D) Egypt
    E) Tunisia

47. Sufism is—
    A) a Muslim tradition that follows descendants of Muhammad.
    B) the government of modern-day Iran.
    C) Islamic mysticism.
    D) a Muslim tradition that follows the Qur'an.
    E) Islamic law.

48. The word *dhimmi* refers to—
    A) Muslims living in a Hindu state.
    B) Muslims in a Christian state.
    C) Christians and Jews in a Muslim state.
    D) Jews living in a Christian state.
    E) Foreign communities in trading cities.

49. A caravel was—
    A) the transport of goods from place to place, commonly on the Silk Road.
    B) the transport of slaves from place to place.
    C) a type of trading ship used along the West African coast.
    D) a large ship designed in China.
    E) a ship used off the coast of South America by the Spanish.

50. If a state worked to increase exports as well as the supply of precious metals, it is pursuing—
    A) capitalism.
    B) mercantilism.
    C) communism.
    D) socialism.
    E) fascism.

51. Which form of Buddhism is most common among the general population?
    A) Mahayana
    B) Zen
    C) Theravada
    D) Sunni
    E) Orthodox

52. The Yuan Dynasty ruled in the 13th and 14th century and was created by—
    A) Marco Polo.
    B) Kublai Khan.
    C) Genghis Khan.
    D) Zheng He.
    E) Hulegu Khan.

53. The African Songhai Empire—
    A) included Timbuktu.
    B) included Great Zimbabwe.
    C) included Gao.
    D) was located in East Africa.
    E) was located in South Africa.

54. John Locke was responsible for—
    A) government checks and balances.
    B) the Declaration of the Rights of Man.
    C) the social contract theory.
    D) the French educational system.
    E) the Glorious Revolution.

55. What is a dhow?
    A) a religious tax
    B) an Ottoman soldier
    C) a type of seafaring trade ship
    D) a Buddhist religious site
    E) a holy site in Islam

56. The Seneca Falls Conference was attended by which group?
    A) prohibitionists
    B) suffragettes
    C) abolitionists
    D) agriculturalists
    E) philosophers

57. The Taiping Rebellion attempted to do what?
    A) promote Confucianism
    B) end the Qing Dynasty
    C) end the Song Dynasty
    D) introduce a new democratic government
    E) introduce a new communist government

58. The Nuremburg Trials are best described as—
    A) war crimes trials after WWII.
    B) war crimes trials after WWI.
    C) the rules and regulations governing the United Nations.
    D) the creation of the League of Nations.
    E) the laws that defined who was and was not Jewish.

59. Feudalism developed in—
    A) medieval China.
    B) medieval Europe.
    C) medieval Japan.
    D) medieval Korea.
    E) both medieval Japan and Europe.

60. Which of the following is an example of a settler colony?
    A) Australia
    B) Canada
    C) The United States
    D) New Zealand
    E) England

61. The army of what country was responsible for the Rape of Nanjing in 1938?
    A) China
    B) Korea
    C) Japan
    D) Vietnam
    E) The United States

62. Collectivization is—
    A) the transfer of land, farms, and industry to public ownership.
    B) the transfer of labor from free to serf.
    C) the transfer of labor from serf to free.
    D) part of the capitalist economic system.
    E) part of the mercantilist system.

63. Who led the Russian Revolution?
    A) Lenin
    B) Stalin
    C) Trotsky
    D) Alexander II
    E) Rasputin

64. The city of Tikal was built by—
    A) the Inca.
    B) the Maya.
    C) the Aztec.
    D) the Olmec.
    E) the Chavin.

65. What is a theocracy?
   A) a government led by the wealthy elites
   B) a government led by religious authorities
   C) a government led by a dictator
   D) a representative democracy
   E) a military dictatorship

66. Fascism was NOT a system of government in which of the following?
   A) Russia
   B) Japan
   C) Spain
   D) Italy
   E) Brazil

67. The Sand Road is sometimes used to refer to—
   A) land trade in Asia.
   B) land trade in Mesopotamia.
   C) land trade in Africa.
   D) trading ports in East Africa.
   E) trading ports in West Africa.

68. The Middle Passage describes—
   A) the trade routes between Europe and the Americas.
   B) the trade routes in the Indian Ocean.
   C) the route slave ships followed from West Africa to the Americas.
   D) immigrant ships to North America.
   E) indentured servants moving to North America.

69. Choose the best definition of an indentured servant.
   A) a slave with no rights
   B) an apprentice with many rights
   C) someone who pays for his passage with a labor contract lasting several years
   D) someone who becomes a slave through capture in war
   E) a paid servant

70. Jesuit missionaries were most successful in—
   A) Latin America.
   B) Spain.
   C) China.
   D) India.
   E) North Africa.

Free-Response Questions

For questions 1 and 2, write a short essay based on your knowledge of World History. For question 3, write a short essay based on your knowledge and the accompanying historical texts.

1. How has communist China remained the same and changed over time, from the time of the Chinese Revolution to today.

2. Compare the impact of colonialism in India and Latin America.

3. The Mongol conquest led to great destruction, but also created a number of stable kingdoms that supported peace and learning. Using your own knowledge and the passages below, analyze the actions and goals of the Mongolian conquest.

MARCO POLO

Of the origin of the kingdom of the Tartars—of the quarter from whence they came—and of their former subjection to Un-khan, a prince of the north, called also Prester John.

The circumstances under which these Tartars first began to exercise dominion shall now be related. They dwelt in the northern countries of Jorza and Bargu, but without fixed habitations, that is, without towns or fortified places; where there were extensive plains, good pasture, large rivers, and plenty of water. They had no sovereign of their own, and were tributary to a powerful prince, who (as I have been informed) was named in their language, Un-khan, by some thought to have the same signification as Prester John in ours. To him these Tartars paid yearly the tenth part of the increase of their cattle. In time the tribe multiplied so exceedingly that Un-khan, that is to say, Prester John, becoming apprehensive of their strength, conceived the plan of separating them into different bodies, who should take up their abode in distinct tracts of country. With this view also, whenever the occasion presented itself, such as a rebellion in any of the provinces subject to him, he drafted three or four hundred of these people, to be employed on the service of quelling it, and thus their power was gradually diminished. He likewise despatched them on other expeditions, and sent among them some of his principal officers to see that his intentions were carried into effect. At length the Tartars, becoming sensible of the slavery to which he tried to reduce them, resolved to maintain a strict union amongst themselves, and seeing that he planned nothing short of their final ruin, they adopted the measure of leavingthe places they then inhabited, and proceeded north across a wide desert, until they felt assured that the distance afforded them security, when they refused any longer to pay to Un-khan the accustomed tribute.

The following passage describes the court of Kublai Khan in the late 13th century.

It was in the month of November that Kubilai returned to Khanbalik. And there he stayed until February and March, the season of our Easter. Learning that this was one of our principal feasts, he sent for all the Christians and desired them to bring him the book containing the four Gospels. After treating the book to repeated applications of incense with great ceremony, he kissed it devoutly and desired all his barons and lords there present to do the same. This usage he regularly observes on the principle feasts of the Christians, such as Easter and Christmas. And he does likewise on the principle feasts of the Saracens, Jews, and idolaters. Being asked why he did so, he replied: 'There are four prophets who are worshiped and to whom all the world does reverences. The

Christians say that their God was Jesus Christ, the Saracens Mahomet, the Jews Moses, and the idolaters Sakyamuni Burkhan [Buddha] who was the first to be represented as God in the form of an idol. And I do honour and reverence to all four, so that I may be sure of doing it to him who is greatest in heaven and truest; and to him I pray for aid. But on the Great Khan's own showing he regards as truest and best the faith of the Christians, because he declares that it commands nothing that is not full of all goodness and holiness.

THE JOURNEY of WILLIAM of RUBRUCK

The Journey of William of Rubruck to the eastern parts of the world, 1253–55, as narrated by himself, with two accounts of the earlier journey of John of Pian de Carpine.

Nowhere have they fixed dwelling-places, nor do they know where their next will be… For in winter they go down to warmer regions in the south: in summer they go up to cooler towards the north. The pasture lands without water they graze over in winter when there is snow there, for the snow serveth them as water. They set up the dwelling in which they sleep on a circular frame of interlaced sticks converging into a little round hoop on the top, from which projects above a collar as a chimney, and this they cover over with white felt…And they make these houses so large that they are sometimes thirty feet in width. I myself once measured the width between the wheel-tracks of a cart twenty feet, and when the house was on the cart it projected beyond the wheels on either side five feet at least. I have myself counted to one cart twenty-two oxen drawing one house, eleven abreast across the width of the cart, and the other eleven before them.

GENGHIS KHAN

"I am the punishment of God… If you had not committed great sins, God would not have sent a punishment like me upon you."

"The greatest happiness is to scatter your enemy, to drive him before you, to see his cities reduced to ashes, to see those who love him shrouded in tears, and to gather into your bosom his wives and daughters."

"It is not sufficient that I succeed—all others must fail."

IMAGE of the ATTACK on BAGHDAD, 1258

KUYAK KHAN

The reply of Kuyak Khan to a Franciscan friar.

And when you say: "I am a Christian. I pray to God. I arraign and despise others," how do you know who is pleasing to God and to whom He allots His grace? How can you know it, that you speak such words?

Thanks to the power of the Eternal Heaven, all lands have been given to us from sunrise to sunset. How could anyone act other than in accordance with the commands of Heaven? Now your own upright heart must tell you: "We [the Pope and monarchs of Europe] will become subject to you, and will place our powers at your disposal." You in person, at the head of the monarchs, all of you, without exception, must come to tender us service and pay us homage, then only will we

recognize your submission. But if you do not obey the commands of Heaven, and run counter to our orders, we shall know that you are our foe.

Practice Test Two Answer Key
SELECTED-RESPONSE QUESTIONS

1. C
2. D
3. A
4. C
5. C
6. D
7. D
8. E
9. A
10. D
11. E
12. E
13. E
14. D
15. C
16. C
17. B
18. B
19. A
20. C
21. B
22. E
23. C
24. B
25. C
26. B
27. E
28. A
29. C
30. D
31. B
32. D
33. E
34. D
35. D
36. A
37. B
38. C
39. C
40. C
41. C
42. A
43. C
44. B
45. C
46. B
47. C
48. C
49. C
50. B
51. A
52. B
53. C
54. C
55. C
56. B
57. B
58. A
59. E
60. D
61. C
62. A
63. A
64. B
65. B
66. A
67. C
68. C
69. C
70. A

FREE-RESPONSE QUESTIONS

1. How has communist China remained the same and changed over time, from the time of the Chinese Revolution to today.

At the time of the Chinese Revolution, much of the Chinese population lived rurally and worked in agriculture. There had been foreign communities in China, for instance, in Shanghai; however, these were no longer present by the time of the Chinese Revolution. The nation had suffered horribly since the first invasion by Japan, and continued to throughout World War II. After the war, the nationalist government was quite weak and the civil war ended quickly with a communist victory.

The communist government of the new People's Republic of China set about implementing their social and economic goals and policies almost at once. Mao's Great Leap Forward, introduced in the 1950s was designed to create a modern, loyal and obedient communist state. The goals of the Great Leap Forward included additional industrialization, the collectivization of agriculture, an end to private property, and an end to any potential resistance or rebellion. While the government certainly hoped to create a successful state, the result was a widespread famine, at least in part, manufactured by the activity of the state. Between 18 and 45 million died within just a few years between 1958 and 1961 as the result of the Great Leap Forward. The failure of the Great Leap Forward caused Mao to lose power within China; however, he regained this during the Cultural Revolution.

The Cultural Revolution, beginning in 1966, sought to eliminate western influences through the use of re-education and other policies, including prison camps, youth organizations, and a purge of moderate official. Forced labor was common and a more agricultural lifestyle was idealized. After Mao's death in 1976, the party distanced itself from the Cultural Revolution, recognizing the harm it had called.

Faced with overpopulation and economic challenges, China introduced a one-child policy in 1979. While some exceptions were allowed, this policy dramatically reduced population growth. Today, the policy has been relaxed even more; however, the lasting effects have caused new problems. There are concerns about the number of dependents in an aging population, as well as gender imbalances.

Economic change in China began in the late 1970s, under the leadership of Deng Xiaoping. The first modifications allowed for trade with the west, with the means of production under government control. Gradually, property right s increased, and today, individuals and corporations may hold control of means of production. Towns are encouraged to open factories for export and foreign countries are welcomed as investors in Chinese industry. Far more of the population now works in business or industry, rather than agriculture.

While economic restrictions have loosened, political ones remain quite strict. Chinese nationals can and often do travel, but still live with substantial restrictions regarding speaking out against their government, criticizing the government or exercising freedom of speech or religion.

Today, China is one of the most economically successful nations; however, its people still lack basic protections or freedoms. Prison camps, forced labor and poor work conditions remain common in China. Without these personal freedoms, China remains a step away from western nations, and slightly outside of the international community.

2. COMPARE THE IMPACT OF COLONIALISM IN INDIA AND LATIN AMERICA.

Both the Latin American countries and India experienced colonialism, but each was under the control of a different colonial power and had distinctly different experiences with imperialism. These experiences have altered the development of nations in both regions, creating close ties in some cases and political struggles in others.

The modern states of India, Pakistan and Bangladesh make up the Indian sub-continent. These were all part of the colonial Raj of the British Empire. The Indian sub-continent had a long history, valuable resources, including cotton and spices, and an equally long history of conquest. In ancient times, Alexander the Great reached India before turning back, and during the 13th century, the Mongols conquered much of the region.

The British conquest of India was based on a desire for trading rights and was originally handled not by the state, but by the British East India Company, incorporated in 1600. Britain, over time, established a treaty-based trade monopoly in India. Violence occurred on Indian soil between the British and French during the 18th century Seven-Year' War. While the original trade monopoly was secured voluntarily through treaties, by the middle of the 18th century, the British East India Company relied upon military force to secure control of India. By the 19th century, the British East India Company acted not only as a commercial force, but an administrative one. Following a rebellion in India in 1857, the British nationalized the British East India Company, making India a British colony. The structures put in place under the company remained.

Once the state was under the control of the crown, efforts were made to keep it peaceful and stable, rewarding and educating locals, often in Britain. Local laws and traditions were allowed to remain, rather than being replaced with western ones. Industry, education and infrastructure were developed under the British, with many locals involved in the process. Notably, the British favored Hindus over Muslims for civil service positions. India became independent after World War II; however, Indian language, culture and religion continued throughout the British occupation of India.

The Spanish were primarily responsible for the settlement of Latin America after Columbus' arrival in the Americas. Conditions in the Americas were very different than those in India. While the religion and culture of India remained intact, the native cultures of the Americas were largely destroyed by colonialism.

First and foremost, native populations in the Americas simply didn't survive the colonization process. Many native groups were warrior cultures, and fought hard against the invaders. Faced with better-armed troops on horseback, many died in battle. Even more devastating was the impact of disease, including smallpox. Finally, the Spaniards put the natives to work in mines and on farms, in unacceptable working conditions, typically without the time or ability to care for their own land or families. Mortality was high. Additionally, the Spanish typically did not travel with wives and families, so married and had children with native women. The mestizo or mixed-race class grew, but the native beliefs, practices and language died out.

The Spanish offered only one path to survival for natives. They could not thrive in Spanish society with their own beliefs and language. Survival required that they accommodate the Spanish by learning their language and converting to Christianity. Some elements of traditional practice remain in Latin American Catholicism; however, the religions of the Aztec and other groups disappeared rapidly.

Both Latin America and India experienced colonialism. India was, fundamentally, a valuable trading partner. It had entered into the partnership voluntarily initially, and there was no expectation of the destruction of the people or their culture. The opposite was true in Latin America. The native peoples were enslaved, with no opportunity for advancement or ability to preserve their own culture. Those who lived did so because they assimilated their new culture.

3. THE MONGOL CONQUEST LED TO GREAT DESTRUCTION, BUT ALSO CREATED A NUMBER OF STABLE KINGDOMS THAT SUPPORTED PEACE AND LEARNING. USING YOUR OWN KNOWLEDGE AND THE PASSAGES BELOW, ANALYZE THE ACTIONS AND GOALS OF THE MONGOLIAN CONQUEST.

In the late 12th and early 13th century, the Mongolian army, under the control and leadership of Genghis Khan, took over much of the known world. The Mongolians were a pastoral people, particularly known for their skill on horseback. They lived in relatively small groups, ruled by local leaders. They were nomadic, following their animals. Today, life in parts of Mongolia remains relatively similar, as people still use the traditional yurts and still follow their animals. Genghis Khan was the son of one of these leaders. They were not literate and relatively little is known of the origins of the Mongolian peoples. Many of the stories that circulated later, like the story of Prester John told by Marco Polo, were legend and myth, rather than history.

Before his death in 1227, Genghis Khan had gained control of large areas of East Asia, extending into the Eastern parts of Europe in the west and into China toward the east. After this death, his successors continued these campaigns, sacking Baghdad in 1258 and eventually establishing wide-ranging empires from Moghul India to the Yuan Dynasty.

The Mongolians are commonly known for their armies and their brutality. Cities that offered any resistance were sacked and destroyed, as you can see in the manuscript illustration of the sack of Baghdad. In many cases, civilians, including both women and children were killed or enslaved. Taking the wives and children of a fallen enemy further humiliated him, as noted in the quote from Genghis Khan about gathering them to his bosom. Those cities that surrendered and opened their gates to the Mongol army were typically spared and generally relatively well-treated. The enemies of the Khan were not. Harsh and brutal retribution occurred to those who opposed him, including nobles.

While Genghis Khan is most commonly remembered for his brutality, he was, for his people, a relatively humane ruler. He implemented laws that improved the food supply and condemned the kidnapping of women. He introduced improved record-keeping procedures and protected trade. The later Mongolian empires created stable, elegant and tolerant kingdoms, implementing parts of the local cultures in ways that worked best for them. Under later Mongolian rulers, the Silk Road grew and flourished during the Pax Mongolica.

Later rulers were particularly known for their willingness to adapt, a behavior already seen in Genghis Khan's action as a ruler. Marco Polo, who lived in the court of Kublai Khan in Yuan Dynasty China, recorded his willingness to embrace and explore different religions. The reader should, in this, recognize the cultural relativism. We have no reason to believe that Kublai Khan favored Christianity over Buddhism or Islam, but Marco Polo certainly did. The various Mongol Khans had interactions with Christians, including representatives of the papacy, but would only consider a vassal relationship with these entities. For the Khans, they were the head of the universe and all others, including the Catholic Church, were to provide service to them.

Eventually, the smaller empires fell, one after another. Genghis Khan divided his empire after his death, and the smaller empires could not retain control. While today the Mongolian nation remains, even the final traces of the Mongol empire, the Moghul state of India, eventually fell to the British.

CHAPTER NINE
Practice Test Three

Selected-Response Questions

Read the question, and then choose the most correct answer.

1. Minarets and calligraphy are associated with—
   A) Hinduism.
   B) Buddhism.
   C) North Africa.
   D) Islam.
   E) Mesoamerica.

2. Kabuki Theater developed in—
   A) Latin America.
   B) China.
   C) Korea.
   D) Japan.
   E) French Indochina.

3. Which of the following contributed to Nazi ideologies in the Holocaust?
   A) Darwinism
   B) Christianity
   C) Judaism
   D) Social Darwinism
   E) Marxism

4. Which of the following is not a similarity of the Haitian, US, and French Revolutions?
   A) a declaration of human rights
   B) the desire for personal freedom
   C) the desire for increased rights for the working classes
   D) violence
   E) leadership by the well-educated upper middle class or elites

5. Creoles were—
   A) individuals with Spanish and native blood.
   B) long-term Spanish settlers.
   C) new Spanish settlers.
   D) Europeans born in Latin America.
   E) individuals with both European and African blood.

6. *Vodun* is an example of—
   A) Shamanism.
   B) Christianity.
   C) Animism.
   D) Daoism.
   E) Syncretism.

7. In which of the following regions and periods did women have the greatest personal freedom?
   A) pre-WWI Britain
   B) the Soviet Union after the Russian Revolution
   C) China in 1800
   D) the United States in 1850
   E) Iran in 1981

8. Choose the answer that is NOT an example of xenophobia.
   A) White Australia policies
   B) US reservations for Native Americans
   C) religious tolerance in the Mongol Empire
   D) immigration limits on Chinese immigrants in the United States
   E) refusal to allow Jewish immigrants early in the Holocaust

9. What is the Hajj?
   A) daily Islamic prayer
   B) fasting during Ramadan
   C) rules about contact between men and women
   D) religious pilgrimage to Mecca
   E) religious pilgrimage to Medina

10. What was the Marshall Plan?
    A) a plan to destroy Nazi Germany
    B) a plan to defeat Japan in World War II
    C) a plan to rebuild defeated countries after World War II
    D) a plan to help Britain rebuild after World War I
    E) a plan to defeat communism in Vietnam

11. How was the Cuban Missile Crisis resolved?
    A) The US bombed Cuba.
    B) The US bombed the Soviet Union.
    C) The Soviets removed the missiles.
    D) The US aimed missiles at Cuba.
    E) The Cold War began.

12. The stupa is an architectural form associated with—
    A) Hinduism.
    B) Buddhism.
    C) Islam.
    D) Hare Krishna.
    E) Christianity.

13. Labor unions developed—
    A) under communism.
    B) prior to the revolutions of 1848.
    C) after the revolutions of 1848.
    D) early in the Industrial Revolution.
    E) after World War I.

14. During the Partition of India, what independent states were created?
    A) India and Pakistan
    B) a united India
    C) India, Afghanistan, and Bangladesh
    D) India, Pakistan, Bangladesh, and Afghanistan
    E) India, Pakistan, and Bangladesh

15. The Mughal Empire had a _____ majority and _____ ruling minority.
    A) Buddhist, Hindu
    B) Hindu, Muslim
    C) Muslim, Hindu
    D) Hindu, Mongol
    E) Hindu, Buddhist

16. In which of the following countries has religion played the smallest role?
    A) Russia
    B) China
    C) Britain
    D) Germany
    E) India

17. Tanks were first used in what war?
    A) World War I
    B) World War II
    C) Vietnam
    D) Korea
    E) The Boer War

18. While Germany was known for *blitzkrieg* warfare, Japan used—
    A) the atomic bomb.
    B) Kamikaze pilots.
    C) land forces.
    D) trench warfare.
    E) submarine warfare.

19. Population demographics are skewed and unusual in China because of—
    A) starvation in the 1950s.
    B) the impact of the Rape of Nanjing in 1938.
    C) restrictive population policies in place since the 1970s.
    D) lack of access to contraception.
    E) lack of access to health care.

20. Between the 12th century and the middle of the 19th, Japan was ruled by—
    A) the Meiji Restoration.
    B) Samurai.
    C) a shogun.
    D) an emperor.
    E) an elected leader.

21. What facilitated the spread of Buddhism, Christianity, and later, Islam?
    A) missionaries
    B) emperors
    C) monks
    D) traders
    E) written texts

22. What event in East Asia do some scholars use to mark the beginning of World War II?
    A) the Rape of Nanjing
    B) the Japanese takeover of Korea
    C) the Japanese invasion of China
    D) the French takeover of Vietnam
    E) the Chinese Revolution

23. By the beginning of World War II, Korea was—
    A) under Chinese control.
    B) under British control.
    C) under French control.
    D) independent.
    E) under Japanese control.

24. Why did the Silk Road eventually fall out of use?
    A) It was slow.
    B) It was dangerous.
    C) There were better, safer roads.
    D) Sea travel was faster and more practical.
    E) Trade stopped.

25. During the colonial period, Vietnam was under the control of—
    A) France.
    B) Britain.
    C) the United States.
    D) China.
    E) Japan.

26. Which of the following is an example of large-scale architecture designed to illustrate the power of the ruler?
    A) the Ziggurat of Ur
    B) the Palace of Versailles
    C) the Stupa at Borobudur
    D) the Parthenon
    E) Hagia Sophia

27. Lady Murasaki's *Tale of Genji* is—
    A) a defense of women's rights.
    B) epic poetry.
    C) the first novel.
    D) written in Chinese.
    E) a play.

28. Ibn Battuta, Marco Polo and Zheng He did NOT visit what location?
    A) China
    B) Baghdad
    C) India
    D) South America
    E) Africa

29. The epic of Malinke Sundiata is about—
    A) a mythological hero.
    B) the founder of the empire of Mali.
    C) the history of Mali.
    D) a deity worshipped in Mali.
    E) the founding of the city of Ur.

30. The city of Timbuktu is commonly—
    A) associated with the founding of Islam.
    B) associated with the Ottoman Empire.
    C) associated with trade and education.
    D) associated with the slave trade.
    E) located in East Africa.

31. How did the Black Death or bubonic plague spread?
    A) Sick people travelled for pilgrimages.
    B) Rats carrying fleas travelled on trading ships.
    C) Rats ran along the Silk Road.
    D) Infested furs transmitted the disease around the world.
    E) People transmitted it from person to person.

32. In what way did the slave trade differ substantially after 1500?
- **A)** It decreased substantially.
- **B)** It increased immensely.
- **C)** Slaves were now from Africa, rather than Southeast Asia.
- **D)** Slave traders were now local, rather than foreigners.
- **E)** Slaves had more rights than before.

33. Slaves in ancient Greece were most commonly—
- **A)** prisoners of war.
- **B)** Africans.
- **C)** Greeks.
- **D)** Turks.
- **E)** Europeans.

34. Which of the following best describes the status of women in ancient Rome?
- **A)** They had limited legal rights and powers.
- **B)** They had full citizen rights.
- **C)** They were isolated and unable to go in public.
- **D)** They lived publicly, but had limited legal rights.
- **E)** They were not allowed to be educated.

35. The Estates General refers to—
- **A)** The French Revolution.
- **B)** The French assembly.
- **C)** Napoleon's empire.
- **D)** the empire of Napoleon III.
- **E)** the conference that met to write the constitution.

36. The technology of porcelain-making developed in—
- **A)** India.
- **B)** Mesopotamia.
- **C)** China.
- **D)** Japan.
- **E)** Mesoamerica.

37. What innovation was necessary to support domestication of plants?
- **A)** the plow
- **B)** the wheel
- **C)** animal harnesses
- **D)** carriages
- **E)** food storage, like pottery

38. Specialization of labor occurred—
- **A)** prior to the introduction of agriculture.
- **B)** not long after the introduction of agriculture.
- **C)** after the introduction of writing.
- **D)** when humans developed religion.
- **E)** after the industrial revolution.

39. What is a *quipu*?
- **A)** Mayan writing
- **B)** Incan record keeping
- **C)** Aztec writing
- **D)** Olmec record keeping
- **E)** Chavin writing

40. Napoleon's empire included which of the following regions?
- **A)** Italy
- **B)** Egypt
- **C)** Algeria
- **D)** Russia
- **E)** Morocco

41. Works of art from all over the world are in museums in the United States and Western Europe. Many of these were collected in the 19th century. What allowed these countries to acquire so much ancient art from varied regions?
    A) imperialism
    B) the discovery of the Americas
    C) mercantilism
    D) capitalism
    E) widespread migration

42. Large numbers of Chinese immigrants entered the United States in the middle of the 19th century. What is the primary reason for Chinese immigration in this period?
    A) They sought political freedom.
    B) They worked on the railroad construction projects.
    C) They were considered desirable immigrants.
    D) They had communities in West Coast cities.
    E) They were forced migrations.

43. What is subsistence agriculture?
    A) agriculture on a large scale, i.e., with significant surplus
    B) agriculture on a small scale, i.e., without surplus
    C) ancient agriculture techniques
    D) the use of modern agricultural techniques
    E) hunting and gathering

44. Prior to the industrial revolution, what was the primary industry in India?
    A) silk production
    B) cotton production
    C) rice production
    D) wheat production
    E) subsistence farming

45. The first factories produced—
    A) textiles.
    B) steel.
    C) coal.
    D) iron.
    E) steam engines.

46. Which of the following countries was the last to industrialize?
    A) Britain
    B) Germany
    C) China
    D) Russia
    E) the United States

47. Of the following, choose the best definition of feudalism.
    A) In a feudal system, individuals owe loyalty and military service to a lord or noble, but farm their own land.
    B) Individuals owe loyalty and labor to the lord, farming both his land and a small plot rented from the lord.
    C) A feudal system is ruled by the Church.
    D) A feudal system is a type of monarchy, led by a king.
    E) A feudal system embraces slavery, with no personal freedom.

48. What was the *Lusitania*?
- **A)** a German submarine
- **B)** a British plane
- **C)** a British passenger ship
- **D)** a German trading vessel
- **E)** a German city

49. The Nine Classics of Confucianism, calligraphy, and poetry were essential for—
- **A)** Chinese emperors.
- **B)** Chinese concubines.
- **C)** Chinese civil servants.
- **D)** Chinese merchants.
- **E)** Chinese nobility.

50. Apartheid was—
- **A)** a type of slavery.
- **B)** strict racial segregation associated with South Africa.
- **C)** trading practices in West Africa.
- **D)** a form of colonial government.
- **E)** rebellion against colonial government.

51. The Great Depression did NOT—
- **A)** lead to significant inflation in Germany.
- **B)** impact countries around the world.
- **C)** impact Russia with the same intensity.
- **D)** lead to the New Deal in the United States.
- **E)** involve the stock market crash.

52. Fascist governments can be characterized as—
- **A)** theocracies.
- **B)** monarchies.
- **C)** oligarchies.
- **D)** authoritarian.
- **E)** military.

53. The *encomienda* system was:
- **A)** a forced labor system employed in Latin America.
- **B)** a traditional Inca labor system.
- **C)** a form of feudalism.
- **D)** a political system employed in Spain.
- **E)** religious persecution in Spain.

54. Choose the best description of Spanish attitudes toward native peoples in South America.
- **A)** They viewed them as subhuman.
- **B)** They viewed them as a potential labor force.
- **C)** They wanted to destroy them.
- **D)** They avoided any form of interaction.
- **E)** They did not attempt to convert them to Christianity.

55. Which of the following is an example of syncretism?
- **A)** Latin American traditions involving saints and processions
- **B)** Protestant church services
- **C)** decoration in Roman Catholic churches in Europe
- **D)** the reuse of Byzantine churches as mosques
- **E)** the immigration of Puritans from England

56. The Ganges River is closely associated with what religion?
    A) Buddhism
    B) Hinduism
    C) Christianity
    D) Judaism
    E) Islam

57. The Taj Mahal was built by—
    A) the builders of Mohenjo-Daro.
    B) Asoka.
    C) Malinke Sundiata.
    D) a Mogul emperor.
    E) Alexander the Great.

58. The city of Rome fell to:
    A) Julius Caesar
    B) the Britons
    C) the Goths
    D) the Mongols
    E) the Saxons

59. How did the Byzantine Empire affect Russia?
    A) The Russians adopted the Orthodox Church.
    B) The Byzantine Empire protected Russian from the Ottomans.
    C) The Byzantine Empire conquered Russia.
    D) The Byzantine Empire fought Russia.
    E) The Byzantine Empire did not affect Russia.

60. The Protestant Reformation began in—
    A) Italy.
    B) France.
    C) Switzerland.
    D) Germany.
    E) Britain.

61. The Vietnam war is an example of—
    A) the Marshall Plan.
    B) containment.
    C) communism.
    D) contamination.
    E) the Domino Effect.

62. Following the discovery of the New World, Spain and Portugal were the primary explorers of the Atlantic. How was the Atlantic region divided between them?
    A) Spain gained control of West Africa, Portugal the Americas.
    B) They each controlled what they could win.
    C) Portugal controlled West Africa, Spain the Americas.
    D) Portugal had trading rights and Spain colonization.
    E) Both had to have the permission of the Catholic Church to colonize.

63. At what point did the Byzantine Empire reach its height?
    A) Around 400 CE.
    B) Around 550 CE.
    C) Around 750 CE.
    D) Around 1000 CE.
    E) Around 1400 CE.

64. Where did the conquests of Alexander the Great stop?
    A) Persia
    B) India
    C) China
    D) Egypt
    E) Mali

65. The city of Mohenjo-Daro was located—
    A) in the Ganges River Valley.
    B) in the Indus River Valley.
    C) in the Tigris River Valley.
    D) in the Euphrates River Valley.
    E) in the Yellow River Valley.

66. After Britain, which nation was the next to embrace industrialization?
    A) Germany
    B) the United States
    C) France
    D) Russia
    E) Japan

67. Which of the following events in the last half-century was impacted by religious fundamentalism?
    A) Indian independence
    B) the Vietnam War
    C) the attack on the World Trade Center on 9/11
    D) the Korean War
    E) the Cold War

68. Which country supported the colonists during the American Revolution?
    A) Britain
    B) Canada
    C) Mexico
    D) Spain
    E) France

69. Which of the following colonial states gained its freedom through violent rebellion?
    A) Algeria
    B) India
    C) Pakistan
    D) Bangladesh
    E) Nigeria

70. The World Health Organization (WHO) is—
    A) part of the League of Nations.
    B) part of the United Nations.
    C) a global humanitarian organization.
    D) run by the United States.
    E) a direct result of World War II.

Free-Response Questions

For questions 1 and 2, write a short essay based on your knowledge of World History. For question 3, write a short essay based on your knowledge and the accompanying historical texts.

1. How have interactions between the United States and other western powers and Japan changed over time, and how have the cultural differences and values remained the same?

2. Both Russia and China had communist revolutions in the 20th century. Compare and contrast the impact of this on each nation's citizens.

3. The Heian Period in Classical Japan is a time of remarkable learning, art, and culture. The passages below illustrate more about this society, including the role of women. Analyze how these works relate to one another and to the culture of Heian Japan.

SEI SHONAGAN

The Beauty of the Seasons: 986–1000 CE

In spring it is the dawn that is most beautiful. As the light creeps over the hills, their outlines are dyed a faint red and wisps of purplish cloud trail over them.

In summer the nights. Not only when the moon shines, but on dark nights too, as the fireflies flit to and fro, and even when it rains, how beautiful it is!

In autumn the evenings, when the glittering sun sinks close to the edge of the hills and the crows fly back to their nests in threes and fours and twos; more charming still is a file of wild geese, like specks in the distant sky. When the sun has set, one's heart is moved by the sound of the wind and the hum of the insects.

In winter the early mornings. It is beautiful indeed when snow has fallen during the night, but splendid too when the ground is white with frost; or even when there is no snow or frost, but it is simply very cold and the attendants hurry from room to room stirring up the fires and bringing charcoal, how well this fits the season's mood! But as noon approaches and the cold wears off, no one bothers to keep the braziers alight, and soon nothing remains but piles of white ashes.

Women in Court

I cannot bear men who believe that women serving in the Palace are bound to be frivolous and wicked. Yet I suppose their prejudice is understandable. After all, women at Court do not spend their time hiding modestly behind fans and screens, but walk about, looking openly at people they chance to meet. Yes, they see everyone face to face, not only ladies-in-waiting like themselves but even Their Imperial Majesties (whose august names I hardly dare mention), High Court Nobles, senior courtiers, and other gentlemen of high rank. In the presence of such exalted personages the women in the Palace are all equally brazen. Small wonder that the young men regard them as immodest! Yet are the gentlemen themselves any less so? They are not exactly bashful when it comes to looking at the great people in the Palace. No, everyone at Court is much the same in this respect.

LADY MURASAKI
THE TALE OF GENJI

Tô no Chûjô nodded. "It may be difficult when someone you are especially fond of, someone beautiful and charming, has been guilty of an indiscretion, but magnanimity produces wonders. They may not always work, but generosity and reasonableness and patience do on the whole seem best."

FUJIWARA NO MICHINAGA

Fujiwara no Michinaga (966-1027) composed the following when one of his daughters became an imperial consort.

This world, I think,

Is indeed my world,

Like the full moon

I shine,

Uncovered by any cloud!

LOTUS SUTRA

I preach with ever the same voice, always taking Enlightenment as my text. For this is the same for all; no partiality is in it, neither hatred nor affection. I am inexorable, bear no love or hatred towards anyone, and proclaim the Law to all creatures without distinction, to the one as well as the other.

I regenerate the whole world like a cloud shedding its water without distinction. I have the same feelings for the high-born as for the low, for the moral as for the immoral, for the depraved as for those who observe the rules of good conduct, for those of sectarian views and unsound tenets as for those whose views are sound and true. I preach the Law to the inferior in mental culture as well as to those of superior understanding. Untouched by weariness, I spread in season the rain of the Law.

Practice Test Three Answer Key
SELECTED-RESPONSE QUESTIONS

1. D	25. A	49. C
2. D	26. B	50. B
3. D	27. C	51. C
4. E	28. D	52. D
5. D	29. B	53. A
6. E	30. C	54. B
7. B	31. B	55. A
8. C	32. B	56. B
9. D	33. A	57. D
10. C	34. D	58. C
11. C	35. B	59. A
12. B	36. C	60. D
13. C	37. E	61. B
14. E	38. B	62. C
15. B	39. B	63. D
16. B	40. A	64. B
17. A	41. A	65. B
18. B	42. B	66. B
19. C	43. B	67. C
20. C	44. B	68. E
21. D	45. A	69. A
22. C	46. C	70. C
23. E	47. B	
24. D	48. C	

FREE-RESPONSE QUESTIONS

1. How have interactions between the United States and other western powers and Japan changed over time and how have the cultural differences and values remained the same?

Following a long history of isolationism, Japan began regular contact with western powers under the Meiji Restoration in the middle of the 19th century. Japan began an intensive program of modernization at this time, including both the creation of a western-style army and navy and modernizing relatively traditional industries, including the production of porcelain and silk. Between 1868, when the emperor was restored to power, and 1912, Japan changed dramatically. By 1912, it had technology, a military, industry, and infrastructure comparable to those in Western Europe. Japan had already fought and won two wars, one against Russia.

The empire was organized around the emperor; however, actual political power was in the hands of a small elite. Nonetheless, the cult surrounding the emperor formed a critical basis for Japanese civilization. The ideology of loyalty, sacrifice and honor is an essential one to understand later Japanese actions, including aggressive expansionism and the strict discipline of the Japanese military. While there was a cult of the emperor, Japan took repeated steps toward representative democracy early in the 20th century, including universal male suffrage.

As Japan extended its reach early in the 20th century, European powers pushed back, preventing the advancement of the Japanese as a colonial power. After a period of economic recession around the end of World War I, slightly earlier than the Great Depression reached America and Europe, Japan began aggressive action against China. This aggression reached remarkable levels, including horrifying brutality against civilians in Nanjing. The Japanese continued their aggressive plan of expansion, moving outward as World War II began. The Japanese army and pilots were known for their bravery, even in the face of invincible odds. This was supported by the cult of the emperor and the traditional values of Japanese society.

Eventually, this push outward and campaign of aggression led to the bombing of Pearl Harbor. With this, America entered World War II and eventually, with the atomic bomb, defeated Japan. After the war, the west, and America in particular, rebuilt Japan, focusing on Japanese industry. The occupation of Japan continued until 1952; however, America and Japan have remained close since that time. The goal of the occupation was to create a state that was economically strong and stable, but which relied upon outside powers for defense and could not rebuild militarily.

Concerns about Japan's remilitarization were overwhelmed by containment plans for communism, as the Chinese communists created the People's Republic of China. When the final treaties were signed, they were remarkably favorable to the Japanese, with limited penalties for their war crimes. Beginning in 1960, the Japanese have actively worked to embrace Japanese culture, while still thriving in a westernized marketplace.

2. **COMPARE THE IMPACT OF THE COMMUNIST REVOLUTIONS IN RUSSIA AND CHINA ON THE PEOPLE OF THESE COUNTRIES.**

During the course of the 20th century, both Russia and China experienced communist revolutions, leading to communist systems of government. The revolutions themselves were quite different, but the results held some significant similarities. In more recent history, the two countries have diverged significantly, leading to a distinctly different experience for the population of each country.

The Russian Revolution lasted approximately two years, and was quite violent. After a number of battles, the victory went to the Bolsheviks. Relatively quickly, Vladimir Lenin established a stable government; however, after his death, conditions in Russia were volatile. There were several years of conflict in the communist party, followed by the victory of Josef Stalin.

Under Stalin, the state was strictly authoritarian. There was no room for or tolerance for variation of opinion or ideology. Broad campaigns began to destroy all potential opponents. In some cases, this took the form of murder, with individuals arrested and killed or sent to prison camps, while in others the process was less clear cut.

In the Ukraine, Stalin instituted harsh policies regarding wheat quotas. These quotas had to be met before the people were fed or even had seed grain for the next year. This process, called the holodomor, is often considered a genocide. Millions died of starvation in the Ukraine, even as grain was grown and available.

Conditions in the Soviet Union remained quite harsh under Stalin's rule. Following Stalin's death, there was still relatively little room for opposition. The country was fully industrialized, but the quality of life was quite poor for much of the population. Economic reforms, beginning with perestroika, led to a progressive loosening of restrictions and eventually, the collapse of the Soviet Union.

The Chinese Revolution was a slower process, beginning as a civil war in the years prior to World War II, followed by a break during the war years. After the war, the civil war came to an end rather quickly, with a victory by the communist party. While Stalin had focused on heavy industry, Mao Zedong was primarily concerned with agriculture.

During the "Great Leap Forward" farms were collectivized and grouped into giant facilities. Workers took their meals in dining halls, and lacked any personal incentive for hard work. This failed, miserably, eventually leading to a reversal. While a poor harvest was the result of this, mass starvation also occurred, with events very much like those in the Ukraine in the 1930s. Millions died of starvation, even though, in the cities, warehouses of food were available.

Just as Stalin had culled the intellectuals and westerners, Mao's government did the same. Some were killed outright and many others were sent to re-education camps. The economy was primarily agricultural. Smaller farms took the place after the failure of the "Great Leap Forward" with some ability for individuals to improve their lot in life.

While the Soviet Union collapsed rather than successfully relaxing the economic tenets of communism, China has followed a very different path. China has kept some of the principles of the communist state, including the authoritarianism embraced under Mao, but has relaxed elements of its economic policy, allowing for private property and ownership, including the ownership of factories. The Chinese authorities have sought out western investors and China has, in the last 20 years, become an economic powerhouse. For many people in China, this has provided an improved standard of living, particularly as the working population decreases; however, many in the countryside remain agricultural.

3. Heian Japan marks the end of the classical period in Japanese history. It was a period of remarkable culture, particularly among the elite and it was a time of creative energy, with a new, particularly Japanese identity developing. The Japanese were distancing themselves from Chinese culture and working to create a uniquely Japanese culture, including the incorporation of Pure Land Buddhism. Perhaps most interestingly, this is a period of significant creativity for women, with many women writing about their experiences and lives.

During the Heian period, many women remained relatively isolated. Their actions were controlled by social norms and they typically hid their faces behind large fans or silk and bamboo screens. In court, however, women shed their fans and walked openly, as recorded in the diaries of Sei Shonagan. This woman, like others of the court, was a poet. Whether openly or behind the scenes, women in Heian Japan wielded social power and many were well-educated, with the ability to write poetry. Reciting and writing poetry was considered an attractive trait. While marriages were typically arranged for political gain, affairs were well-tolerated, as shown by the passage by Lady Murasaki. Children born outside of marriage were not considered illegitimate. The first novel, the Tale of Genji by Lady Murasaki, was written by a noblewoman during this time. Her novel illustrates the significant role women played in Heian society, as well as the lively and educated society in which they lived.

In Confucian China, daughters were considered a burden, but in the families of Heian Japan, daughters provided potential access to the imperial family and the only means of social improvement. Before and after this period, female children were frequently exposed at birth, but during this time, daughters were desirable. . They could be married or become concubines, potentially bearing a son to the imperial family. The culture was uxorial with men commonly living with their wives after marriage, providing the wife's family with significant control of her children. The verse written by one of the Fujiwara illustrates this. His daughter has brought honor to his family. Japanese women began to appear, not only in society, but in art, as shown in the illustration of the Tale of Genji.

The growing role of women was supported by the changing religious views of the time. Buddhism was embraced, but integrated aspects of traditional Japanese religion,

Shintoism. The strong appreciation of beauty and nature expressed by Sei Shonagan reflects this syncretism. It is also visible in the lotus sutra, a particularly popular sutra during this period. Texts supported the idea that women could become Buddhas without being reborn as men. In this, men and women were equal.

The relative egalitarianism of Heian Japan ended with introduction of the Shogunate and military rule. Women lost their freedom and most were no longer educated. Obedience was valued over the elegant ability to compose poetry at will and recite traditional verses. The writings of women of this time, written in kana, or Japanese script, remain accessible, providing an image into a window of Japanese culture so very different from the culture that followed.

CHAPTER TEN
Practice Test Four

Selected-Response Questions
Read the question, and then choose the most correct answer.

1. The story of Romulus and Remus explains—
   A) the founding of Athens.
   B) the founding of Rome.
   C) the existence of the Roman Senate.
   D) the power of the Roman Emperor.
   E) the spread of the Roman Empire.

2. Which of the following did not support the transmission of diseases on a large scale?
   A) Bantu migrations
   B) the Columbian Exchange
   C) the Silk Road
   D) the Indian Ocean Trade Network
   E) Mediterranean trade

3. Read the following passage and choose the correct term for what is presented in the passage.

   "If anyone, no matter who, were given the opportunity of choosing from amongst all the nations in the world the set of beliefs which he thought best, he would inevitably—after careful considerations of their relative merits—choose that of his own country. Everyone without exception believes his own native customs, and the religion he was brought up in, to be the best."

   – Herodotus, *the Histories*

   A) historiography
   B) cultural relativism
   C) historical fact
   D) personal narrative
   E) global history

4. What does the phrase "white man's burden" refer to?
   A) the costs of trade
   B) the expense of providing food and shelter
   C) the burden of colonizing and westernizing "primitive" peoples
   D) the costs of mining natural resources
   E) the need to industrialize western nations

5. The image shown below is from the tomb of whom?

   A) Qin Shi Huang
   B) Wu Zetian
   C) Zheng Hi
   D) Cixi
   E) Mao Zedong

6. Which European nation was particularly known for the strength of its navy?
   A) Spain
   B) France
   C) Germany
   D) Britain
   E) The Netherlands

7. What did Phoenician traders export?
   A) cyprus wood
   B) cedar wood
   C) cotton
   D) silk
   E) porcelain

8. Which empire included large territorial holdings in Europe, Northern Africa, and Western Asia?
   A) the Byzantine empire
   B) the British empire
   C) the Ottoman empire
   D) the Napoleonic empire
   E) the Roman empire

9. The most stable country in Latin America through the 20th century was—
   A) Nicaragua.
   B) Chile.
   C) Brazil.
   D) Mexico.
   E) Peru.

10. NAFTA is an example of—
    A) a defense alliance.
    B) a trade agreement.
    C) an unequal treaty.
    D) a colonial agreement.
    E) a global organization.

11. Who controlled trade on the Indian Ocean Trade Network?
    A) the traders
    B) the Chinese
    C) the Indians
    D) the British
    E) the pirates

12. Piracy was common in—
    A) the Mediterranean.
    B) the Indian ocean.
    C) the Atlantic.
    D) the Pacific.
    E) the Caribbean.

13. What movement supported the revolutions of 1848?
    A) communism
    B) Marxism
    C) socialism
    D) capitalism
    E) mercantilism

14. Which of the following is an example of a theocracy?
    A) Iran
    B) Iraq
    C) Saudi Arabia
    D) Italy
    E) France

15. The United States backed which world leader in the 20th century?
    A) the Shah of Iran
    B) Adolf Hitler
    C) Benito Mussolini
    D) Margaret Thatcher
    E) Tony Blair

16. What is a special economic zone?
    A) a region with lower taxes
    B) a region with higher taxes
    C) a colonial agreement allowing for trade
    D) an unequal trade treaty
    E) a region in China designed to encourage foreign investment

17. How does the Jamaica Letter, written by Simon Bolivar, differ from other declarations of natural rights?
    A) It did not allow for natural rights.
    B) It did not allow for personal freedoms.
    C) It believed a period of dictatorship was necessary.
    D) It supported a democratic government.
    E) It attempted to create a free state.

18. Japan pursued a policy of _____ until the middle of the 19th century.
    A) mercantilism
    B) isolationism
    C) capitalism
    D) imperialism
    E) Marxism

19. The Crusades did NOT—
    A) result in lasting land gains.
    B) provide new learning to the west.
    C) offer an option for young men to reduce violence in Europe.
    D) provide religious indulgences.
    E) offer the opportunity to gain personal wealth.

20. The Heian Period marks—
    A) the beginning of the Shogunate.
    B) the end of the Shogunate.
    C) the beginning of Classical Japan.
    D) the beginning of the Meiji Restoration.
    E) the end of Classical Japan.

21. Which of the following is not commonly correlated with industrialization?
    A) literacy
    B) high birth rate
    C) steam power
    D) internal combustion engines
    E) lower birth rate

22. Prior to the introduction of domesticated plants and animals, humans—
    A) lived in large groups.
    B) built permanent settlements.
    C) had clear social hierarchy.
    D) were hunter-gatherers.
    E) were pastoralists.

23. How was Wu Zetian unusual?
    A) He was a civil servant.
    B) She was a poet.
    C) She ruled as Empress, with full political power.
    D) He explored much of the world.
    E) She wrote the first novel.

24. The colony of Australia was originally established—
    A) as a settlement colony.
    B) as a penal colony.
    C) as a French colony.
    D) as a plantation economy.
    E) as an American colony.

25. Educated native elites often returned to their home country and—
    A) assisted the colonial forces.
    B) served as bureaucrats.
    C) worked for independence.
    D) served in the military.
    E) immigrated to the colonial power.

26. Which of the following is NOT an example of colonial troops serving the colonial power?
    A) ANZAC
    B) Canadian troops serving in World War I
    C) Indian troops serving the British East Indies Company
    D) Algerian troops resisting the French
    E) Canadian troops serving in World War II

27. William Smith paid for his passage by signing a labor contract to work under a blacksmith in the colonies. He will owe four years of labor, but expects to be a qualified smith at the end of his time. What is this an example of?
    A) serfdom
    B) chattel slavery
    C) indentured servitude
    D) forced migration
    E) involuntary service

28. Higher birth rates were more common in—
    A) agricultural societies.
    B) hunter-gatherer societies.
    C) industrialized societies.
    D) communist states.
    E) developed nations.

29. The Manhattan Project refers to—
    A) the sale of Manhattan to the Dutch.
    B) the development of the atomic bomb.
    C) the settlement of Manhattan.
    D) the urbanization of Manhattan.
    E) the creation of Wall Street.

30. Science and learning thrived under—
    A) the Islamic caliphates.
    B) Europe after the fall of Rome.
    C) Europe under Charlemagne.
    D) China during the Warring States period.
    E) China during the Cultural Revolution.

31. Which of the following was responsible for many significant inventions, including paper money, gunpowder, and printing?
    A) China
    B) the Umayyad Caliphate
    C) India
    D) Japan
    E) the Ottoman Empire

32. What 15th-century invention revolutionized Europe?
    A) the steam engine
    B) the spinning jenny
    C) the printing press
    D) the damask loom
    E) the flying buttress

33. Egyptian pyramids served what function?
    A) ritual spaces
    B) burial spaces
    C) palaces
    D) symbols of power
    E) living spaces

34. *Cuneiform* and hieroglyphics are both examples of what?
    A) types of art
    B) mathematical tools
    C) epic poems
    D) types of writing
    E) types of buildings

35. The _____ is to China as the _____ is to India.
    A) Stupa, Pagoda
    B) Mosque, Stupa
    C) Pagoda, Stupa
    D) Mosque, Minaret
    E) Minaret, Stupa

36. Which of the following cities provides insights into both Muslim and Christian history?
    A) Athens
    B) Baghdad
    C) Timbuktu
    D) Istanbul
    E) Venice

37. Which of the following is NOT a common trait of Islam and Judaism?
    A) use of a written religious text
    B) reverence for prophets of God
    C) a requirement of a religious pilgrimage to Mecca
    D) holy sites in Jerusalem
    E) a traditionally patriarchal culture

38. Choose the best description of early trade networks in the Americas.
    A) They were large and well-organized.
    B) They were minimal and local.
    C) They traded large scale goods.
    D) There was no trade in the Americas.
    E) They traded with European explorers.

39. The Phoenicians were responsible for what achievement?
    A) *Cuneiform*
    B) hieroglyphs
    C) pictograms
    D) phonetic alphabet
    E) the dhow

40. What distinctive architectural form has developed in various locations around the world, independently?
    A) the stupa
    B) the minaret
    C) the gothic cathedral
    D) the skyscraper
    E) the stepped pyramid

41. The Spanish Inquisition was—
    A) an attempt to weed out heresy in the Catholic Church.
    B) an attempt to reduce abuses within the Church.
    C) a response to the Protestant Reformation.
    D) a response to the discovery of the Americas.
    E) devised by King Ferdinand and Queen Isabella.

42. How did the Phoenician trade network end?
    A) The Phoenicians were defeated by Rome.
    B) The Phoenicians died from disease.
    C) The Phoenicians settled a new land.
    D) The Phoenicians stopped trading.
    E) The Phoenicians were defeated by Athens.

43. The Taiping Rebellion hoped to overthrow the Qing Dynasty and—
    A) establish Daoism
    B) establish Buddhism
    C) establish Confucianism
    D) establish Christianity
    E) establish Islam

44. Areas of Africa that are were not successfully converted to either Islam or Christianity practice what?
    A) Vodun
    B) Buddhism
    C) Hinduism
    D) Shamanism
    E) daoism

45. Rome idolized the culture of—
    A) Britain
    B) Phoenicia
    C) the Iliad
    D) Egypt
    E) Greece

46. What is asceticism?
    A) self-denial
    B) self-indulgence
    C) self-harm
    D) isolation
    E) a religious tradition

47. Plato and Aristotle are examples of what?
    A) Greek playwrights
    B) Greek epic poets
    C) Greek ship builders
    D) Greek philosophers
    E) Greek politicians

48. When did contact between Russia and Europe begin?
    A) after the Russian Revolution
    B) during World War I
    C) with the reign of Peter the Great
    D) with the reign of Catherine the Great
    E) with the reign of Alexander II

49. Which of the following cities had the closest ties to the Byzantine Empire?
    A) Venice
    B) Paris
    C) London
    D) Rome
    E) Baghdad

50. Sugar plantations were most commonly located where?
    A) India
    B) South America
    C) the Caribbean
    D) North America
    E) Central America

51. Christian monasticism has its origins where?
    A) Britain
    B) Italy
    C) Greece
    D) Egypt
    E) Jerusalem

52. The Yin-Yang symbol is part of what tradition?
    A) Confucianism
    B) Buddhism
    C) daoism
    D) Hinduism
    E) Islam

53. The *encomienda* system is most similar to which of the following?
    A) mercantilism
    B) Marxism
    C) chattel slavery
    D) manorialism
    E) authoritarianism

54. What criteria was used to divide India when it was partitioned?
    A) language
    B) ethnicity
    C) natural boundaries
    D) religion
    E) colonial boundaries

55. How did political stability impact trade along the Silk Road?
    A) Stable imperial rule allowed for easier trade and travel.
    B) Political instability made trading more profitable.
    C) Political stability led traders to use sea routes.
    D) Political conditions did not impact the trade routes.
    E) Political instability led to a lack of international trade.

56. Of the following, identify the primary source.
    A) a novel about the Byzantine empire
    B) a diary of a lady of the court during the French Revolution
    C) a historical textbook about the Russian Revolution
    D) a movie made about the Chinese Revolution
    E) a documentary about the French Revolution

57. What is eremitism?
   A) self-denial
   B) self-isolation
   C) self-flagellation
   D) self-immolation
   E) self-discipline

58. Choose the answer that presents events in the correct chronology:
   A) the French Revolution, the American Revolution, the Industrial Revolution, WWI
   B) the American Revolution, the French Revolution, Napoleon, WWI
   C) the French Revolution, Napoleon, the American Revolution, WWI
   D) Napoleon, the invention of the steam engine, WWI, the invention of the automobile
   E) the Rape of Nanjing, WWI, the Great Depression, WWII

59. Choose the best definition for nepotism.
   A) awarding jobs based on merit
   B) awarding jobs based on test scores
   C) awarding jobs based on personal connections
   D) awarding jobs based on bribery
   E) awarding jobs based on a combination of merit and scores

60. In the Chinese family, traditionally, who holds authority?
   A) the mother
   B) the grandmother
   C) the father
   D) the children
   E) the manorial lord

61. Where was the conference held that divided the city of Berlin and other lands near the end of WWII?
   A) Berlin
   B) Dresden
   C) Paris
   D) Yalta
   E) Athens

62. The Glorious Revolution occurred where?
   A) France
   B) North America
   C) Haiti
   D) Britain
   E) Jamaica

63. The Boxer Rebellion was opposed to what?
   A) foreign influences
   B) Chinese imperialism
   C) Japanese imperialism
   D) Korean imperialism
   E) Buddhism

64. What Roman general conquered modern-day France and portions of Britain?
   A) Trajan
   B) Julius Caesar
   C) Nero
   D) Caligula
   E) Augustus

65. The Ottoman Empire did NOT recognize which of the following religions?
   A) Orthodox Christianity
   B) Judaism
   C) Sunni Islam
   D) Shi'a Islam
   E) Armenian Christians

66. Between 1915 and 1922, Turkey forced Armenian Christians from their homes, forced them to march into the desert, killed many, and forcibly kidnapped and converted Armenian children. This is an example of:
    - **F)** a. Religious persecution
    - **G)** b. Holodomor
    - **H)** c. Holocaust
    - **I)** d. Genocide
    - **J)** e. Fascism

67. What international incident set off World War I?
    - **A)** the invasion of Poland
    - **B)** the attack on Serbia
    - **C)** the assassination of Archduke Ferdinand
    - **D)** the attack on Belgium
    - **E)** the attack on Russia

68. Where was the city of Persepolis?
    - **A)** Greece
    - **B)** Turkey
    - **C)** Phoenicia
    - **D)** Syria
    - **E)** Persia

69. What South American country has been ruled by a monarch?
    - **A)** Chile
    - **B)** Peru
    - **C)** Brazil
    - **D)** Colombia
    - **E)** Uruguay

70. Which African nation retained its independence?
    - **A)** Zaire
    - **B)** Nigeria
    - **C)** Ethiopia
    - **D)** South Africa
    - **E)** Mali

Free Response Questions

For questions 1 and 2, write a short essay based on your knowledge of World History. For question 3, write a short essay based on your knowledge and the accompanying historical texts.

1. How has Islam changed or remained the same, in terms of action, expectation, beliefs, and values, since its inception in 622 CE?

2. Compare the Abbasid Caliphate to Western European society in the Middle Ages.

3. The following passages describe the actions of Europeans with regard to Africans, including the experiences of a British traveler, a discussion of slave ships, and explanations of white burden. Analyze these passages and consider how these texts reflect changing views of Africa over time.

RICHARD EDEN

DECADES OF THE NEW WORLD, 1555

Touching the manners and nature of the people, this may seem strange, that their princes and noblemen used to pounce and raise their skins with pretty knots in diverse forms, as it were branched damask, thinking that to be a decent ornament. And albeit they go in manner all naked, yet are many of them, and especially their women, in manner laden with collars, bracelets, hoops and chains, either of gold, copper, or ivory. I myself have one of their bracelets of ivory, weighing two pound and six ounces of troy weight, which make eight and thirty ounces. This one of their women did wear upon her arm. It is made of one whole piece of the biggest part of the tooth, turned and somewhat carved, with a hole in the midst, wherein they put their hands to wear it on their arm. Some have on every arm one, and as many on their legs, wherewith some of them are so galled that, although they are in manner made lame thereby, yet will they by no means leave them off. Some wear also on their legs great shackles of bright copper, which they think to be no less comely. They wear also collars, bracelets, garlands and girdles, of certain blue stones like beads. Likewise, some of their women wear on their bare arms certain foresleeves made of the plates of beaten gold. On their fingers also they wear rings, made of golden wires, with a knot or wreath, like unto that which children make in a ring of a rush. Among other things of gold, that our men bought of them for exchange of their wares, were certain dog-chains and collars.

They are very wary people in their bargaining, and will not lose one spark of gold of any value. They use weights and measures, and are very circumspect in occupying the same. They that shall have to do with them, must use them gently; for they will not traffic or bring in any wares, if they be evil used.

SLAVE TRADE DOCUMENTS

John Barbot traveled at least twice to the West Coast of Africa (in 1678 and 1682) for the French Royal African Company.

Those sold by the Blacks are for the most part prisoners of war, taken either in fight, or pursuit, or in the incursions they make into their enemies territories; others stolen away by their own countrymen; and some there are, who will sell their own children, kindred, or neighbours. This has been often seen, and to compass it, they desire the person they intend to sell, to help them in carrying something to the factory by way of trade, and when there, the person so deluded, not understanding the language, is old and deliver'd up as a slave, notwithstanding all his resistance, and exclaiming against the treachery....

The kings are so absolute, that upon any slight pretense of offences committed by their subjects, they order them to be sold for slaves, without regard to rank, or possession....

Alexander Falconbridge, a surgeon aboard slave ships and later the governor of a British colony for freed slaves in Sierra Leone, gives this account of the Middle Passage.

From the time of the arrival of the ships to their departure, which is usually about three months, scarce a day passes without some Negroes being purchased and carried on board; sometimes in small and sometimes in large numbers. The whole number taken on board depends on circumstances. In a voyage I once made, our stock of merchandise was exhausted in the purchase of about 380 Negroes, which was expected to have procured 500...

The men Negroes, on being brought aboard the ship, are immediately fastened together, two and two, by handcuffs on their wrists and by irons riveted on their legs. They are then sent down between the decks and placed in an apartment partitioned off for that purpose. The women also are placed in a separate apartment between the decks, but without being ironed. An adjoining room on the same deck is appointed for the boys. Thus they are all placed in different apartments.

But at the same time, however, they are frequently stowed so close, as to admit of no other position than lying on their sides. Nor with the height between decks, unless directly under the grating, permit the indulgence of an erect posture; especially where there are platforms, which is generally the case. These platforms are a kind of shelf, about eight or nine feet in breadth, extending from the side of the ship toward the centre. They are placed nearly midway between the decks, at the distance of two or three feet from each deck. Upon these the Negroes are stowed in the same manner as they are on the deck underneath.

In each of the apartments are placed three or four large buckets, of a conical form, nearly two feet in diameter at the bottom and only one foot at the top and in depth of about twenty-eight inches, to which, when necessary, the Negroes have recourse. It often happens that those who are placed at a distance from the buckets, in endeavoring to get to them, tumble over their companions, in consequence of their being shackled. These accidents, although unavoidable, are productive of continual quarrels in which some of them are always bruised. In this distressed situation, unable to proceed and prevented from getting to the tubs, they desist from the attempt; and as the necessities of nature are not to be resisted, ease themselves as they lie. This becomes a fresh source of boils and disturbances and tends to render the condition of the poor captive wretches still more uncomfortable. The nuisance arising from these circumstances is not infrequently increased by the tubs being too small for the purpose intended and their being emptied but once every day. The rule for doing so, however, varies in different ships according to the attention paid to the health and convenience of the slaves by the captain. . . .

Upon the Negroes refusing to take sustenance, I have seen coals of fire, glowing hot, put on a shovel and placed so near their lips as to scorch and burn them. And this has been accompanied with threats of forcing them to swallow the coals if they any longer persisted in refusing to eat. These means have generally had the desired effect. I have also been credibly informed that a certain captain in the slave-trade, poured melted lead on such of his Negroes as obstinately refused their food. . . .

THE WHITE MAN'S BURDEN

This poem is symbolic of the imperial adventure, expressing the European—here, British—belief that non-European countries needed European "guidance" in the form of paternalism, one facet of colonialism.

Take up the White Man's burden—

Send forth the best ye breed—

Go bind your sons to exile

To serve your captives' need;

To wait in heavy harness,

On fluttered folk and wild—

Your new-caught, sullen peoples,

Half-devil and half-child.

Take up the White Man's Burden—

In patience to abide,

To veil the threat of terror

And check the show of pride;

By open speech and simple,

An hundred times made plain.

To seek another's profit,

And work another's gain.

Take up the White Man's burden—

The following response to Kipling's poem The White Man's Burden, was written in 1903 by the British journalist Edward Morel based on his experiences in the Belgian Congo; it highlighted the abuse suffered in Africa due to European colonialism.

It is [the Africans] who carry the 'Black man's burden'. They have not withered away before the white man's occupation. Indeed ... Africa has ultimately absorbed within itself every Caucasian and, for that matter, every Semitic invader, too. In hewing out for himself a fixed abode in Africa, the white man has massacred the African in heaps. The African has survived, and it is well for the white settlers that he has....

What the partial occupation of his soil by the white man has failed to do; what the mapping out of European political 'spheres of influence' has failed to do; what the Maxim and the rifle, the slave gang, labour in the bowels of the earth and the lash, have failed to do; what imported measles, smallpox and syphilis have failed to do; whatever the overseas slave trade failed to do, the power of modern capitalistic exploitation, assisted by modern engines of destruction, may yet succeed in accomplishing.

Practice Test Four Answer Key
SELECTED-RESPONSE QUESTIONS

1. B
2. A
3. B
4. C
5. A
6. D
7. B
8. E
9. D
10. B
11. A
12. E
13. B
14. A
15. A
16. E
17. C
18. B
19. A
20. E
21. B
22. D
23. C
24. B
25. C
26. D
27. C
28. A
29. B
30. A
31. A
32. C
33. B
34. D
35. C
36. D
37. C
38. B
39. D
40. E
41. A
42. A
43. D
44. D
45. E
46. A
47. D
48. C
49. A
50. C
51. D
52. C
53. D
54. D
55. A
56. B
57. B
58. B
59. C
60. C
61. D
62. D
63. A
64. B
65. D
66. D
67. C
68. E
69. C
70. C

FREE-RESPONSE QUESTIONS

1. How has Islam changed or remained the same, in terms of action, expectation, beliefs, and values, since its inception in 622 CE?

Islam was founded by the prophet Muhammad in 622 CE. During the course of his lifetime, Muhammad experienced a number of prophetic visions and experiences, recorded in the written text, the Qur'an. The Qur'an provides a clear guide to life and conduct for Muslims.

Because it is a strongly text-based faith, some aspects of Islamic faith have remained steady throughout time. The Five Pillars of Islam, including the hajj, or pilgrimage to Mecca, donations to the poor, and regular, five times-a-day prayer are unchanging throughout Islam, regardless of where you go or the branch of Islam. The reasoned moderation encouraged in these pillars is also consistent. For instance, pregnant women are not expected to fast during Ramadan, but may make a charitable donation or postpone their fast to a more appropriate time in their lives. The fundamental practices of the faith demonstrate continuity.

Islam has, however, changed significantly. While there was only one branch of Islam originally, today there are two, often in conflict with one another. Shi'a Islam has traditionally been associated with fundamentalism; however, it is more accurate to recognize Shi' as a tradition directly descended from Muhammad and his family members, with clear allegiances to individual spiritual leaders. Sunni Islam has traditionally been considered more moderate and changeable, but today, Sunni Islam is associated with particularly violent political movements in the Middle East.

The role and status of women has also changed in Islamic society. Traditionally, in many Islamic cultures, women lived a relatively public life. They assisted in family businesses, sold goods at market and otherwise participated in the world around them. There is no evidence that they wore the niqab, or black covering over the body, head and face. While the Qur'an speaks of modesty for both men and women, this attire is not required by Islam, but is often required by the Islamic state, for instance, the Taliban government formerly in power in Afghanistan. In many regions, women are denied education, when traditionally many women were quite educated. The first degree-granting university, founded in Muslim North Africa, was the work of a female scholar and there are noted female poets, doctors and mystics in Islamic tradition.

Another clear change in the Islamic faith is the treatment of foreigners. Traditionally, Islam accepted individuals of other religions, first those religions of the book, Judaism and Christianity, but later Hinduism as well. Individuals were free to practice their own faiths, but were required to pay an additional tax. Today, that tolerance is dissipating in many Islamic countries, particularly those embracing Sharia or Islamic law. While Islam was an expansionist religion, spreading rapidly along trade routes, this spread did not involve forced conversions. Acts of terror, like the 9/11 attack and other actions of Al-Quaeda, are not in line with the teachings of the Qur'an.

Islam has retained the traditional practices of prayer, pilgrimage and fasting, but has, in many modern Islamic countries, set aside its traditions of learning, tolerance, and support for women that existed historically. For centuries, Islam protected the knowledge of the classical world, created works of art and helped the world move forward into a brighter and more scientific world. Today, fundamentalist movements, including the Taliban and ISIS, have replaced knowledge and learning with destruction to their own lands, monuments and people.

2. COMPARE THE ABBASID CALIPHATE TO WESTERN EUROPEAN SOCIETY IN THE MIDDLE AGES.

The world of the Middle Ages encompasses both Western Europe and the empires further east including the Islamic Caliphate. The experiences and environments of these two regions were utterly different during this period.

The Abbasid Caliphate was the largest Islamic state during the period we commonly define as medieval or the Middle Ages. From around 750 onward, the Abbasid Caliphate created a culturally and intellectually rich empire, known for its learning. In 767, the Abbasids founded the city of Baghdad, later to become a key stop along the Silk Road and a noted center of trade. While the political power of the Abbasid Caliphate was relatively short-lived, it retained cultural and religious power for much longer.

The period from the founding of Islam through the sack of the city by the Mongols in 1258 is commonly referred to as the Golden Age of Islam. The Abbasid Caliphate is at the center of that period, culturally. The government invested in and sponsored learning. They set up hospitals and universities, required medical licenses for doctors, translated classical texts and established lasting trade relations.

After the sack of Baghdad in 1258, the Abbasid Caliphate regained power; however, the Golden Age had come to an end. The Caliphate itself formally came to an end as the region fell under Ottoman control in the 15th century.

While the Abbasid Caliphate was building universities and studying science, the west was fundamentally still, during the Early Middle Ages, in a period often called the dark ages. Literacy was uncommon and technology nearly unknown. Much of the learning of the classical world had been entirely lost and this was a period of significant decline. Cities had shrunk or disappeared, and the Church had little influence in many areas. A few larger local rulers managed to organize to stop the Islamic push into Europe at the French border. Only gradually, in the 9th century, did civilization begin to return to the region. Under Charlemagne, many converted to Christianity and new churches were built, along with monasteries and schools in the cities to train priests. Slowly and gradually, the cities grew. Nonetheless, access to books was minimal and there were few surviving classical texts.

With the support of the Church, the Crusades began. There were several reasons for the Crusades, both pragmatic and religious. Most importantly, however, the wars for control of Jerusalem and surrounding lands brought Christians into close contact with

Muslims. While there were no lasting gains of land in the Crusades and no real financial or spiritual gains, the contact between Christians and Muslims brought something critically important to Europe; learning. The classical texts, scientific learning, education and medicine of the Arab world dramatically changed science, learning and even theology in Europe. After this time, the universities grew and blossomed. More men entered the church and the universities and more books were copied and produced.

The cultural interactions of the Crusades helped bring Europe into the High Middle Ages, marked by soaring cathedrals and theology influenced by Aristotelian ideals. While this time was the end of the Golden Age of Islam that was the result of invaders from the East, rather than the Crusades. Both the Golden Age of Islam and the Europe in the High Middle Ages and Renaissance embraced learning and intellectual endeavors as part of a newer, more modern world.

3. THE FOLLOWING PASSAGES DESCRIBE THE ACTIONS OF EUROPEANS WITH REGARD TO AFRICANS, INCLUDING THE EXPERIENCES OF A BRITISH TRAVELER, A DISCUSSION OF SLAVE SHIPS, AND EXPLANATIONS OF WHITE BURDEN. ANALYZE THESE PASSAGES AND CONSIDER HOW THESE TEXTS REFLECT CHANGING VIEWS OF AFRICA OVER TIME.

In the ancient and medieval world, Africa made up only one part of a broad trading network. Coastal cities were active trading ports, while towns inland were stops along the Sand Road through Africa. While there was a slave trade, it was relatively small in scope. After the discovery of the Americas, that trade in slaves along the West Coast of Africa increased immensely, destroying the population in some parts of Africa. While attitudes turned against slavery over time, the overall perception of Africa did not change for quite some time. The damage of slavery, colonialism and imperialism remains in Africa even today.

European explorers, like the British Richard Eden, shared his own descriptions of Africans; however, there is no disrespect in his text. These are traders, and even, in his telling, good ones. He was an explorer sharing stories of his explorations and the people he met. The 16th century wholly predates the British desire for imperialism or colonialism. This is clear in Eden's description.

By the late 17th century, slavery was well-established, with huge numbers of slaves captured, kidnapped and sent overseas. While the majority of the slave traders were Portuguese, other Europeans were certainly involved and aware of the slave trade. The European observer identifies those responsible for kidnapping, but does not condemn the act of slavery. He does identify the actions of those who kidnapped their neighbors and associates as treachery, but not the actions of the European slave traders. By the middle of the 18th century, the abolitionist movement was growing, in part, thanks to texts like this one. Alexander Falconbridge wrote his own experiences as a doctor on a slave ship, sharing the inhuman and horrifying conditions on the ship. Published texts like this helped to ban slavery in Britain. While some spoke out against slavery, slavery and imperialism are two distinct and different issues.

The slave trade required a belief, fundamentally, that Africans were less human than people of European origin. While Europe eventually deemed slavery unacceptable and immoral, by the time this occurred, the era of imperialism was beginning. European countries divided up Africa into a number of colonies, each governed somewhat differently. Rudyard Kipling's The White Man's Burden is the epitome of the European attitude in this period. Efforts to colonize, settle and civilize Africa were economically successful, but were also an attempt to illustrate and prove the very quality of European society over African. While interactions between Europeans in Africa were typically peaceful, local people were certainly involved in and damaged by violent conflicts, like the Boer War, as well as by the lasting impact of colonialism in a direct way. Apartheid in South Africa, in which the white population direly limited the rights of Africans through the 1980s and into the 1990s is perhaps the best example of this.

Finally, The Black Man's Burden, written in response to Kipling's poem, provides an end statement to the era of imperialism. This shows the costs of imperialism. Even today, these costs remain as ethnic groups and different regions battle with one another and countries struggle to establish peaceful and stable governments.

APPENDIX
Sample Essays

Prompt One: The Impact of Disease

Compare the process of disease transmission and its impact during the Black Death to the impact of small pox on the Americas after the arrival of Europeans.

LOW-SCORING ESSAY

Both the Black Death and smallpox killed large numbers of people. The Black Death did so relatively quickly, while exposure to smallpox took significantly longer. There are a number of differences between the two diseases; however, both medically and historically.

The Black Death is a bacteria, commonly called bubonic plague. It caused a number of different symptoms, including large blisters. The Black Death was actually not typically easily caught from person-to-person. In most cases, the Black Death was transmitted through infected fleas, carried on rats by trading vessels, then spread over land, along the Silk Road. The Black Death had a relatively high fatality rate and killed 30 to 40 percent of the population of areas it reached, travelling through much of Asia, Africa, and Europe within just a few years. This is not the fatality rate of those that caught the disease, but rather the population overall.

Smallpox was a relatively common disease in Europe, Asia and Africa. While it was rather dangerous, many Europeans already had some immunity to the illness and it was not at all uncommon. Smallpox existed consistently, rather than appearing in a broad, fatal wave that spread across multiple countries. This was not true for Americans. The disease did not exist in the Americas and destroyed many Native American populations when they were exposed to it. The disease arrived in the Americas with European colonists, brought over by carriers on ships. This happened multiple times, prior to the introduction of vaccination for smallpox.

If people had not travelled, the risk of these illnesses would have been less. It is possible that they would have quickly died out, killing the portion of the population without natural immunity or the ability to survive. Today, smallpox has been obliterated thanks to vaccination campaigns and bubonic plague is rare and treatable.

AVERAGE-SCORING ESSAY

Disease has frequently decimated human populations, altered lives and presented struggles, economically, medically and historically. Two of the most significant illnesses to strike humanity and cause historical impact are the Black Death and smallpox. The Black Death is a bacterial illness, caused by the transmission of the Yersinia Pestis bacteria. Smallpox is a viral illness, not unlike chicken pox, with several variations, some more or less dangerous.

The Black Death arrived in a fast and fatal rush in the middle of the 14th century, killing as much as 40 percent of the population from China to London to Baghdad and beyond. It moved quickly, taking only a few years to wreak havoc on the world. The path of the Black Death directly follows the trade paths of the late Middle Ages. It killed indiscriminately, taking both the rich and poor. With no understanding of how the disease was spread, there was no option for containment. The Yersinia Pestis bacteria is carried by fleas. Those fleas were carried by traders throughout the known world. They rode on rats in trading ships and on furs in the Silk Road, before finding and biting unwitting hosts.

Smallpox is a much more common illness. In some forms, it was quite mild, causing minor scarring, but no serious risk of death. In the most common form, it was fatal as much as 30 percent of the time, and almost certainly, more likely to be fatal for those in poor health. Some variations were fatal as much as 90 percent of the time. While worrisome, many in Europe had some natural immunities or had already survived a mild case of smallpox or a similar illness, to smallpox and survived it, perhaps with scars. This relatively common illness travelled to the Americas during the Columbian Exchange. The populations of the Americas had no natural immunity and almost certainly died at a much higher rate than Europeans, particularly after forced labor had physically weakened groups. In North America, smallpox blankets were intentionally provided to Native American groups with the hope of triggering infection.

Trade provided access to new foods, goods and labor. It also allowed bacteria and viruses to easily travel from place to place. For bubonic plague, this meant on rat hosts or furs, while smallpox travelled in human hosts or items they had handled, like smallpox blankets. The Silk Road, the Indian Ocean Trade Network and other trade routes spread the Black Death. Bubonic plague recurred later; however, it was not as prevalent, nor as widespread. Smallpox remained a scourge in Europe until the beginning of inoculation; however, its toll remained relatively low. This is not true in the Americas, where, eventually, smallpox and other European diseases wiped out native populations.

HIGH-SCORING ESSAY

Trade routes, like the Silk Road and, later, the Columbian Exchange, moved both goods and people long distances relatively efficiently. It was an even more efficient means to move diseases, like the Black Death and smallpox, across land, seas and oceans. While there are distinct differences in the pandemic of the Black Death and the epidemic of smallpox, both illnesses devastated populations and changed the demographics and landscape of entire regions.

In the 1340s, the Yersinia Pestis bacteria began to spread, moving outward from isolated communities in China. The Y.Pestis bacteria travels in fleas and was likely, at this time, carried on furs being exported out of the region. This bacteria can cause three different forms of plague. The most common is bubonic plague, causing large boils and killing approximately 60 percent of its victims. Other variations include pneumonic plague, which impacted the respiratory system, and septicemic plague, which affected the gut. Both have a near 100 percent mortality rate. Once Y.Pestis had reached more heavily inhabited areas, it spread quickly, with infected fleas finding rat hosts on merchant ships and caravans. The Black Death killed as much as 30 to 40 percent of the population of Europe in total, and similar numbers in other regions. For Europe, the Black Death and the dramatically lower population helped to bring an end to feudalism and welcome the new opportunities of the Renaissance. It is fair to assert that the Black Death ushered in a new and better age for many in Europe, rife with opportunity to gain land, pursue new employment and even become wealthier. Later waves of pandemic plague occurred, but without the severity of the Black Death.

Smallpox was a relatively common viral illness in Europe and other parts of Africa and Asia. The illness was well-known, but varied from quite mild to deadly, depending upon the variation. The most common strains had an overall mortality rate around 30 percent once contracted; however, in Europe and other parts of the "old world" many people likely had some natural immunity, either through genetic advantages or exposure to similar illnesses, like cowpox. Isolation measures were well understood quite early, limiting the danger of widespread contagion from smallpox in Europe. The same was not true when smallpox made its way from the "old world" to the Americas. Initially, it is most likely that smallpox arrived accidentally, as a sailor became ill on the ship or goods contaminated with fluid from smallpox reached American shores. With no natural immunity and depleted immune systems from harsh forced labor, smallpox and other European illnesses spread rapidly through Native American populations. While this early exposure was unintentional, later, smallpox was used as a biological weapon against native groups in North America. European settlers provided infected blankets to Native American tribes in the hopes of creating a smallpox epidemic. While the pandemic of the Black Death helped to create a newer, better Europe, smallpox and similar epidemics among Native Americans simply destroyed these populations, contributing substantially to the utter decimation of many groups. Faced with war, forced labor and a loss of land, the loss of population from an epidemic disease like smallpox was simply impossible.

While these two illnesses both have relatively high mortality rates and struck populations quite hard, the final impact on the individual populations was dramatically different. Europe came out of the Black Death to welcome a new era of experience, opportunity and learning in the early modern world. On the other side of the world, smallpox, influenza and measles destroyed entire cultures and civilizations, turning once great Native American cities into ghost towns and leaving only a few survivors behind in their wake.

Prompt Two: Continuity and Change over Time

Analyze how the role of Christianity in society and government has changed from the time of Constantine to today.

LOW-SCORING ESSAY

Christianity has been the dominant religion in the western world since around 350 CE. It has changed over time, and has grown, as missionaries spread Christianity into Africa and the Americas.

Prior to the time of Constantine, Christianity was illegal and Christians were persecuted. Once Constantine accepted Christianity, churches were built and efforts were made to send out missionaries. The church grew and grew, but many of the leaders of the church were immoral. Because of this, the Reformation began, creating new churches based on the text of the Christian Bible, rather than Church tradition. Some countries, like much of Germany and Britain, converted to Protestantism. Others, like Italy and Spain, did not.

Christianity came to the Americas with settlers. In South America, that meant Spanish Catholics, while in North America, early settlers were Protestants. The founders of the Constitution acknowledged this Protestant tradition, but created a separation of church and state. That separation remains today, and is popular in other western democracies and Christian countries. This is better because it allows people to practice their religion without persecution.

Today, there are a lot of different Christian denominations. Some are very traditional, while others are quite modern. Traditional denominations maintain standard church services and may focus more attention on traditional values or even really old-fashioned ones. Modern services use newer music casual clothing and are often less formal than traditional services. The beliefs may vary, though, as belief and the type of service aren't always related to one another. In this way, Christianity has adapted to the modern world.

AVERAGE-SCORING ESSAY

Christianity was accepted by the Emperor Constantine and has grown since then to become a worldwide church. Jesus died in 33 CE, but it took around 300 more years for Christianity to become an accepted and well-organized religion and eventually, a force that ruled Europe. The Church was later divided, but the faith remained important. Today, Christianity, particularly Protestant Christianity, is growing.

In the first centuries of Christianity, Christians were persecuted by the Romans, limiting their political ability and authority. It is only after Constantine's conversion that the Church developed political power; however, during the Dark Ages, there was little political order or government. Christianity continued in the Byzantine Empire and North Africa. The Church helped to support the growing power of empire, as Charlemagne defeated various pagan groups and forced them to convert. Christianity spread rapidly from that time and was soon the dominant religion of Europe. The Church remained involved in government throughout the Middle Ages, even supporting the Crusades. The Church provided the only path to literacy, the only source of a university education and controlled rulers with threats of excommunication.

The Protestant Reformation divided the Church into a number of splintering smaller churches, including all sorts of Protestant denominations. This weakened the political power of the church and caused a number of conflicts. In practice, this provided a new incentive to read, new abilities for personal gain and new freedom for political rulers. Without the active presence of the Catholic Church, science was able to grow and thrive in many European countries.

The Enlightenment altered the impact of Christianity in Western society, creating a separation, for the first time, between religion and government. This spread and was embraced as part of an Enlightened government. Religion became a progressively more private and less public issue following the Enlightenment and became less prominent in society. While, throughout the 19th century and early 20th century, many were churchgoers, the church itself was less powerful. It had become a social tool rather than a political one. Many faiths took steps to modernize to meet the needs of their congregations.

Late in the 20th century, interest in devout and literal forms of religion, called fundamentalist Christianity, grew. Fundamentalist Christianity rejects many of the ideals of the Enlightenment and seeks a more active role for the church in government. These denominations reject modern social values, the role of the state and believe in a return to more traditional morality. While these are often associated with religion in the United States, evangelical movements are also growing in parts of Africa and South America.

HIGH-SCORING ESSAY

In the West, Christianity has shaped the world over time, just as the world has shaped the faith. From a small and persecuted religion, it grew into a force that controlled Europe, was divided by Reformation, and reshaped itself to meet the needs of a more modern world. Missionaries and trade spread the message of Christianity, and the faith adapted to the needs of local populations over time.

Christianity has its origins in the Jewish faith and finds its origin story, the Crucifixion, in the history of the Roman Empire; however, it is not a religion of the Roman Empire. Christianity developed in the hidden catacombs of the Empire, but was not accepted until the time of Constantine. For a short while, Christianity was flexible, without set texts or rituals and appealed, largely, to the lower classes. This changed as it became an accepted religion, embraced by the Roman state. Doctrine and acceptable belief were defined and the church split forming the Eastern Orthodox and Western Catholic churches. When Rome fell, Christianity remained.

In the early Byzantine Empire, the church was an intrinsic part of the ruling society, and as the Byzantine Empire spread, so too did the Orthodox Church. In the west, as learning and civilization remained in decline, the church remained, but was relatively small and weak. It gradually spread, through the efforts of monks, and by 800, it once again secured a clear relationship with government. The Church provided authority when it crowned Charlemagne Holy Roman Emperor. Later kings throughout Europe were crowned by their bishops, providing them with a means to authority from the Church. The Church was the sole source for education, authority, information, and more during this period, both in the East and West.

While the Church had been a key source of stability throughout the Middle Ages and Early Renaissance, in 1517, the Reformation began. The Church was, by this time, corrupt and battling a number of significant problems, including nepotism and the sale of indulgences. Martin Luther challenged many of these problems with the Church, originally intending to reform from within, rather than create a new church entirely; however, these challenges led to the creation of Protestantism, with its many denominations and varied beliefs. Protestantism weakened the position of the papacy, provided individuals with a new path to personal salvation, and altered the political climate of many countries and their relationships with one another. Now, a much wider range of religious options existed within a single faith, creating a much more multifaceted religion.

The influence of both Catholicism and Protestantism weakened as the Enlightenment progressed. The number of regular church goers decreased, and churches gradually changed their services to better accommodate their communities. In small communities, churches often remained a center of activity, filling a social function as well as a religious one. While the importance of religion decreased from the middle of the 18th century onward, by the late 20th century, the evangelical movement brought new life to Christianity. Evangelical Christianity favors a literal interpretation of the Bible, a return to a strong involvement of religion in government and has strong missionary tendencies. It is spreading rapidly, not entirely unlike the Church in a much earlier time.

Document-Based Questions

Analyze these documents and consider the causes of the French Revolution and how the royal family, and Marie Antoinette in particular, were involved in that Revolution.

This collection of documents all relates to the French Revolution. Several are specific to Marie Antoinette who, in the popular press, bore the responsibility for many of the problems connected to the aristocracy and condition of the French people.

MARIE ANTOINETTE: LETTER to her MOTHER, 1773

On Tuesday I had a fête which I shall never forget all my life. We made our entrance into Paris. As for honors, we received all that we could possibly imagine; but they, though very well in their way, were not what touched me most. What was really affecting was the tenderness and earnestness of the poor people, who, in spite of the taxes with which they are overwhelmed, were transported with joy at seeing us. When we went to walk in the Tuileries, there was so vast a crowd that we were three-quarters of an hour without being able to move either forward or backward. The dauphin and I gave repeated orders to the Guards not to beat any one, which had a very good effect. Such excellent order was kept the whole day that, in spite of the enormous crowd which followed us everywhere, not a person was hurt. When we returned from our walk we went up to an open terrace and stayed there half an hour. I cannot describe to you, my dear mamma, the transports of joy and affection which every one exhibited towards us.

MADAME CAMPAN: *MEMOIRS of the PRIVATE LIFE of MARIE ANTOINETTE*, 1818

In order to describe the queen's private service intelligibly, it must be recollected that service of every kind was honor, and had not any other denomination. To do the honors of the service, was to present the service to an officer of superior rank, who happened to arrive at the moment it was about to be performed: thus, supposing the queen asked for a glass of water, the servant of the chamber handed to the first woman a silver gilt waiter, upon which were placed a covered goblet and a small decanter; but should the lady of honor come in, the first woman was obliged to present the waiter to her, and if Madame or the Countess d'Artois came in at the moment, the waiter went again from the lady of honor into the hands of the princess, before it reached the queen.

ABBE SIEYES: WHAT IS the THIRD ESTATE?

Public functions may be classified equally well, in the present state of affairs, under four recognized heads; the sword, the robe, the church and the administration. It would be superfluous to take them up one by one, for the purpose of showing that everywhere the Third Estate attends to nineteen-twentieths of them, with this distinction; that it is laden with all that which is really painful, with all the burdens which the privileged classes refuse to carry. Do we give the Third Estate credit for this? That this might come about, it would be necessary that the Third Estate should refuse to fill these places, or that it should be less ready to exercise their functions. The facts are well known. Meanwhile they have dared to impose a prohibition upon the order of the Third Estate. They have said to it: "Whatever may be your services, whatever may be your abilities, you shall go thus far; you may not pass beyond!" Certain rare exceptions, properly regarded, are but a mockery, and the terms which are indulged in on such occasions, one insult the more.

If this exclusion is a social crime against the Third Estate; if it is a veritable act of hostility, could it perhaps be said that it is useful to the public weal? Alas! who is ignorant of the effects of monopoly? If it discourages those whom it rejects, is it not well known that it tends to render less able those whom it favors? Is it not understood that every employment from which free competition is removed, becomes dear and less effective?

THE TENNIS COURT OATH, JUNE 1789

The National Assembly, considering that it has been called to establish the constitution of the realm, to bring about the regeneration of public order, and to maintain the true principles of monarchy; nothing may prevent it from continuing its deliberations in any place it is forced to establish itself; and, finally, the National Assembly exists wherever its members are gathered.

Decrees that all members of this assembly immediately take a solemn oath never to separate, and to reassemble wherever circumstances require, until the constitution of the realm is established and fixed upon solid foundations; and that said oath having been sworn, all members and each one individually confirm this unwavering resolution with his signature.

DECLARATION of the RIGHTS of MAN, 1789

Articles:

1. Men are born and remain free and equal in rights. Social distinctions may be founded only upon the general good.

2. The aim of all political association is the preservation of the natural and imprescriptible rights of man. These rights are liberty, property, security, and resistance to oppression.

3. The principle of all sovereignty resides essentially in the nation. No body nor individual may exercise any authority which does not proceed directly from the nation.

4. Liberty consists in the freedom to do everything which injures no one else; hence the exercise of the natural rights of each man has no limits except those which assure to the other members of the society the enjoyment of the same rights. These limits can only be determined by law.

5. Law can only prohibit such actions as are hurtful to society. Nothing may be prevented which is not forbidden by law, and no one may be forced to do anything not provided for by law.

6. Law is the expression of the general will. Every citizen has a right to participate personally, or through his representative, in its foundation. It must be the same for all, whether it protects or punishes. All citizens, being equal in the eyes of the law, are equally eligible to all dignities and to all public positions and occupations, according to their abilities, and without distinction except that of their virtues and talents.

7. No person shall be accused, arrested, or imprisoned except in the cases and according to the forms prescribed by law. Any one soliciting, transmitting, executing, or causing to be executed, any arbitrary order, shall be punished. But any citizen summoned or arrested in virtue of the law shall submit without delay, as resistance constitutes an offense.

8. The law shall provide for such punishments only as are strictly and obviously necessary, and no one shall suffer punishment except it be legally inflicted in virtue of a law passed and promulgated before the commission of the offense.

9. As all persons are held innocent until they shall have been declared guilty, if arrest shall be deemed indispensable, all harshness not essential to the securing of the prisoner's person shall be severely repressed by law.

10. No one shall be disquieted on account of his opinions, including his religious views, provided their manifestation does not disturb the public order established by law.

11. The free communication of ideas and opinions is one of the most precious of the rights of man. Every citizen may, accordingly, speak, write, and print with

freedom, but shall be responsible for such abuses of this freedom as shall be defined by law.

12. The security of the rights of man and of the citizen requires public military forces. These forces are, therefore, established for the good of all and not for the personal advantage of those to whom they shall be intrusted.

13. A common contribution is essential for the maintenance of the public forces and for the cost of administration. This should be equitably distributed among all the citizens in proportion to their means.

14. All the citizens have a right to decide, either personally or by their representatives, as to the necessity of the public contribution; to grant this freely; to know to what uses it is put; and to fix the proportion, the mode of assessment and of collection and the duration of the taxes.

15. Society has the right to require of every public agent an account of his administration.

16. A society in which the observance of the law is not assured, nor the separation of powers defined, has no constitution at all.

17. Since property is an inviolable and sacred right, no one shall be deprived thereof except where public necessity, legally determined, shall clearly demand it, and then only on condition that the owner shall have been previously and equitably indemnified.

EDMUND BURKE: THE DEATH of MARIE ANTOINETTE

It is now sixteen or seventeen years since I saw the queen of France, then the dauphiness, at Versailles; and surely never lighted on this orb, which she hardly seemed to touch, a more delightful vision. I saw her just above the horizon, decorating and cheering the elevated sphere she had just begun to move in, glittering like the morning star full of life and splendor and joy. 0, what a revolution! and what a heart must I have, to contemplate without emotion that elevation and that fall! Little did I dream, when she added titles of veneration to those of enthusiastic, distant, respectful love, that she should ever be obliged to carry the sharp antidote against disgrace concealed in that bosom; little did I dream that I should have lived to see such disasters fallen upon her, in a nation of gallant men, in a nation of men of honor, and of cavaliers! I thought ten thousand swords must have leaped from their scabbards, to avenge even a look that threatened her with insult.

LAMARTINE: THE DEATH of MARIE ANTOINETTE

The Queen, after having written and prayed, slept soundly for some hours. On her waking, Bault's daughter dressed her and adjusted her hair with more neatness than on other days. Marie Antoinette wore a white gown, a white handkerchief covered her shoulders, a white cap her hair; a black ribbon bound this cap round her temples .... The cries, the looks, the laughter, the jests of the people overwhelmed her with humiliation; her colour, changing continually from purple to paleness, betrayed her agitation .... On reaching the scaffold she inadvertently trod on the executioner's foot. "Pardon me," she said, courteously. She knelt for an instant and uttered a half-audible prayer; then rising and glancing towards the towers of the Temple, "Adieu, once again, my children," she said; "I go to rejoin your father."—LAMARTINE.

GABRIELLI: THE EXECUTION of MARIE ANTOINETTE

At 11am, she was led out of the prison, her hands bound and placed in the back of a cart that would take her to the scaffold on the Place de la Revolution. The way was slow, yet every account of her last journey tells us that she remained calm and composed. And as she reached the scaffold, she stepped down gently and walked easily up the steps. Then, she surrendered herself to her executioners and as preparations were made, every minute must have seemed like an hour.

At 12:15, the blade fell, and her severed head was held high to the joyous cries of the crowd.

THE NATIONAL CONVENTION, 1792

M. Collot d'Herbois. You have just taken a wise resolution, but there is one which you cannot postpone until the morrow, or even until this evening, or indeed for a single instant, without being faithless to the wish of the nation, - that is the abolition of royalty. [Unanimous applause.]

M. Quinette. We are not the judges of royalty; that belongs to the people. Our business is to make a concrete government, and the people will then choose between the old form where there was royalty and that which we shall submit to them. ...

M. Gregoire. Assuredly no one of us would ever propose to retain in France the fatal race of kings; we all know but too well that dynasties have never been anything else than rapacious tribes who lived on nothing, but human flesh. It is necessary completely to reassure the friends of liberty. We must destroy this talisman, whose magic power is still sufficient to stupefy many a man. I move accordingly that you sanction by a solemn law the abolition of royalty.

The entire Assembly rose by a spontaneous movement and passed the motion of Monsieur Gregoire by acclamation.

M. Bazire. I rise to a point of order. . . . It would be a frightful example for the people to see an Assembly commissioned with its dearest interests voting in a moment of enthusiasm. I move that the question be discussed.

M. Gregoire. Surely it is quite unnecessary to discuss what everybody agrees on. Kings are in the moral order what monsters are in the physical. Courts are the workshops of crimes, the lair of tyrants. The history of kings is the martyrology of nations. Since we are all convinced of the truth of this, why discuss it? I demand that my motion be put to vote, and that later it be supplied with a formal justification worthy of the solemnity of the decree.

M. Ducos. The form of your decree would be only the history of the crimes of Louis XVI, a history already but too well known to the French people. I demand that it be drawn up in the simplest terms. There is no need of explanation after the knowledge which has been spread abroad by the events of August 10.

LOW-SCORING ESSAY

Marie Antoinette was the queen of France at the time of the French Revolution. She was quite selfish and continued to spend money even though the country was starving. She did not care about her people and can be blamed for the French Revolution. These documents illustrate the struggles of the French Revolution, from the ridiculous procedures in the French court to the final abolishment of the monarchy.

The first two passages, Marie Antoinette's letter to her mother and Camban's discussion of court protocols serve to show just how very disconnected the court was from the people. Even when, in a moment of kindness, Marie Antoinette insists that no one be hurt, it implies that people normally were. The amount of waste in the court had to have been unreal, given the number of people involved in dressing a single woman.

The Tennis Court Oath, Declaration of the Rights of Man and National Assembly piece all show how important the Revolution was. They set out smart guidelines to create a constitution and agreed that decisions about the monarchy should be made jointly.

The passages describing Marie Antoinette's execution suggest something very different about the Revolution. Marie Antoinette was imprisoned, tried without any proper legal defense, and sentenced to die. Her death is, after a life of parties, quiet only for her. She dies in front of a cheering crowd. Just as the queen died unfairly, so too will the Revolution die, after a Reign of Terror.

AVERAGE-SCORING ESSAY

The French Revolution was a short-lived experiment, forcing a country from absolute monarchy to a republic in just a few short years. This was a violent process and one that took many victims, including Marie Antoinette, along with it. This isn't to say that the monarchy was a good situation, particularly for the lower classes, but that the Revolution was not, in the end, an effective solution.

The French court, as shown in Campan's passage, was an elaborate farce of ritual and routine. A young Austrian princess, Marie Antoinette, entered this court, hopeful and ready to start her new life. She did, as a young woman, care about her people, as expressed in the letter. She was not, as a girl, the woman known for her lavish spending. Even so, Marie Antoinette's spending was not the cause of the Revolution.

The king and Paris parlement summoned the Estates-General, or a meeting of all three estates, to deal with issues of government finance. When they did not comply with his wishes, he attempted to dismiss the Estates-General. The Third Estate refused to depart, taking the Tennis Court oath on the tennis court at the Palace of Versailles. They agreed to remain in session to create a constitution. The Estates became the National Assembly, creating the Declaration of the Rights of Man, based on the U.S. Declaration of Independence. Their work continued, with some conflict between those who wanted a constitutional monarchy and those committed to a republic, as can be seen in the records of the National Assembly.

With the final texts describing Marie Antoinette's death, it becomes clear who won in the Assembly. The former queen has fallen, been imprisoned and has been put to death. Her death is a public spectacle for a country already embroiled in revolution. With her, the monarchy meets its final end. Her children are motherless and her son will die from the conditions of his imprisonment in just a few short years. While her daughter will live out her life, it will be an unhappy one.

The worst days of the revolution are still to come, as many more will lose their lives to the guillotine. The deaths connected to the royal family are among the first blood lost during the revolution, but far from the last. Many more will die during the Reign of Terror.

HIGH-SCORING ESSAY

The modern mythology of Marie Antoinette portrays her as a vain woman, completely removed from the problems of others, maliciously proclaiming "Let them eat cake!". Marie Antoinette never said those words, and as these documents illustrate, can be rightfully portrayed as a victim of her own circumstances, a scapegoat for the aristocracy at a time of revolution. These documents, as well as other evidence from the period, come together to form a picture of a troubled society, a spoiled, but not unkind, queen, and revolutionaries on a path to destruction.

The daughter of Empress Maria Theresa of Austria, as a young girl, Marie Antoinette was particularly noted for her fine character and gentle heart. Her tutors praised her many virtues, even if she was, on occasion, a bit flighty. The letter from the young Dauphine to her mother illustrates that. She worried about the well-being of the people and rejoiced in their joy. She is hopeful, kind, and, not long after her wedding, a much-welcomed addition to the French royal family. Raised in a casual and informal court, the rigor and rules of the French court must have been quite a shock to the young woman. As seen in the passage from Campan's book on Marie Antoinette, the court was highly ritualistic. A very young woman was suddenly thrust, not only into the limelight, but into a world of structure, rules and hierarchy. She had married a stranger and was, relatively early on, already failing at a key marital obligation, providing an heir.

Marie Antoinette made the French court her own, setting fashions from towering high hairstyles to simple muslin dresses suitable for picnics at her private country house. She spent lavishly, threw grand parties, and lived like a queen. As she enjoyed her status and wealth, the people of France were suffering. Eventually, the economic distress in France led to the beginning of Revolution, and the Estates Generale were called. Here, we find the words of the Abbe Sieyes regarding the Third Estate, the peasants and working class of France. He, essentially, states that the Third estate has borne the burdens of the wealthy and the aristocracy. Marie Antoinette personifies those burdens for many. Contemporary publications, including cheap pamphlets, portrayed her in the very worst light.

The French Revolution began with grand goals. The Tennis Court Oath marks the first sign of true power from the Third Estate, as they commit to remain together, working toward a constitution. Initially, the Estates-General worked with the king, but this marks a shift in that relationship. When the king attempted to disband the Estates-General, they refused. The power of the aristocracy was on the decline. The Declaration of the Rights of Man further emphasize the power of the people over royalty and the aristocracy. These rights have nothing to do with birth, so the rights that have traditionally been conferred by noble birth are irrelevant. They are also disconnected from the Church, suggesting the beginning of a newly secular society. The discussions from the National Assembly of 1792 illustrate the end of the monarchy. This is no longer a group committed to a constitutional monarchy, but rather moving rapidly toward republicanism. In this society, there was little room for a queen like Marie Antoinette, granted her position through birth rather than work. She was, fundamentally, a drain on the resources of France, rather than a benefit to it.

The passages by Edmund Burke, LaMartine and Gabrielli mark the end of the Bourbon dynasty, with one final death. Louis XVI had already been executed by guillotine and these passages all deal with Marie Antoinette's death. She was no longer a spoiled young queen. After years in prison, her health was failing, her husband dead and her children in danger. One had even been forced to make false accusations against her. Nonetheless, LaMartine and Gabrielli suggest that she went to the guillotine with grace and courage, revealing the character that her tutors and early letters had suggested. Finally, Burke's passage reflects upon not only her grace and beauty, but also her fall and, eventually, the fall of the French Revolution.

Made in the USA
Monee, IL
20 April 2021